Specialty Competencies in Organizational and Business Consulting Psychology

Series in Specialty Competencies in Professional Psychology

JAY C. THOMAS

Specialty Competencies in Organizational and Business Consulting Psychology

OXFORD
UNIVERSITY PRESS
2010

OXFORD
UNIVERSITY PRESS

Oxford University Press, Inc., publishes works that further
Oxford University's objective of excellence
in research, scholarship, and education.

Oxford New York

Auckland Cape Town Dar es Salaam Hong Kong Karachi
Kuala Lumpur Madrid Melbourne Mexico City Nairobi
New Delhi Shanghai Taipei Toronto

With offices in
Argentina Austria Brazil Chile Czech Republic France Greece
Guatemala Hungary Italy Japan Poland Portugal Singapore
South Korea Switzerland Thailand Turkey Ukraine Vietnam

Published by Oxford University Press, Inc.
198 Madison Avenue, New York, New York 10016
www.oup.com

Oxford is a registered trademark of Oxford University Press

Library of Congress Cataloging-in-Publication data on file
ISBN-13 9780195385496 Paper

9 8 7 6 5 4 3 2 1

Printed in the United States of America
on acid-free paper

ABOUT THE SERIES IN SPECIALTY COMPETENCIES
IN PROFESSIONAL PSYCHOLOGY

This series is intended to describe state-of-the-art functional and foundational competencies in professional psychology across extant and emerging specialty areas. Each book in this series provides a guide to best practices across both core and specialty competencies as defined by a given professional psychology specialty.

The impetus for this series was created by various growing movements in professional psychology during the past 15 years. First, as an applied discipline, psychology is increasingly recognizing the unique and distinct nature among a variety of orientations, modalities, and approaches with regard to professional practice. These specialty areas represent distinct ways of practicing one's profession across various domains of activities that are based on distinct bodies of literature and often addressing differing populations or problems. For example, the American Psychological Association (APA) in 1995 established the Commission on the Recognition of Specialties and Proficiencies in Professional Psychology (CRSPPP) in order to define criteria by which a given specialty could be recognized. The Council of Credentialing Organizations in Professional Psychology (CCOPP), an interorganizational entity, was formed in reaction to the need to establish criteria and principles regarding the types of training programs related to the education, training, and professional development of individuals seeking such specialization. In addition, the Council on Specialties in Professional Psychology (COS) was formed in 1997, independent of APA, to foster communication among the established specialties, in order to offer a unified position to the pubic regarding specialty education and training, credentialing, and practice standards across specialty areas.

Simultaneously, efforts to actually define professional competence regarding psychological practice have also been growing significantly. For example, the APA-sponsored Task Force on Assessment of Competence in Professional Psychology put forth a series of guiding principles for the assessment of competence within professional psychology, based, in part, on a review of competency assessment models developed both within (e.g., Assessment of Competence Workgroup from Competencies Conference—Roberts et al., 2005) and outside (e.g., Accreditation Council for Graduate Medical Education and American Board of Medical Specialties, 2000) the profession of psychology (Kaslow et al., 2007).

Moreover, additional professional organizations in psychology have provided valuable input into this discussion, including various associations primarily interested in the credentialing of professional psychologists, such as the American Board of Professional Psychology (ABPP), the Association of State and Provincial Psychology Boards (ASPBB), and the National Register of Health Service Providers in Psychology. This wide-spread interest and importance of the issue of competency in professional psychology can be especially appreciated given the attention and collaboration afforded to this effort by international groups, including the Canadian Psychological Association and the International Congress on Licensure, Certification, and Credentialing in Professional Psychology.

Each volume in the series is devoted to a specific specialty and provides a definition, description, and development timeline of that specialty, including its essential and characteristic pattern of activities, as well as its distinctive and unique features. Each set of authors, long-term experts and veterans of a given specialty, were asked to describe that specialty along the lines of both functional and foundational competencies. *Functional competencies* are those common practice activities provided at the specialty level of practice that include, for example, the application of its science base, assessment, intervention, consultation, and where relevant, supervision, management, and teaching. *Foundational competencies* represent core knowledge areas which are integrated and cut across all functional competencies to varying degrees, and dependent upon the specialty, in various ways. These include ethical and legal issues, individual and cultural diversity considerations, interpersonal interactions, and professional identification.

Whereas we realize that each specialty is likely to undergo changes in the future, we wanted to establish a baseline of basic knowledge and principles that comprise a specialty highlighting both its commonalities with other areas of professional psychology, as well as its distinctiveness. We look forward to seeing the dynamics of such changes, as well as the emergence of new specialties in the future.

Originally called "Industrial-Organizational Psychology (I/O)," practitioners of this specialty emanate from varying backgrounds in business-psychology related fields. Although it was one of the original four specialties of the American Board of Professional Psychology (ABPP) established in 1947, as described in chapter 1, the domain of contemporary I/O professional practice can best be thought of as a hybrid across multiple traditions. For this volume in the series, we asked Jay Thomas to describe this particular hybrid model. The original board reflecting the specialty of I/O psychology (the American Board of Industrial and Organizational Psychology) within the greater organization of ABPP (which at the time of this writing encompasses 13 differing specialty boards in professional psychology), was restructured in 2005 and is now called the American Board of Organizational and Business Consulting Psychology (ABOBCP). This name change was made in order to best capture the notion that specialists in this area can be educated and trained (and practice) in related, but somewhat differing traditions. Readers interested in this specialty area within psychology will find this text invaluable as the most current description of the competencies thought important to help define the OBC psychologist.

Arthur M. Nezu
Christine Maguth Nezu

References

Kaslow et al. (2007). Guiding principles and recommendations for the assessment of competence. *Professional Psychology: Research and Practice, 38*, 441–451.

Roberts et al. (2005). Fostering a culture shift: Assessment of competence in the education and careers of professional psychologists. *Professional Psychology: Research and Practice, 36*, 355–361.

ACKNOWLEDGMENTS

I have a number of people to thank for their help in the preparation of this book: Art and Christine Nezu for coming up with the idea for the series and asking me to participate, and an anonymous reviewer who commented on the outline and planned contents. My graduate assistant and student, Heidi Meeke, contributed information used in chapter 10 and provided helpful reviews of other chapters. Another student, Corey Baechel, reviewed several chapters and added immeasurably to them through his questions. My colleague Jon Frew served as reviewer and sounding board. At times he may have thought he was teaching a seminar on context. I owe a debt to many colleagues on the American Board of Organizational and Business Consulting Psychology who have contributed ideas and enhanced my continuing education over the years. This book, and my career, would not have been possible without three outstanding mentors. Gerald V. Barrett, then department chair at the University of Akron met with the new industrial and organizational psychology students on a late August day in 1975 and told us two things: "There is no one best way (to do anything)" and "Do not rely on the received doctrine." During the next 4 years he made sure we would never forget them, but it took me the better part of three and a half decades to understand what he meant. Ralph Alexander taught through modeling that there is no area of knowledge that is irrelevant. Ralph died before I fully recognized his influence and could thank him as he should have been thanked. His rigorous but creative approach combined with Jerry's "no one best way" is the best training any aspiring psychologist could ask for. More recently, my boss, friend, and mentor, Michel Hersen, taught me that one can be headstrong and task oriented, yet still be human. Finally, over the past year my wife has had to contend with a husband who was more distracted (and grouchy) than usual and my children and grandchildren did the same. I appreciate their forbearance.

CONTENTS

PART I

Introduction to Organizational and Business Consulting Psychology

ONE

Hybrid Power

The History of Organizational and Business Consulting Psychology

Organizational and business consulting psychology (OBCP) is a hybrid specialty composed of multiple sets of traditions.

Industrial psychology began almost as soon as psychology had developed enough of a science for it to be applied to industry. As early as the 1890s, Hugo Munsterberg, the German American psychologist, was involved with the selection of street car operators (cf. Koppes, 2007), and by the 1920s, business applications of psychology in employee selection, advertising, and organizational design were thriving. Industrial psychology was one of the four original specialties of the American Board of Professional Psychology (ABPP) in 1947. By the late 1960s, the word "industrial" was recognized as misleading in that psychologists were working at all levels in many types of organizations; hence, the name of the primary professional organization was changed from Division 14 of the American Psychological Association to Industrial and Organizational Psychology in 1973, later Society for Industrial and Organizational Psychology (SIOP) in 1982 (Koppes, 2007). In Europe the specialty includes the appellation "work psychology." Throughout its history, industrial/organizational (I/O) psychology has drawn heavily from the traditions of experimental, social, and differential psychology. There has been a consistent and heavy emphasis on quantification (Zickar & Gibby, 2007).

Consulting psychology has historically also been associated with the application of psychology in organizations. Developing in parallel with I/O psychology, consulting psychology has traditionally had more of a "clinical" flavor, with many practitioners originally trained in clinical or counseling psychology. These traditions permit "knowledge" to be formed via means other than quantification, so some consulting psychologists have been attuned to phenomenological, narrative, or interpretive forms of investigation (Lewin, 1947; Nevis, 1987). Consulting psychologists have been more likely to emphasize services to individuals or groups than have traditional I/O psychologists, who tend to put more emphasis on building or changing processes or systems that subsequently result in changes in work-related behavior or performance. It is fair to say that consulting psychologists have put greater emphasis on licensure and credentialing than I/O psychologists have. Like two siblings who occasionally fight and occasionally play together, the two disciplines have developed concurrently and today are heavily intertwined at the practitioner level. There is overlap in the membership of SIOP and the Society for Consulting Psychology (SCP). Both are divisions of the American Psychological Association (APA). In 2005, the American Board of Industrial and Organizational Psychology, a specialty board of the American Board of Professional Psychology (ABPP) and an original specialty within ABPP, was reconstituted as the American Board of Organizational and Business Consulting Psychology to reflect the fact that specialists may be trained, experienced, and practice in related but somewhat different traditions. In this book, the term *OBC psychologist* will be used to reflect the hybrid practice. The terms *I/O psychology* and *consulting psychology* will be used when referring specifically to the discipline.

Competencies and Outcomes

Competencies are the knowledge, abilities, skills, and other characteristics (KSAOs) that are needed to perform well in a task, job, or profession. They are often associated with the activities the professional performs (Rodolfa et al., 2005). This emphasis on KSAOs and activities is incomplete. To get the whole picture we begin with the outcomes the psychologist, or the psychologist's client, is seeking to achieve. In logic modeling (Frechtling, 2007; McLaughlin & Jordan, 2004), desired longer term and short-term outcomes are identified first, then outputs from the intervention, inputs including resources (time, budget, capability, etc.) are considered. Contextual factors are considered since the culture of the organization can heavily influence the chance of success of various types of interventions. Only then are activities that constitute the intervention specified. Competencies are a form of input that the OBC psychologist brings to the situation and they are only relevant in connection with the goals of the consultation. For example, a psychologist may spend a good deal of time, effort, and money developing expertise in a statistical analysis methodology—say, time series analysis—and thus this would be considered a competency of the psychologist. But it is not a requisite competency unless the goals of the consultation and resources available call for its use: a question about change over time and a minimum of 100 or so data points. Similarly, a psychologist may be very good at observing group processes or identifying training needs, but these competencies come into play only if the situation calls for them.

Table 1.1 lists the competencies identified by professional organizations as germane to OBC psychology (APA, 2007; Education and Training Committee, 2002; SIOP, 1998). It is a long list and few, if any, psychologists have all of these competencies in their repertoire. In fact, most practitioners will be limited to reliance on a relative few. Ask an OBC psychologist what he or she does and a likely answer might be "I work in employee selection"; "I do organizational development"; or "Most of my work is coaching and individual assessment." Their brochures and websites may list a half dozen or so activities, more only if several consultants work in the same group. My goal in writing this book is to put the competencies into a context. By concentrating on clients' objectives rather than activities, the OBC psychologist gains flexibility in providing services. For example, an employee selection program may be intended to increase job performance among a class of workers. However, a tight labor market may mean few qualified workers are available and thus require that emphasis be placed on creating a more comprehensive training program or redesigning the job to achieve the same objective. The results may not be exactly similar, but resources are not infinite. The competent OBC psychologist finds a way either to reach the goal or to convince the client that there is a need to recalibrate aspirations.

The ABPP bases its specialty certifications on competencies. Candidates are expected to demonstrate that they are competent in their specialty area through education, practice samples, and examinations. ABPP distinguishes between foundational and functional competencies. *Functional competencies* represent the day-to-day activities, presumably with intended outcomes, provided by a specialist psychologist. *Foundational competencies* represent those aspects of practice that cut across functions and activities and, taken as a whole, make a psychologist a psychologist as opposed to another type of professional. ABPP (2007, p. 7) defines functional and foundational competencies as shown in Table 1.2.

Roldofa et al. (2005) envision a cube model with functional and foundational competencies laid out at right angles to one another and stages of professional development providing depth to the cube. Their list of

TABLE 1.1 Competencies and Proficiencies Recommended by the American Board of Professional Psychology (ABPP), the Society for Consulting Psychology, the American Psychological Association, and the Society for Industrial and Organizational Psychology

ABPP COMPETENCIES (FUNC = FUNCTIONAL; FOUND = FOUNDATIONAL)	PROFICIENCIES FROM THE STANDARDS FOR DOCTORAL TRAINING IN CONSULTING PSYCHOLOGY (APA DIVISION 13, 2002)	COMPETENCIES FROM GUIDELINES FOR EDUCATION AND TRAINING AT THE DOCTORAL AND POSTDOCTORAL LEVELS IN CONSULTING PSYCHOLOGY/ORGANIZATIONAL CONSULTING PSYCHOLOGY (APA, 2007)	PROFICIENCIES FROM THE STANDARDS FOR DOCTORAL TRAINING IN INDUSTRIAL/ ORGANIZATIONAL (I/O) PSYCHOLOGY (APA DIVISION 14, 1998)	PRIMARY CHAPTER
	Education and Training Committee, Div. 13 (2002).	*American Psychological Association (2007)*	*Society of Industrial/ Organizational Psychologists (1999).*	
Ethics and legal foundations (Found)	Ethics	Professional ethics and standards: Awareness of relevant ethical principles: i.e., confidentiality, culture-centered awareness/ understanding guanxi as they apply in the OCP context.	Ethical, legal, and professional contexts of I/O psychology	12
Science Base and Application (Func)	Research and evaluation	Research methods and statistics	Research methods	2
Science Base and Application (Func)	Research and evaluation	Process consultation/Action research	Statistical methods/data analysis	2, 9
	Primarily Individual-Level Core Competencies:		*Listed out of order to fit with Division 13 Standards*	
Assessment, Intervention, Consultation (all Func)	Individual assessment of purposes of career and vocational assessment	Individual assessment of purposes of career and vocational assessment	Career development	6, 9

Assessment (Func)	Individual assessment for purposes of employee selection or development	Individual assessment for purposes of employee selection or development	Personnel recruitment, selection, and placement	6, 9
Assessment (Func)	Job analysis for purposes of individual assessment	Job analysis and culture/diversity as found in race, ethnicity, gender (women/men), sexual orientation, disability status, socioeconomic status, national heritage, industry, education, job/role calibrations for purposes of individual assessment	Job/task analysis and classification	4
Intervention, Consultation (Func) Interpersonal Interactions (Found)	Executive and individual coaching	Executive and individual coaching	Leadership and management	7
Intervention, Consultation, some Assessment (all Func) Interpersonal Interactions (Found)	Individual-level intervention for job- and career-related problems	Individual-level intervention for job- and career-related problems	Performance appraisal and feedback	7, 5
	Primarily Group-Level Core Competencies:			
Consultation (Func) Science Base and Application (Func)	Assessment of functional and dysfunctional group behavior	Assessment of functional and dysfunctional group behavior	Small group theory and team processes	9
Assessment, Consultation, Intervention (Func)	Assessment and development of teams	Assessment and development of teams with attention to diversity (here and after used to refer to the full range of diversity variables) considerations	Training: Theory, program design, and evaluation	7, 9

(Continued)

TABLE 1.1 **Competencies and Proficiencies Recommended by the American Board of Professional Psychology (ABPP), the Society for Consulting Psychology, the American Psychological Association, and the Society for Industrial and Organizational Psychology (*Continued*)**

ABPP COMPETENCIES (FUNC = FUNCTIONAL; FOUND = FOUNDATIONAL)	PROFICIENCIES FROM THE STANDARDS FOR DOCTORAL TRAINING IN CONSULTING PSYCHOLOGY (APA DIVISION 13, 2002)	COMPETENCIES FROM GUIDELINES FOR EDUCATION AND TRAINING AT THE DOCTORAL AND POSTDOCTORAL LEVELS IN CONSULTING PSYCHOLOGY/ORGANIZATIONAL CONSULTING PSYCHOLOGY (APA, 2007)	PROFICIENCIES FROM THE STANDARDS FOR DOCTORAL TRAINING IN INDUSTRIAL/ORGANIZATIONAL PSYCHOLOGY (APA DIVISION 14, 1998)	PRIMARY CHAPTER
Intervention, Consultation (Func)	Creating group-level teams in organizations (e.g., self-directed work groups)	Creating group-level teams in organizations (e.g., self-directed work groups)	Work motivation	8
Assessment, Consultation, Intervention (Func)	Intergroup assessment and intervention	Intergroup assessment and intervention		9
Assessment, Consultation, Intervention (Func)	Group boundary assessment and intervention	Group boundary assessment and intervention		9
Individual and Cultural Diversity (Found), Science Base and Application (Found)	Identity group (racial, gender, ethnic) management in the organizational context	Identity group (racial, gender, ethnic, age, nationality, sexual orientation, life span, disability groups, social prejudice, culture, religion, belief systems, organizational hierarchy role)	Individual differences	12, 4, 5, 6, 8, 9
	Primarily Organizational/Systemic-Level Core Competencies:			
Assessment (Func)	Organizational diagnosis, including systemic assessment of the entire organization or large component parts of the organization	Organizational diagnosis, including systemic assessment of the entire organization or large component parts of the organization and diversity cohorts within the organization's stakeholder groups		9

Assessment (Func)	Attitude, climate, and satisfaction surveys	Attitude, climate, and satisfaction surveys, including portioned profiles representing work units, organizational-level groups, diversity/multicultural groups, and upfront/nonnegotiable announcements of ethical commitments, especially confidentiality		8,9
Assessment, Consultation (Func)	Evaluation of corporate management philosophy, organizational culture, and nature of systemic stressors	Evaluation of corporate management philosophy, organizational culture, and nature of systemic stressors	Health and stress in organizations	9
Supervision and Management (Func)	Workflow and project planning activities	Workflow and project planning activities (e.g., Gantt charts, PERT (Program Evaluation Review Technique) charts, fishbone diagrams		10
Assessment (Func)	Identification of aggregate performance measures	Identification of aggregate performance measures, charting and plotting measures		4, 10
Assessment, Consultation (Func) Individual and Cultural Diversity (Found)	Assessment of organizational values and management practices	Assessment of organizational values and management practices and philosophy/policy	Organizational theory	9
Interventions, Consultation (Func)	Organizational-level interventions	Organizational-level interventions, collating data, portioning data, intervention design	Organizational development	9
Interventions, Consultation (Func)	Change management of organizational systems	Change management of organizational systems		9
Science Base and Applications (Func)			Consumer behavior	9 (some)

(Continued)

TABLE 1.1 Competencies and Proficiencies Recommended by the American Board of Professional Psychology (ABPP), the Society for Consulting Psychology, the American Psychological Association, and the Society for Industrial and Organizational Psychology (*Continued*)

ABPP COMPETENCIES (FUNC = FUNCTIONAL; FOUND = FOUNDATIONAL)	PROFICIENCIES FROM THE STANDARDS FOR DOCTORAL TRAINING IN CONSULTING PSYCHOLOGY (APA DIVISION 13, 2002)	COMPETENCIES FROM GUIDELINES FOR EDUCATION AND TRAINING AT THE DOCTORAL AND POSTDOCTORAL LEVELS IN CONSULTING PSYCHOLOGY/ORGANIZATIONAL CONSULTING PSYCHOLOGY (APA, 2007)	PROFICIENCIES FROM THE STANDARDS FOR DOCTORAL TRAINING IN INDUSTRIAL/ ORGANIZATIONAL (I/O) PSYCHOLOGY (APA DIVISION 14, 1998)	PRIMARY CHAPTER
Assessment (Func)			Criterion theory and development	4
Science Base and Applications (Func)			Human performance/human factors	4, 8
Assessment (Func)			Job evaluation and compensation	8
Science Base and Applications, Consultation (Func)			Judgment and decision making	8
			Internship	N/A

OCP = organizational consulting psychology; I/O = industrial/organizational.

Note: Adapted from the American Board of Organizational and Business Consulting Psychology. (2008). *Examination manual.* Chapel Hill, NC: American Board of Professional Psychology.

Sources:

American Psychological Association. (2007). Guidelines for education and training at the doctoral and postdoctoral levels in consulting psychology/organizational consulting psychology. *American Psychologist, 62*(9), 980—992.

Education and Training Committee, Division 13, Society of Consulting Psychology, American Psychological Association. (2002). Principles for education and training at the doctoral and postdoctoral level in consulting psychology/organizational. *Consulting Psychology Journal: Practice and Research, 54*(4), 213—222.

Society for Industrial and Organizational Psychology. (1998). *Guidelines for education and training at the doctoral level in industrial/organizational psychology.* Dayton, OH: Author.

foundational competencies is slightly different from those of the ABPP, including reflective practice/self-assessment, scientific knowledge and methods, relationships, and interdisciplinary systems, as well as ethical standards/policy issues and individual and cultural diversity. Regardless of which list is relied on, we can expect that a properly trained doctoral-level professional psychologist should possess most of the foundational competencies needed for any established specialty, with some modification allowed for differences in the context and scope of practice. The functional competencies differ from one specialty to another; skills in, say, assessment may not effectively transfer from one specialty to another. If a psychologist changes or adds a new specialty, a critical question is how the new competencies were developed and applied. The context is always important. It is noteworthy that the Society for Consulting Psychology has demarcated the various competencies in its list as being at the individual, group, or organizational level. A psychologist who is capable at one level may not have the same capacity at another level.

These lists are useful to accreditors, regulators, and credentialing groups. The psychologist in practice probably does not think in these terms so much as asking the question "Am I competent to take on this task?" The approach of this book is to describe the various fields of OBC psychology from the point of view of (1) what is known or believed; (2) what standards

TABLE 1.2 **ABPP's functional and foundational competencies**

FUNCTIONAL COMPETENCIES

Assessment. Defining, diagnosing, and conceptualizing problems and issues associated with individuals, groups, and/or organizations.

Intervention. Developing, implementing, and evaluating interventions designed to produce positive change.

Consultation. Providing expert guidance or professional assistance to a consultee's needs or goals.

Science Base and Application. Producing, consuming, or communicating scientific theory and knowledge relevant to areas of professional practice.

Supervision and Management. The guidance, direction, and monitoring of trainees, residents, staff, or programs.

Teaching. Formal teaching (including workshops, coursework, and presentations) related to the specialty.

FOUNDATIONAL COMPETENCIES

Ethics and Legal Foundations. Awareness and application of appropriate ethical and legal practice requirements.

Individual and Cultural Diversity. Awareness and sensitivity in working with diverse individuals, groups, and communities who represent various cultural and personal background and characteristics.

Interpersonal Interactions. Ability to relate effectively and meaningfully with individuals, groups, and/or communities, and the ability to function effectively in interdisciplinary systems.

Professional Identification. Practice conducted within the boundaries of competencies, including involvement in the profession and the specialty in particular. Continuing development as a psychologist specialist. Advocacy for the profession.

exist, if any, for practice within a domain; (3) what should the psychologist be able to do to help the client organization reach its goals; and (4) what about this role is different from the roles of other psychologists and other professionals.

The Psychologist as Technologist

The services we provide are intended to achieve objectives, typically more than one objective. We use science and a little art to design assessments and interventions to achieve these goals; in short, we have a technology. I prefer the terms *technology* and *technologist* to scientist-practitioner and similar labels that convey little meaning about what the psychologist does that benefits the client. Some authors (e.g., Blanton, 2000) dislike the term *technologist* because to them it implies that the psychologist is a technician who applies the same techniques over and over. On the contrary, a technologist solves problems, often using whatever science applies but equally often being ahead of science (Petroski, 2003). The analogy with engineering is apt. Petroski points out that engineers were developing steam engines long before thermodynamics was developed as a branch of physics. Indeed, the development of the engines propelled the development of the science. Necessity may be the mother of invention; and invention, in turn, may beget science. Quoting a design text, Petroski says, "Engineers use science to solve their problems if the science is available. But available or not, the problem must be solved, and whatever form the solution takes under these conditions is called engineering" (Z. M. Lewalski, quoted in Petroski, 2003, p. 241). The psychologist consultant is in many ways like the engineer. A given assignment may require approaches and solutions that the science of psychology has not yet addressed, or if addressed, not yet resolved. The technologist recognizes that no design is ever perfect and there is no optimal solution to any problem that involves multiple objectives. Because the technologist is concerned with solving problems, a whole range of research and investigative techniques open up beyond the standard methods for determining causation and association prevalent in psychology. The technologist models a solution, tries it out, and tinkers with it until it seems to work well enough. When the solution fails or has unexpected effects, the technologist performs failure analysis to determine what went wrong to avoid the same scenario the next time (Petroski, 1985). The competent psychologist strives to find workable solutions that achieve the client's goals as well as possible given resources, budget, timelines, culture, and other situational factors. There are no universal "best practices."

All authors hope that their work stands up to the test of time. In psychology in general and OBCP in particular, there are numerous journals, technical and research reports, books, and other media published around the world that have the potential to change the field every year—more than one person or a team can keep up with. To make matters worse, for at least the past half-century the field has been pushed and pulled by fads and fashions, only some of which are relevant a decade later (Dunnette, 1966). Other trends, such as the emphasis on quality in the 1980s and 90s, have an impact, then fade from prominence while leaving an imprint on the field. However, over long stretches of time the framework of practice remains relatively stable. For that reason I have chosen to rely mostly on references from classic sources or major integrative sources such as the *Annual Review of Psychology*, handbooks, and other edited works rather than rely as heavily on individual papers as I might in a theoretical piece, textbook, or literature review. In places in the book are examples drawn from my experience or the experiences of other OBC psychologists. These are intended as examples, not proofs. In general, I assume that the reader has a reasonably strong background in the science of psychology, methodology, and related foundational areas. In OBC psychology the skills to practice generally are developed after graduate school (Silzer, Erickson, Robinson, & Cober, 2008; Somerville, 1998), so when possible I have included occasional tables, checklists, or procedures that help translate foundational knowledge into functional capacity. These do not represent the only way to accomplish a particular goal. Somerville (1998) notes that the large consulting firms tend to develop their own ways of accomplishing the tasks of an OBC psychologist, so it is likely that readers will either have or develop their own versions of these methods. Within our hybrid discipline there are few standard ways of doing anything; if there is one constant in competent practice, it is that the context guides the solution.

TWO

Conceptual and Scientific Foundations

[handwritten annotation:] Fundamental issue w/ a system is identify up its boundary. subsystems

Since the work of Lewin (1947) and, more formally, Katz and Kahn (1966, 1978), organizational theory has used force field analysis and systems theory as conceptual frameworks for understanding the development, evolution, and effects of changes in organizations. Theories originating in social psychology have influenced concepts of small work group and team dynamics. At the individual level, several theories of personality, cognition, human abilities, and attribution are influential. There is, however, no universally recognized conceptual framework for groups and individuals. What is recognized is the need to examine the situation. The OBC psychologist must be an expert at job or work analysis and in comprehending organizational culture and climate. Some forms of work done by OBC psychologists are constrained by legal and professional standards. Other forms of work have not been regulated to this degree.

Research Methods

Because I/O psychology was rooted in employee testing and the use of research to inform practices, there has always been a tradition comparable to what clinicians call evidence-based practice. The specialty of OBCP encompasses a number of empirical traditions. Research methods in active use range from full-experiments and quasi-experiments to field studies. Action research was developed in the 1940s and is still a mainstay of organizational development, particularly in Europe (Gustavsen, 2008). *Action research* involves the consultant working with the client organization to gather information through surveys, focus groups, interviews, or other means; analyzing the information; and using it to plan the next phase of change. The focus is on using the information to support the change effort rather than collecting data for long-term scientific purposes.

Although both quantitative and qualitative methods are used, studies that supply numerical data are clearly more abundant in the research journals. There seems to be an antiquated belief still current that equates quantitative data, however derived, with greater scientific rigor (Blanton, 2000). Designs used in other areas of psychology such as single-subject designs (cf. Barlow & Nock, 2009; Barlow, Nock, & Hersen, 2009) are rarely encountered even though they could be very useful, particularly in studying individual development efforts. For those who insist on applying statistical methods to single-case or small sample studies, randomization tests are well established and proven (Edgington & Onghena, 2007; Todman & Dugard, 2001); they just have not been widely used in I/O or consulting psychology.

Experimental laboratory research has influenced many theories in organizational psychology, including motivation and goal setting, training methods, influence processes, and others. Although highly influential through the 1970s, the ecological validity and consequent generalizability of results from lab experiments became questioned as they challenged common practice and common sense. For example, several theories that stemmed from studies of undergraduates seemed to indicate that extrinsic reinforcers (e.g., pay for performance) were not only ineffective but were contra-effective (Rynes, Gerhart, & Parks, 2005). Today it is the studies that are questioned, not the practices.

Laboratory experiments may still be useful, provided some means of determining how to estimate the generalizability of experimental studies is established. Campbell (1986) provides five criteria:

1. Empirical results obtained in the field are identical to those obtained in the laboratory.

2. The direction of empirical relationships is the same as those found in the laboratory.

3. The conclusions drawn about a specific question are the same for field studies as they are for laboratory studies.

4. The existence of a particular phenomenon can demonstrated in the laboratory as well as the field.

5. Data from the laboratory can be used to justify or support the application of a particular practice or program in an operational setting. (p. 270)

Campbell states that although most people consider ecological validity to apply to the first criterion, he believes that numbers 3 and 5 are the most useful conceptualization because it is so rare to obtain an exact replication from the laboratory to the field. Indeed, the reason laboratory studies are done in the first place is to gain an element of control over extraneous factors that reduce the effect to be observed. Therefore, laboratory results should almost always provide greater effect sizes than field studies can produce.

Industrial and organizational psychologists continue to place the bulk of their bets on surveys and self-report. A study of the contents over the first decade of *Organizational Research Methods* found that surveys were the most popular research technique used in about a third of the articles (Aguinis, Pierce, Bosco, & Muslin, 2009). This reliance on surveys continues to increase (Aguinis et al., 2009) even though it is widely established that the results can be misleading due to variations in question wording, format, context (Schwartz, 1999), and the influence of faulty memories and emotions (Stone et al., 2001). This is not to say that self-report should not be used, but it should rarely be the exclusive means of information gathering in a study or in practice. Many survey-based studies ignore sampling strategies. The researchers send out several hundred surveys, get back a couple of hundred and subject the data to the most sophisticated analyses even though descriptive statistics would be more informative. Doing sophisticated analyses on survey data with 25%–35% return rates, even when this is comparable to return rates obtained in other studies, is not appropriate (Freedman, Pisani, & Purves, 2007). Matching mediocrity is not a path to competence or relevance (Smith, 2006); that is, choosing a methodology or analytical method simply because others use it is not an effective research practice. Studies useful for both research and practice incorporate more than one measurement technique, pay attention to sampling issues, and employ interpretable analytic methods.

Statistical Analysis

Spector (2001) described statistical analysis procedures that are most popular in I/O psychology. Most are based on correlation/regression methods, including bivariate correlations, partial correlation, multiple regression, moderated regression, mediation tests, and logistic regression. Analysis of variance is used often enough to mention, but it does not hold the central place in industrial/organizational psychology that it does in experimental psychology. Factor analysis, including confirmatory factor analysis, is an analysis family of which I/O psychologists should have at least basic familiarity. Recently, structural equation modeling (SEM) has become very popular, although its use in studies probably exceeds its usefulness. Hierarchical linear modeling (HLM) is useful in that it allows for controlling for category or block membership—for example, a study may examine employee attitudes and organizational outcomes in a company with several locations. HLM allows for examining the location effect in the most unbiased manner (Bickel, 2007). The final method in Spector's treatment is item response theory (IRT). IRT has found its use in evaluating test fairness at the item level and in the purpose it was originally developed for: adaptive testing. Adaptive testing is unusual in that it is one of the few applications in psychology of Bayesian probability theory as trait estimates are adjusted based on prior information of the difficulty levels of items passed and failed by the individual examinee and future items are chosen based on these estimates.

Spector and other writers (e.g., Blanton, 2000; Peterson, 2009; Thomas, 2008) have lamented the tendency of journal editors and reviewers to demand the most sophisticated analyses possible, even when the required analysis provides no additional understanding and often obfuscates the results. Most researchers are university faculty and the reward contingencies are much different for them than for practitioners. Unfortunately, this results in a large body of work being published that is essentially irrelevant to practice (Blanton, 2000), and I would add, to real life.

The competent practitioner needs to know statistics at some level, but the degree and nature of skills vary depending on the nature of the work in which the OBC psychologist engages. Those who develop and select instruments using criterion-related validation methodology need a high level of expertise in psychometrics and many of the methods Spector listed. Research with immediate application uses surveys, interviews, focus groups, and observation. Specialists must have a strong background in psychometrics, information gathering and integration, and the capability of using and understanding statistical procedures. Overall, as practitioners they need to be able to conduct appropriately sized and targeted studies aimed at producing usable results in the spirit of Patton's (2009) concept of utilization-focused evaluation—that is, paying more attention to the practical use of research data than on the internal validity of evaluation studies. Those who try to keep up with the literature need a basic understanding of these statistical procedures but need not be capable of performing them. Competence requires an understanding of the strengths and limits of statistical theory, particularly the severe logical limitations of significance testing (Gigerenzer, 1993, 2008; Thomas, 2008; Wilkinson and the Task Force on Statistical Inference, 1999).

Qualitative research methods are widely used by practitioners. For example, interviews and focus groups are used extensively in consumer research and action research. A few journals such as *Consulting Psychology: Research and Practice* and *Organizational Dynamics* publish some qualitative studies, usually case studies, but generally qualitative research lies outside the mainstream of research. Given the usage in application, this neglect of qualitative methods is unfortunate. This could change; a recent edited handbook on research methods in I/O psychology contains two chapters on qualitative methods (Rogelberg, 2004), which is more attention than other handbooks in the field have paid to the methods. With the exception of engineering psychologists, psychologists in general pay little attention to the analysis of errors with the intent to understand their origins and prevention. Techniques such as failure analysis and root cause analysis (cf. Dekker, 2006; Heuvel et al., 2009) are extensively used in industry, transportation, hospitals, and even schools. With a tradition of collecting critical incidents, this seems a natural methodology for OBC psychologists to adopt. It has the advantage of preparing them for working with interdisciplinary teams on important problems. Since psychologists are ethically bound to use methods they are competent in, it makes sense to increase the attention to these techniques in training programs for OBC psychologists.

Cascio and Aguinis (2008) examined the topics studied by I/O psychologists over a 45-year period, from January 1963 to May 2007, as published in *Personnel Psychology* and the *Journal of Applied Psychology*. They found that those journals tend to publish in much the same areas, as shown in Table 2.1. They also examined trends in *human capital*, an updated term for human resources, and found little overlap between the published research in I/O psychology and these trends. Cascio and Aguinis concluded that several factors need to change if I/O psychology is to achieve its goals of increasing influence with leading executives, policy makers, and politicians. A survey of organizational consulting psychologists by Blanton (2000) found that, as a group, these professionals saw the research literature as having little relevance to their daily work.

OBC psychologists are not alone in finding the research that supposedly underlies the field to be lacking in relevance and its ability to guide the practitioner. Our colleagues in the other disciplines of professional psychology have debated the same issue (cf. Persons & Silberschatz, 1998; Truax & Thomas, 2003). The idea of evidence-based practice has stirred a large controversy, with a special APA task force reporting in 2006 that science should drive practice, but that practitioners need to be able to adapt

TABLE 2.1 **Top Five Topics of Articles Published in Two Leading Industrial/Organizational Psychology Journals 1963–2007**

TOPIC	PERSONNEL PSYCHOLOGY	JOURNAL OF APPLIED PSYCHOLOGY
	% of articles	*% of articles*
Methodology- psychometric issues	21	22
Predictors of performance	20	13
Work motivation and attitudes	12	16
Performance measurement-work outcomes	11	10
Leader influences	7	6
Human factors-applied experimental psychology	0	9

Source: Cascio, W. F., & Aguinis, H. (2008). Research in industrial and organizational psychology from 1963 to 2007: Changes, choices, and trends. *Journal of Applied Psychology, 93*(5), 1062–1081.

it to the needs of their clients (APA Task Force on Evidence-Based Practice, 2006). A similar approach would be helpful in OBC psychology, but researchers need to focus more on studying relevant topics (Aguinis & Cascio, 2008).

Developing Research Competence

Graduate programs develop research competence. However, competence in research and related skills are not all one needs to be a competent, practicing OBC psychologist. The SIOP Professional Practice Committee surveyed members on professional practice and development activities (Silzer et al., 2008). They divided respondents into four categories: full-time practitioners ($n = 594$), part-time practitioners ($n = 96$), occasional practitioners who spend a day or less per week in practice ($n = 180$), and nonpractitioners ($n = 89$). Silzer et al. found that full-time practitioners said their most important activities are these:

- Consulting and advising clients
- Building relationships
- Managing work projects and administrative activities
- Implementing and delivering programs and/or tools
- Developing and designing systems, methods, and/or programs

The least important activities were

- Writing for a scientific journal
- Teaching courses or training programs
- Writing reports, articles, chapters
- Conducting primary research and data analysis

Proficiency in the latter group was gained in graduate school. Proficiency in actual consulting activities is learned on the job and through self-learning; the only professional activity that was reported as learned in graduate school was "Conducting selection and development assessments" (51%). Different from other fields of professional psychology, the concept of "supervision" as used in those fields does not exist in OBC psychology. OBC psychologists may have bosses and mentors who teach them the ropes and guide them to competence and success, but clinical-type supervision is never discussed in the literature and does not appear in the Silzer et al. survey.

PART II

Functional Competency—
Assessment for
Personnel Decisions

THREE

Legal and Professional Standards Related to Assessment and Personnel Decisions

No other area of practice in organizational and business consulting psychology is as contentious as the development, validation, and collection of information used in personnel decisions. The competent OBC psychologist working in this arena must be cognizant of laws, regulations, court cases, and professional standards. This chapter outlines this area of knowledge but does not attempt to provide a definitive presentation of all these areas.

Laws and Regulations Affecting Personnel Decisions

Tiffin (1943) noted that "recent social legislation" (p. 3) placed limits on employers that were unheard of even 10 years earlier. Tiffin had it easy compared to the myriad laws, regulations, executive orders, and court decisions faced by anyone working today in the human resources field. These rules emanate from all layers of jurisdiction from cities and counties to states and the federal government. These laws prohibit discrimination on the basis of race, gender, ethnic or national origin, age, and disability. There are, however, subtle differences in how each of these read and are administered. Some states and cities add other factors such as sexual orientation. Psychologists working with multinational organizations will also need to know the legal limits in each country or jurisdiction in which the organization recruits or places employees. Laws and regulations in many jurisdictions can be found on websites of enforcement agencies. For example, the U.S. Equal Employment Opportunity Commission lists the "laws prohibiting discrimination" as well as provides definitions of harassment, retaliation, and responsibilities of employers (http://eeoc.gov/, down-loaded October 6, 2008). This site also provides links to comparable sites covering laws in the European Union, the United Kingdom, Canada, and Hong Kong. The major U.S. laws relating to discrimination are shown in Table 3.1. Laws, regulations, and court decisions in the states can be found on websites managed by each state and often private organizations or foundations. For example, laws, regulations, and court decisions of California and Oregon can be found on www.eeolaw.org/ (downloaded October 6, 2008). A comprehensive treatment of discrimination law as it applies to employment is provided by Landy (2005). In addition, readers are encouraged to read the column "On the Legal Front" by Art Gutman and Eric Dunleavy, which appears in *The Industrial-Organizational Psychologist (TIP)*, the quarterly newsletter of the Society for Industrial and Organizational Psychology (SIOP). Current and past issues of *TIP* may be downloaded at SIOP.org. The laws and court decisions from all the jurisdictions in which an OBC psychologist may work form a complex body of knowledge that changes—sometime subtly, sometimes drastically—with actions from legislative bodies and the courts.

The level of competency required of the psychologist varies depending upon each one's role. All OCB psychologists need to have a basic understanding of the primary discrimination and equal employment laws[1] as well as the basics of laws relating to family leave and harassment. Psychologists who develop procedures for employment decisions, including hiring, firing, and promotion, must have a deeper working knowledge of issues relating to adverse impact and affirmative action. Those who have administrative responsibility for human resources must have even broader knowledge encompassing wage and hour laws, conditions of work, safety, and other matters beyond the scope of this book. Regardless of the role of the psychologist, it is necessary to maintain a boundary and not step into the role of proffering legal advice. Clients may wish to know if a particular action is "legal," is defensible, or will keep them "out of trouble." Based on the principle that telling people they may not rob banks is not the practice of law, it seems reasonable that the psychologist may describe how the services or technology have fit legal requirements or how the same issue has been dealt with in the past. However, a definitive answer must come from an

---

[1]   To simplify the writing, unless otherwise stated, I am going to refer to "laws" as including the various laws, regulations, and court decisions. This is consistent with everyday usage but is formally incorrect. Unfortunately, attempting to be formally correct results in an unreadable document, so I trust the reader can parcel out the meaning in this section.

TABLE 3.1 **The Major United States Laws on Discrimination**

LAW	COVERAGE	COMMENT
Title VII of the Civil Rights Act of 1964 (Title VII), which prohibits employment discrimination based on race, color, religion, sex, or national origin.	"…cover all private employers, state and local governments, and education institutions that employ 15 or more individuals. These laws also cover private and public employment agencies, labor organizations, and joint labor management committees controlling apprenticeship and training."	
The Equal Pay Act of 1963 (EPA), which protects men and women who perform substantially equal work in the same establishment from sex-based wage discrimination.	"… covers all employers who are covered by the Federal Wage and Hour Law (the Fair Labor Standards Act). Virtually all employers are subject to the provisions of this Act."	
The Age Discrimination in Employment Act of 1967 (ADEA), which protects individuals who are 40 years of age or older.	"… covers all private employers with 20 or more employees, state and local governments (including school districts), employment agencies and labor organizations."	
Title I and Title V of the Americans with Disabilities Act of 1990 (ADA), which prohibit employment discrimination against qualified individuals with disabilities in the private sector, and in state and local governments.	…"cover all private employers, state and local governments, and education institutions that employ 15 or more individuals. These laws also cover private and public employment agencies, labor organizations, and joint labor management committees controlling apprenticeship and training."	Recently updated in the Americans with Disabilities Act Amendments Act of 2008. Changes the law to counter some court findings by changing the definition of disability, major life activities, and the rights of those "regarded to have a disability".
Sections 501 and 505 of the Rehabilitation Act of 1973, which prohibit discrimination against qualified individuals with disabilities who work in the federal government.		
The Civil Rights Act of 1991, which, among other things, provides monetary damages in cases of intentional employment discrimination.		This act also bans the use of racial norming.

Note: Descriptions of laws and coverage taken verbatim from U.S. Equal Opportunity Commission, http://eeoc.gov/, downloaded October 6, 2008.

attorney who knows the intricacy of the laws in all of the jurisdictions that may be involved. I posed the question of where the role boundaries are to an I/O psychologist who is also an attorney, Gerald V. Barrett, he replied that attorneys typically do not have the mathematical, scientific, or even labor law background to fully understand the concepts and precedents in discrimination law, much less those related to psychometrics, validation strategies, and statistical analyses (G. V. Barrett, personal communication, October 17, 2008). Thus, the psychologist may have to take on the role of instructor and interpreter. In addition, Barrett agrees that it is reasonable to describe similar cases in which a company prevailed over a plaintiff. Presumably the psychologist would also include discussions of cases when the plaintiff prevailed. When it comes to a psychologist testifying in court as an expert witness, Barrett points out that different judges will have different standards for role boundaries.

Professional Standards

All psychologists working in the area of employment decision making should be intimately familiar with regulatory and professional standards. These include the federally produced Uniform Guidelines on Employee Selection Procedures (1978), the *Standards for Educational and Psychological Testing* (American Educational Research Association, American Psychological Association, & National Council on Measurement in Education, 1999), the Society for Industrial and Organizational Psychology's (2003) *Principles for the Validation and Use of Personnel Selection Measures*, the APA's *Report of the Task Force on Test User Qualifications* (APA, 2000), and the APA's (n.d.) *Rights and Responsibilities of Test Takers: Guidelines and Expectations*. An excellent background on the history, contents, disagreements, deficiencies, and positive qualities of most of these documents is provided by Jeanneret (2005).

UNIFORM GUIDELINES ON EMPLOYEE
SELECTION PROCEDURES

The Uniform Guidelines were adopted in 1978 and reflect the professional, political, and legal climate of the time. Being three decades old they are somewhat out of date in all three of those arenas. They do, however, provide some degree of uniformity across federal agencies. Prior to the Uniform Guidelines, each agency had its own set of standards or guidelines and these often conflicted with one another. In 1979 a set of Questions and Answers (Q & As) was published; generally these are included in discussions of the Uniform Guidelines. Jeanneret (2005) points out that the Uniform Guidelines do not cover all federal discrimination laws. The Age Discrimination Act of 1967, sections 501, 503, and 504 of the Rehabilitation Act of 1973 (regarding disability), and the Americans with Disabilities Act of 1991 are not included, nor are the Americans with Disabilities Act Amendments of 2008.

Jeanneret (2005) parsed the Uniform Guidelines and pointed to the most critical sections. Some of the most significant or interesting aspects are these:

- Discrimination and adverse impact. The definition of discrimination is that there is unjustifiable adverse impact. Adverse impact is explained as occurring when the selection ratio of a protected group is 80% that of the group with the highest selection ratio. Usually this is expected to be the nonprotected group (i.e., white males), but this is not always the case. The four-fifths (80%) rule is not logical on a number of counts and is often contravened by those bringing suit. At best it is a weak guideline for employers to keep an eye on.

- Fairness. If technically feasible, there should be an investigation into the fairness of a selection procedure. Under the Uniform Guidelines, such investigations are to be conducted using moderated multiple regression methods. Jeanneret (2005) points out that there have been no consistent research findings of slope or intercept differences comparing African American or Latino groups relative to whites on cognitive tests and job performance.

- Cutoff scores. The Uniform Guidelines state that cutoff scores should normally be set "so as to be reasonable and consistent with normal expectations of acceptable proficiency within the work force" (§5H). Jeanneret (2005) concludes that this implies that professional judgment is needed in setting such cutoffs.

- The bottom line. The Uniform Guidelines adopted an approach to adverse impact based on the bottom line, that is, the selection ratios after all hiring procedures have been completed. Only if adverse impact occurred did the individual components need to be subjected to review. However, the Supreme Court in *Connecticut v. Teal* (1982) determined that if any component of a selection system showed adverse impact, even if the bottom line did not, then the component was subject to review.

- Alternative selection procedure. If there are two selection procedures that can be shown to have substantially equal validity, the employer is to use the one with less adverse impact. Jeanneret (2005) notes that this has become more complicated with the passage of the Civil Rights Act of 1991, but in any event, there are problems with the definition of the terms *substantially equal validity* and *lesser adverse impact* as well as practicalities of utilizing some alternative procedures.

- Job-relatedness and business necessity. A procedure may be job related, that is, there is validity evidence supporting its use, or the procedure may be required by business necessity. This is often determined by laws and regulations. For example, nurses may be required to hold a nursing license in the state.

- Validity. For demonstrating the job relatedness of a selection procedure there needs to be acceptable validity evidence. The Uniform Guidelines describe the various types of evidence that would be acceptable. These are based on earlier version of the *Standards* and make no mention of the *Principles*. The OBC psychologist must be able to justify validity evidence for a procedure and generally should be able to explain why a method that differs from the Guidelines was used and can be relied upon.

STANDARDS FOR EDUCATIONAL AND PSYCHOLOGICAL TESTING

The *Standards* were published to permit "the evaluation of tests, testing practices, and the effects of test use" (AERA, APA, & NCME, 1999, p. 2). They provide a number of standards for a variety of uses; however, the *Standards* are careful to point out that judging the adequacy of a test does not require the literal satisfaction of every standard. The standards are presented in three parts. Test construction, evaluation, and documentation describe psychometric standards such as evidence for validity, reliability, and precision of measurement, norms, and documentation. It is reasonable to infer that any psychologists using tests should be able to comprehend the material in Part 1. Part 2 is concerned with fairness in testing. Various definitions of fairness are presented; a competent OBC psychologist should understand the rationales and problems with each of these. There are also standards on testing people from diverse linguistic backgrounds and testing people with disabilities. Part 3 is dedicated to testing applications, of which employment and credentialing constitute a chapter. Another application, testing for program evaluation and public policy may be relevant for some OBC psychology-related work. The other standards for psychological testing and assessment are largely oriented to clinical applications but may apply if the psychologist is doing career counseling or assessment for developmental purposes.

PRINCIPLES FOR THE VALIDATION AND USE
OF PERSONNEL SELECTION MEASURES

The *Principles* were issued by SIOP in 2003. The current document is the fourth edition. The content of the *Principles* is aspirational in character, rather than setting standards, and is intended to be "taken in its entirety rather than considered as a list of separately enumerated principles" (SIOP, 2003, p. 1). Further, the *Principles* do not interpret statutes, regulations, or case law. The document does provide

1. principles regarding the conduct of selection and validation research

2. principles regarding the application and use of selection procedures

3. information for those responsible for authorizing or implementing validation efforts

4. information for those who evaluate the adequacy and appropriateness of selection procedures (SIOP, 2003, p. 1)

The *Principles* provide guidance and do not replace appropriate training, are not exhaustive, and should not be seen as an attempt to "freeze" the field or prevent creative applications in the future.

It is difficult to summarize a document that is intended to be taken in its entirety. Jeanneret (2005) noted five critical areas: the analysis of work, validation, generalizing validity evidence, fairness and bias, and operational considerations. OBC psychologists working in the realm of employee decision making, including selection, assessment, appraisal, promotion, and termination, need to know the *Principles* and be able to describe how their work fits the framework within the *Principles*. Since litigation is common over the decisions that result from such decision systems, the psychologist must be highly detail oriented and clear about what was done and not done.

REPORT OF THE TASK FORCE ON
TEST USER QUALIFICATIONS

APA formed a task force on test user qualifications because there was some evidence that some test users were not qualified to appropriately select, administer, and interpret tests. The guidelines are aspirational because they are targeted to what APA considers the optimal use of tests. The guidelines provide generic qualifications and specific qualifications for "optimal use of tests in particular settings or for specific purposes" (APA, 2000, p. 8), which the guidelines term "contexts."

Generic Qualifications   The generic qualifications cover knowledge and skills that we would expect any properly trained psychologist to possess by the time he or she earns the doctorate. The guidelines cover several aspects of test usage:

1. Psychometric and measurement knowledge, including classical test theory and item response theory, when appropriate, and basic statistics

2. Selection of appropriate tests, including validity concerns

3. Administration procedures, including rights of test takers

4. Ethnic, racial, cultural, gender, age, and linguistic variables

5. Testing individuals with disabilities

Specific Guidelines for the Employment Context   The guidelines distinguish among testing for classification, description (i.e., assessment of current KSAOs), prediction, intervention planning, and tracking (of employees over time, as in criterion-related validation studies). To successfully fulfill these purposes the psychologist needs knowledge of and competencies in job analysis, identification of job families and clusters, labor agreements, federal and state laws, professional standards, performance measurement and the degree to which criteria may be dynamic, and the potential effects of the testing on the individuals. The guidelines indicate that these competencies are likely to be acquired in an integrated program of study targeted to testing in the employment context and through supervision.

RIGHTS AND RESPONSIBILITIES OF TEST
TAKERS: GUIDELINES AND EXPECTATIONS

This short document outlines the rights and responsibilities of test takers and also provides guidelines for testing professionals on how to ensure that test takers receive their rights and meet their responsibilities. The guidelines cover similar material as chapters in the *Standards* but are updated and do not provide specific standards. The guidelines tend to be procedural, making them useful to the professional in ensuring that the testing process is properly managed. The guidelines seem most appropriate for educational and clinical testing, but there are a number of features that

OBC psychologists should attend to in designing a testing program. For example, there are test taker rights guidelines about informing test takers of planned use of test results, general information about the appropriateness of the test for the purpose, how questions from test takers will be handled, how and when results will be available and at what cost, and that accommodations can be made for those with disabilities. The guidelines for professionals on test taker responsibilities provide potentially useful procedural guidance on how test takers should be instructed of their responsibilities prior to the test.

FOUR

Task Analysis, Job Analysis and Job Modeling

Assessment in OBCP is different in a very important way from assessment in other psychological specialties; at least two different types of assessments are required. At a minimum, the OBC psychologist has to assess both the job and the person. Indeed, in general, the first sign of an incompetent OBC psychologist would be performing assessments of people or designing an intervention without first analyzing the position or situation.[1] Contrast this with assessment assignments in other specialties: a clinical psychologist may be asked to assess cognitive and personality functioning as a means of diagnosing personality, cognitive, or mental disorders; a forensic psychologist may be asked to assess an accused person's competence to stand trial or assess an inmate in a prison regarding risks if released to the general population; or a clinical neuropsychologist may be requested to evaluate cognitive functioning and possible need for rehabilitation services for a patient with a traumatic brain injury. In all of these cases the environment is assumed and deviations below normal functioning may be of primary interest, although areas of strength are also noted. The OCB psychologist may be faced with a task of assessing people for fit in a constrained situation with the recognition that those who are deemed to be poor fits may well thrive in a different position and no dysfunction or pathology is implied.

---

[1] The exception would be doing assessments for career development counseling because in that activity the objective is to determine the sorts of environment a person might best fit and because the environmental assessments have commonly already been conducted and published.

A simple example can illustrate this dual assessment paradigm. A company offers specialized data and information services to other organizations, including custom designed integrated databases and web interfaces. Certain employees act in both sales and project manager roles: they make initial contact with a potential customer; assess the customer's wants and needs; outline and price a suitable system; and manage the development, implementation, and servicing of the product. To be successful in this position a person must have capabilities in sales including being personable and able to generate a feeling in the customer that the person is amiable and competent. The person must know how to design databases, interfaces, and related programs; how to estimate development and implementation time both for costing and delivery estimates; and be able to manage the development process as done by multiple engineers or computer programmers. This simple analysis indicates that certain personality factors may be important, that technical expertise must be assessed, and that project planning and management skills must be determined. Depending on the size of the company, labor market, and other factors, the organization may use a strategy of hiring people who already have all of these characteristics or it may have to hire people who have the potential to develop these competencies and train or develop them. The choice of strategy influences the assessment process. In the first instance it may make sense to assess existing skills through a simulation or knowledge test. In the second case the psychologist may need to rely on measures of ability to assess potential. Of course the actual decisions are more complex and require more systematic evaluation and knowledge of the methods of assessment of both jobs and of people. The remainder of this chapter concentrates on methods of job analysis and job modeling and the primary types of assessment apt to be employed by an OCB psychologist. It is important to remember that all of this work takes place in a framework of technological, financial, legal, and social constraints.

The earliest industrial psychologists recognized the need for an analysis of the job for which they were to help select employees. For much of the 20th century the emphasis was on "the" job or a family of jobs. For example, a factory may employ people in several mechanic positions, and these positions may even form one or more lines of progression over a career; a new employee may begin as a mechanic helper then progress into a specialty such as diesel mechanic, hydraulic systems mechanic, machine repair, and so on. All of these may require similar forms and levels of mechanical aptitude and so could be treated as essentially similar in a job family.

With rapid technological and social change it has become necessary to often go beyond the existing job or job family with the consequence that OCB psychologists may perform their analysis at larger clusters of jobs and may analyze jobs that do not yet exist. In addition, traditional job analysis can be expensive and time-consuming so it frequently makes sense to combine as many functions as possible in a given analysis. At a minimum the job analysis may inform both the employee selection and training processes. In large organizations the OCB psychologist may be performing job modeling, which combines the analysis of positions, workforce planning and analysis, and strategic planning (Schippmann, 1999). In large-scale endeavors the psychologist may need to interface with human resource professionals, managers from many functions, and even labor economists.

Task Analysis

A task analysis provides a step-by-step description of how to perform a task. It includes a description of the conditions in which the task is performed (e.g., extremes of temperature, timing factors, time of day), references referred to, performance standards, and the other information listed in Table 4.1. For example, a task might be "Rotates tires on commercial trucks." A step might be "Torques lug nuts to 50 foot pounds." In addition to providing input to training programs and procedures, a task analysis might be useful in identifying common points of errors or hazards present on the job and needed tools or other resources. For instance, the lug nut example indicates that the mechanics must have a torque wrench available and that it be calibrated so that 50 foot pounds of torque can be easily read. The task analysis would reveal that training to use certain tools or following critical procedures may be needed to ensure that the task is successfully completed. A critical aspect of any task analysis is the selection of *subject matter experts* (SME; commonly pronounced "smee"). SMEs need to be experienced and knowledgeable guides to the task. They must also be competent communicators and cooperative. One danger the analyst must watch out for is a tendency of supervisors to assign the most expendable members of their crews to be SMEs. The most expendable crew member is often the least experienced or the least capable, hardly fulfilling the "expert" part of SME. Outside of training program development, task analyses are relatively uncommon activities for the OBC psychologist. They are more commonly part of the work of an engineering psychologist.

TABLE 4.1 **Job Analysis Information for Training Program Development, Job Design, or Content Oriented Assessments**

The following list is information to be routinely collected prior to developing a content valid selection system and for use in guiding the development of training programs.

1. Tasks performed on the job.

2. Materials, tools, equipment used to perform the tasks.
   Identifying the materials, tools, and equipment often highlights knowledge, skills, or abilities needed to perform the job. As a simple example, a Commercial Vehicle Enforcement Officer (CVEO) may have to check tire pressures using a tire pressure gauge. This, in turn, would require sufficient manual dexterity and acuity of vision to use the gauge.

3. Communications and interpersonal contact.
   With whom do people on the job interact and in what manner (e.g., CVEO interacts with supervisor, co-workers, truck drivers, public, state patrol officers, judges, etc.). Different groups and types of contact may place different behavioral demands on a person. Samples of written communication should be collected (e.g., citations).

4. Documents and other written material used.
   These include manuals, instructions, specifications, regulations, job aids, electronic support systems, computer interfaces/programs. This establishes what sorts of documents job incumbents have to be able to read. Samples of the most important or most commonly used materials should be taken and a readability analysis conducted to determine reading difficulty.

5. Hazards and safety precautions encountered on the job.
   These may help identify or justify a knowledge, skill, or ability (KSA) as being needed for job performance.

6. Consequences of errors.
   This can easily establish the criticality or business necessity of KSAs.

7. Knowledge, skills, and abilities required.
   Also document when these are acquired (e.g., pre-hire, during training, after extended experience). Depending on the job, physical abilities may also be assessed.

8. Standards of performance (when applicable and available).

Job Analysis

Job analysis is performed to determine what people do in the job and what knowledge, skills, abilities, and other characteristics (KSAOs) are required to do the job well. There is some confusion inherent in distinguishing between what is a knowledge, a skill, or an ability, so KSAOs are now often lumped together as "competencies." In addition a comprehensive job analysis will often gather additional information depending on the purpose behind doing the analysis.

From the job analysis we can determine the following:

- Recruitment strategies for new personnel (sometimes)
- Selection methods for hiring successful employees

- Criteria for measuring job success
- Changes in job design to make people more productive and/or satisfied (sometimes)
- Job families and career paths useful for career planning, succession planning (sometimes) (Job families are jobs that require similar abilities and skills.)
- Determining compensation strategies and levels
- Motivational components present in the job situation or which might work for the people in the job (sometimes)

Although a "job" is an abstract concept, the job exists within a context of an organization, its culture, the workplace environment, and other factors that may vary from one situation to another. For this reason the SIOP *Principles* use the term *analysis of work.*

There are many forms of job analysis. Schippmann (1999) lists 15 prominent models that are in current use. A recent variation on job analysis, *competency modeling,* puts less emphasis on tasks and functions and more on worker-oriented constructs. Although widely discussed in the human resources field, competency modeling has a number of deficiencies that must be remedied in each use (Markus, Cooper-Thomas, & Allpress, 2005; Shippmann et al., 2000). Each job analysis model was developed to satisfy somewhat different objectives yet are typically used in a range of applications. It is unlikely that the typical practitioner would have expertise in each of these. They do share components in common and all OCB psychologists should have at least basic knowledge of these and expert levels of expertise in the methods most applicable for the type of practice they engage in. According to Schippmann, all job analysis models can be arranged using two sets of two continua. The first is worker-oriented versus job-oriented (McCormick, 1976, 1979). A worker-oriented analysis concentrates on the characteristics required of the worker. For example, in the database job described earlier an analysis might lead to the hypotheses that a successful employee would have an above average level of extroversion, a high numerical relations ability, knowledge of certain programming techniques, and know-how to write a sales agreement (remember this is a simple example). A job-oriented analysis concentrates on what is actually done on the job, such as calls on customers, prepares budget, uses Adobe Dreamweaver to design webpage, creates database using Oracle. A job-oriented analysis will also examine the conditions under which the job is performed just as is done in a task analysis. These range from physical (temperature, time of day, pace) to social (alone, with others, via teleconference), and other factors. A worker-oriented analysis has the advantage of permitting direct inferences to personal characteristics. Many worker-oriented analysis questionnaires will identify cognitive abilities or personality factors that appear to be related to job performance. Job-oriented analyses can require a somewhat greater inferential leap. Does calling on customers require an extroverted personality or elevated social skills? Such analyses do have the advantage of providing information useful for training and development purposes (we could train the budgeting process) and can highlight opportunities for job redesign or safety improvements.

The second pair of continua identified by Schippmann (1999) involve whether the analysis is conducted relying on rational (qualitative) methods or empirical (quantitative) approaches. The former methods include interviews, focus groups, and observation by the analyst. These methods can be especially useful in gaining an understanding of the position and the people in it. The empirical methods predominantly consist of questionnaire-based techniques.

Depending on the purpose of the analysis the focus might be on job-specific analyses—that is, a job as it exists within a particular organization or context—or an analysis of a job or occupation as it commonly is done in many organizations. Job-specific analyses are described by Harvey, Anderson, Baranowski, and Morath (2007). Their approach is similar to that previously shown in Table 4.1, but they are not concerned with tasks as the unit of analysis. They do develop task lists to guide the rest of the analysis and for the development of job specific questionnaires. Harvey et al. provide detailed instructions for developing these lists and accompanying surveys. The surveys typically ask how frequently each task is performed and how important the task is. Rating of the difficulty of each task is often added by other analysts. One note of caution: The lists are often made up using information from analyses of similar jobs at other sites. It is important to make sure that the tasks are actually performed at the new site. One consultant was embarrassed to discover that certain highly rated tasks were not performed by the employees on site; the tasks were so important that specialists were called in to do them.

An all-purpose rational technique that should be in every OCB psychologist's repertoire is the *critical incident technique (CIT)* (Flanagan, 1954). This method is useful in job-specific analyses and task analyses. Critical incidents are examples of extremely effective or ineffective job behaviors. These are collected from many people in a position to know firsthand about such incidents using the following four questions adapted from McCormick (1979):

1. What led up to the incident?
2. What exactly did the person do that was so effective (or ineffective)?
3. What were the consequences of the behavior?
4. Were the consequences within the control of the person?

Ideally a great number of critical incidents are collected and content analyzed for common factors or themes relating to performance. Harvey et al. (2007) describe a workshop-based method that requires far fewer incidents, but it must be done in conjunction with other techniques. It should be noted that the performance may or may not be due to an individual's competence or motivation. Fitts, for example, found that the design of cockpit controls confused pilots and led to crashes of U.S. Army Air Force planes in World War II (Dekker, 2006). Changing the design of the controls so they could not easily be confused was a more robust solution than changing training, selection, or discipline systems.

Rational methods can be time-consuming and may be expensive. They can also be impractical for those working in very large organizations, particularly firms with locations around the world. Regardless, the competent OCB psychologist should be able to justify why these methods were or were not used and how the psychologist is convinced the job analysis information is credible.

Schippmann's empirical dimension is primarily characterized by the use of surveys. Job analysis surveys may be custom made for the project, or standardized instruments may be employed. One of the most common of the latter is the *Position Analysis Questionnaire (PAQ)*, originally developed by McCormick, Jeanneret, and Meacham (1969) and since refined and revised several times. Use of an instrument such as the PAQ allows for preexisting information to be incorporated into the job analysis, a technique Peterson and Jeanneret (2007) refer to as the deductive method of job analysis. The PAQ can be used for traditional job analysis purposes as well as compensation analyses and a variation can be used for obtaining information useful for career development. PAQ data have been obtained from hundreds of thousands of jobs, thus providing an extensive database for comparative purposes. They provide information on expected abilities, skills, knowledge, and other personal characteristics as well as educational and training levels. The data also provide information useful for compensation studies. It is possible to conduct a complete analysis using just survey methods, although when possible I prefer to include job observation and interviews with experts and job incumbents to augment the information and create a context for understanding the position in the organization.

The Occupational Information Network (O*NET) is the replacement for the *Dictionary of Occupational Titles* (DOT; U.S. Department of Labor, 1991). The DOT was based on extensive nationally conducted job analyses that provided job descriptions, qualifications, and ratings on data, people, and things for thousands of jobs. With the O*NET the information available was expanded to include more information so that the following categories are now included (Peterson & Jeanneret, 2007):

- Worker requirements (including basic skills, cross-functional skills, knowledge, education)

- Experience requirements (level of education, training, experience, licensing)

- Occupational requirements (generalized work activities, work context, organizational context)

- Occupation-specific requirements (occupational knowledge; occupational skills; tasks, duties, machines, tools, and equipment)

- Occupation characteristics (labor market, occupational outlook, wages)

- Worker characteristics (abilities, interests and work values, work styles)

Much of the information in the O*NET was obtained using PAQ-like surveys, and anyone gathering occupational information may obtain survey materials from the O*NET center (Peterson & Jeanneret, 2007). Anyone doing a job analysis should start with the O*NET. It is especially useful when analyzing a job prior to performing an individual assessment. One must confirm the information for the specific organization since the information is generic. Much of the information on requisite business and consulting skills for OBC psychologists in chapter 10 was taken from the O*NET.

Since both rational and empirical methods can be effective but have limitations, some models of job analysis integrate both methods. Such hybrid models (Brannick, Levine, & Morgeson, 2007; Schippmann, 1999) can be especially useful since they provide both comparative quantitative information and the richness obtained through qualitative techniques. The ultimate choice of technique will depend on the type of job being analyzed and the purpose of the analysis. A resource for templates for job analyses of a variety of jobs is Prien, Goodstein, Goodstein, and Gamble (2009). Much of the job analysis work I have performed has been intended to guide training program development, job design, and the development of content-oriented selection or assessment procedures in technical jobs. Table 4.1 describes the job analysis methods I have found most useful for these purposes. The information can be gathered through a variety of means, including the following:

- Individual interviews with job incumbents
- Group interviews with job incumbents
- Interviews with supervisors, managers, subordinates, customers, and staff (e.g., training personnel)
- Critical incidents
- Questionnaires based on the interviews
- Standardized questionnaires
- Job element surveys
- Observation by the job analyst
- Measurements taken by the job analyst
- Review of archival materials, documents, and similar materials

Although some organizations will emphasize one method over another, well-done job analyses usually include three or more of these methods.

LEGAL REQUIREMENTS FOR JOB ANALYSIS

The Uniform Federal Guidelines on Employee Selection Procedures describe several aspects of job analysis information that should be documented. Table 4.2 summarizes these. The "status" column may be used to record the current status of job analysis information for a particular job.

JOB DESCRIPTIONS

Job descriptions are a common product of a job analysis. They are not as ubiquitous as a few years ago, with some organizations finding them overly confining and leading to a lack of flexibility. However, they do have their uses in designing organizations, staffing, and reducing role ambiguity. The format of job descriptions varies across organizations, but a few general principles apply. Brannick et al. (2007, p. 179) list four components that should be included in a job description:

1. Identifiers (job title plus other classifying information)
2. Summary (mission or objective statement)
3. Duties and tasks (what, why, how)

TABLE 4.2 **Summary of the Job Analysis Requirements of the Uniform Guidelines Requirements**

REQUIREMENT	CRITICALITY OF THE INFORMATION	STATUS; USED TO RECORD THE CURRENT STATUS OF JOB ANALYSIS INFORMATION FOR A PARTICULAR JOB
Description of the method used to analyze the job is provided	Essential	_____
The work *behavior* should be completely described	Essential	_____
- associated tasks	Essential	_____
- work products	Essential	_____
Measures of criticality and/or importance of the work behavior should be provided	Essential	_____
- method of determining criticality/importance described	Essential	_____
Operational definition of each knowledge, skill, ability	Essential	_____
Relationship between each KSA and work behavior	Essential	_____
- method used to determine relationship of KSAs to work behavior	Essential	_____
Work situation described		_____
- setting in which work behavior occurs		_____
- manner in which KSAs are used		_____
Complexity and difficulty of the KSA as used in the work behavior		_____

4. Other information, such as responsibility, including nature of supervision given and received; knowledge, including education experience or other minimum qualifications; and context, such as hazardous working conditions or rotating shift work

Job Modeling

Job analyses work well for describing jobs or job families. Job modeling involves taking the job analysis results and augmenting them with additional information to allow strategic planning of the workforce. A psychologist working in the realm of job modeling may be asked to analyze jobs that do not yet exist or that are changing so substantially that present workers may not be able to perform many of the functions without significant retraining. In some cases the change may be so great that it is unlikely that the employees who currently perform the job will be able to adapt, resulting in replacement of entire categories of the workforce or the reassignment of products or services to another location.

Job modeling is much more directed to the outside world and the future than is traditional job analysis. The OBC psychologist must be able to interact with strategic planners, market researchers, labor force analysts, technical experts, and even authorities on politics and law. For example, dental hygienists traditionally perform such tasks as cleaning teeth, doing minor or preliminary procedures, assisting dentists, and instructing patients in oral hygiene. In recent years some states have enlarged the scope of practice of licensed dental hygienists to include interpreting radiographs (X-rays), performing restorative procedures (filling cavities), and even practicing independently without a dentist on the premises. A large dental services organization in a state considering such a change needs to estimate the effects on practice policies, training, hiring patterns of dentists and hygienists, hiring standards of hygienists, whether trained hygienists will be available for hire, compensation strategies, risk management of professional liabilities, the marketing impact (Will this change allow lower charges and, hence, a larger pool of potential patients? Will current patients accept the change?) and numerous other factors.

Schippmann (1999) describes the process of job modeling as progressing through stages of NOW, WOW, and HOW. NOW involves examining the current macro, micro, and organizational environments in which the organization lives. Analyzing macroenvironments includes examining the social, economic, political/legal, and technological conditions. Microenvironment analysis will include gathering information about market conditions, competitors, customers, and suppliers. The organizational analysis will include the job analysis information along with documentation of current technological, financial, infrastructure, and contextual and cultural factors. Together these create a detailed snapshot of the organization as it is. WOW takes the vision of the organization's leaders and stakeholders to describe what could be. The HOW phase involves developing competitive strategies, strategic initiatives, and functional initiatives. The latter include research and development, purchasing, manufacturing or service delivery, distribution, finance, marketing, sales, and human resources. In this way all of the critical parts of the organization's anatomy are planning and implementing change in coherent and coordinated ways. The OCB psychologist in job modeling thus needs to have the ability to work with the broadest possible spectrum of people found in the business. The psychologist's fullest contribution will come from moving beyond analysis to assisting with the envisioning of the future and facilitating planning and change.

Outcomes of Job Analysis and Job Modeling

The activities of job analysis and job modeling provide documentation used in designing many types of programs. The nature of the reports generated by the analyst will depend on which purposes are most important. It can be expected that most work products from these analysis will emphasize specific job/job family requirements and associated employee characteristics since the most common purposes of job analysis and modeling are to support employee selection, training, and career development programs. Schippmann (1999) presents the structure of the results graphically in an appealing manner using two pyramids. The first is the work pyramid. At its base are the organizational vision, competitive strategy, and strategic business initiatives. The second level consists of work activities and work context. At the peak are required work competencies. The second pyramid addresses the people in the job. At the base are abilities, traits, and interests/values/motivations. The second level is made up of education and training as well as experience. The peak indicates the available competencies. Since both pyramids are capped by common terms it is relatively easy to move from one focus to the other. Whether or not Schippmann's approach or some other rubric is employed, a basic competency of the OBC psychologist is to arrange and present the results of an analysis in a useful manner. There should be clear connections between the job requirements, training needs, and other work factors and the requisite human qualities to be considered in selection, training, and other assessment or intervention.

FIVE

Assessment of Performance

William sells appliances for a locally based company with several stores. As a longtime employee he serves both walk-in customers and contractors who buy in bulk. The latter are given lower prices in exchange for the high volume of appliance purchases. William tracks his success primarily through his commissions and partly from the satisfaction he gets from helping his customers find the best solution for their needs and budgets. Because he has lived in the area his whole life, has a large network of friends, many dating back to his school days, and because he has worked for the store for over 20 years, William has a large number of repeat customers and referrals. This results in a relatively steady level of sales, so even though he does not maximize his revenue since he gives his friends the "contractor discount," he is a consistent performer. Harry, the sales manager, tracks total revenue but is also very interested in maximizing revenue per sale; one of his objectives for the year is to increase this figure by an ambitious percentage. William's use of the contractor discount for his friends brings in repeat business but does not result in the highest dollar value per sale. For this reason Harry does not see William as a high-performing sales person. Beth, the store manager, notes that William is always pleasant and professional, meets customers immediately when they enter the store, is usually willing to stay late or come in on a day off when needed, and helps mentor the younger sales people. She sees William as one of the store's most important employees and dreads the day he retires.

William's situation is an excellent illustration of the problems we encounter when attempting to measure performance. Different people have varying perceptions as to what constitutes success.

Defining and measuring success has plagued OBC psychologists for a century, so much so that the *Criterion Problem* is one of the fundamental issues of the field (Austin & Villanova, 1992). The outcomes from performance measurement activities fall into four main categories: between individual comparisons, within individual comparisons, system maintenance, and documentation (Cleveland, Murphy, & Williams, 1989). Performance measures used for comparing between individuals contribute to decisions on salary, promotion, termination, and similar actions. Those intended for within-individual comparisons are primarily used for identifying training and development needs and giving individual feedback. Performance appraisal systems intended for systems maintenance have outputs involved with goal attainment and clarification, evaluating the personnel system, and identifying organizational development needs. Documentation results in recording personnel decisions, meeting legal requirements, and providing criteria for validation research. This validation related output was less closely related to the documentation factor than the other two.

The activities associated with each of these seem similar, but because of contextual and impact factors they differ in important ways. For criteria used in administrative decision making, a fundamental requirement is meeting the demands of discrimination laws and creating the perception of procedural justice among employees. Administrative criteria must reflect the goals, purpose, and mission of the larger organization. A major concern is that they be fair and be seen as fair by the employees and the organization. The weighting of the components of success may change from time to time as the organization chooses to emphasize different sorts of behavior. For example, in a production job there are two classic criteria: productivity (how much is produced) and quality (how well it is produced). After a certain point these are often in opposition. One can produce more, but with lower overall quality, or one can take time and produce high quality, but less product. An organization may choose to reward productivity at one time and quality at another. In addition, in deciding who might get promoted, the organization might look beyond performance on the current job and instead assess potential for the next job. The latter would not constitute criteria, but employees often confuse performance measurement and the appraisal of potential, leading to feelings of inequity when performance is higher than future potential.

Developmental criteria are used to provide feedback to people about how well they are doing so they can improve. Success might be defined for the individual in terms of the types of assignments they have had, a comparison based on where they are in their career (e.g., rookie vs. seasoned performer), and their aspirations. A research-oriented measure or even an administrative measure may give people little information about how to improve their performance in the near and long term.

Research-oriented criteria differ from the others in that they are not influenced by discrimination law (so long as they are not used in administrative decision making). The quality of a research study is limited by the quality and relevance of the outcome measures the study employs. These criteria may be developed to reflect the researcher's interests and goals rather than those of the organization. In many cases, such as validation research, these coincide, and standards for criteria in such studies represent the union of the two sets. Criteria devised for research may be expensive to gather and tend to target one or a few facets of performance that the researcher is interested in. Understanding some aspect of performance may require the use of very narrow measures. Comparability between studies may require measures that are used in several different organizations but are of little interest to any given organization. Alternatively, some studies, particularly older ones, will use employee comparisons (who is the best worker, next best, etc., down to the worst). These comparisons would have little value for administrative or developmental purposes. (A rank ordering from best to worst might conceivably be used in determining some administrative decisions, such as the order in which layoffs occur, but usually other measures take precedence).

Although performance is often recognized as being multidimensional, administrative decisions often require these dimensions to be reduced to a single composite. There is no single best way to accomplish this (Schmidt & Kaplan, 1971). Schmidt and Kaplan distinguished between judgmental and statistical forms of combination. The former utilizes importance judgments to create a combination of dimensions that represent their utility to the organization. Statistical combinations rely on the results of a numerical analysis such as canonical correlation to obtain weights for dimensions that result in the highest possible relationship of the combination with another set of variables (e.g., predictors). Generally, judgmental combinations are preferred because they represent utilities of the client organization rather than the arbitrary weighting that results from statistical analysis, particularly with relatively small samples (i.e., fewer than thousands of cases). Even with judgmental composites, a good deal of information is lost, especially if the performance dimensions are relatively independent. It may be as important to know why a predictor relates to a form of performance as it is to know the degree of association. In such cases, Schmidt and Kaplan recommend not creating composites at all but concentrating on methods that provide the most understanding.

In considering performance measurement, two key concepts should be kept in mind at all times. First is Wallace's (1965) injunction that the primary use of criteria is for understanding. If we do not understand performance we can not efficiently shape it, and if we do understand it we can devise ever more powerful ways of managing it. The second key concept is Fiske's (1951) principle that criteria ultimately derive from values. A criterion measure has no meaning outside of the value system in which it is used. The OBC psychologist is not in a position to impose values (Harrison, 1974/1968; Kendler, 1993) but can help a client organization become aware of how its values are expressed, or not expressed, in its performance measurement system.

The Theory of Criterion Measurement

CONCEPTUAL AND ACTUAL CRITERIA

The conceptual criterion is the ideal that we would measure if we could. However, doing so is not always practical. For example, we might be interested in success over an entire career, but we don't have 20 to 40 years to wait. So we use a substitute measure, the actual criterion. We assume that the actual criterion is highly correlated with the conceptual criterion. A similar distinction was made by Thorndike (1949), who differentiated between ultimate, intermediate, and immediate criteria. The ultimate criterion is "the final goal of a particular type of selection or training" (Thorndike, 1949, p. 121). The ultimate criterion reflects the career of the individual, at least in the organization in question. It is "complex and always multiple" (p. 121). Immediate criteria are performance measures that are available soon after a person joins an organization. These are often training grades or successful completion of a probationary period. Intermediate criteria are measures that can be obtained after a person has been in the job long enough for behavior and performance to become reasonably stable. Thorndike considered immediate and intermediate criteria to be partial because they necessarily do not reflect all aspects of the ultimate criterion. In other words, they are to some extent deficient because some information is not available and so not included in the measure. Immediate and intermediate criteria may also be contaminated to some degree simply because the weighting of information may not reflect the weights in the ultimate criterion. It is important to be aware of the limitations of data.

CRITERIA FOR CRITERIA

Weitz (1961) discussed criteria for criteria in terms of time, type, and level. These remain important practical considerations and serve as a useful taxonometric scheme. Viswesvaren (2001) elaborated on the literature on criteria for criteria and identified three additional aspects: user acceptability, reliability, and construct validity of the measures.

Time   Consistent with Thorndike's (1949) distinction we need to consider the point in an individual's career at which criterion data are gathered. For most purposes you don't compare the performance of a person who has been on the job for one month with the performance of someone who has years of experience. Usually there is a learning curve (negatively accelerated and often consisting of multiple plateaus) and people differ in the slope of that curve. In addition, during the acquisition of skill, performance may be unstable, changing from day to day. For many purposes it does not make sense to take criterion measures until performance has leveled off and is stable.

Type   There are many different types of performance, each of which is relevant in some circumstances and not relevant in others. There are two basic types of criteria: hard and soft, otherwise known as objective and subjective (Smith, 1976). Most of us would intuitively prefer hard criteria—items such as total sales, amount produced, absenteeism, accidents, and so on. However, these are beset with problems and are difficult to use effectively.

Rothe (1978), in a series of studies over many years, studied productivity in many industrial occupations. These serve to illustrate the problems in hard criteria. He found that productivity varied greatly among individuals from day to day, week to week, and month to month. His examination of the causes of this variation revealed that it was more often due to situation factors (e.g., capacity of the machinery, availability of materials) rather than to differences between individuals. Although these causes of unreliability of criteria are important to know about and must be dealt with, psychologists are often more interested in individual performance and not machine performance. Getting a measure of productivity that takes into account the extra-individual factors in productivity is often too expensive and difficult to be practical. In addition, these sorts of measures are often misleading. For example, in factories, how people are scheduled to machines often makes a big difference in individual productivity. At times supervisors will schedule the best people on the best machines with the intent of maximizing the performance of both. Other times they will assign the best people to the worst machines thinking that those people can make the most of a bad situation. In these cases the productivity of the best people may be below that of the worst performers!

These days there are more jobs outside of factories than in them, but the issues with hard criteria remain. Many organizations use sales as a criterion, but to do so involves taking into account opportunity bias. One insurance company consistently experienced more sales in a few square blocks of Manhattan than in the entire state of Montana. In that company a sales person based in New York City would almost surely have greater productivity than one in Montana just because of the potential sales inherent in the location.

Other types of hard criteria are difficult to work with, even though there is no acceptable substitute. Behaviors that are relatively rare—for example, accidents and detected theft—are hard to work with statistically. You will find in the safety literature that accidents are notoriously hard to predict. This is not necessarily because of poor theorizing or poor measures of traits or behaviors thought to result in accidents, but because accidents tend to be few and far between. Really lousy drivers, for example, may have only two or three accidents in a couple of years, even though their probability of having one at any one time is far higher than that of the average person. Such rare events result in very low reliability and low correlations with other variables.

Overall, hard criteria have much appeal and often excellent face validity, but they present challenges for the creation of reliable and valid performance measures. It's not unusual for a creative and competent OBC psychologist to overcome challenges, but to establish that competence it is necessary that the logic and method be clearly explicated.

Frequently the problems with hard criteria force us to use subjective criteria, usually ratings by supervisors or other people in a position to evaluate performance. Essentially we are asking these people to take into account all of the factors that limit the value of hard criteria and somehow make a judgment of each person's performance. I don't know exactly how people do this, but it does seem to work. While it would be quite difficult to program a computer to computationally make these adjustments, trained raters seem to be able to do so quite readily. The key is training of the raters. Untrained raters tend to give unreliable results, whereas trained raters tend to agree well with one another. More important, the ratings tend to agree well with long-term measures of success.

Soft criterion measures typically take the form of rating scales. The many types of rating scales are covered in many books. Newman, Kinney, and Farr (2004) and Pulakos (2007) provide useful surveys of the most common formats; graphic rating scales, behaviorally anchored scales, behavioral summary scales, and mixed standard scales. The type to use depends on the situation and organizational tradition. Raters must accept the format and it must ideally be easily convertible to allow for feedback. For several decades a good deal of research was conducted to determine the psychometric characteristics of various formats, most notably their resistance to various types of rater error (see Thomas & Meeke, 2010, for a brief discussion of rater errors). Rater errors, such as halo effect, lenience, severity, and others, have not been shown to seriously affect the validity of performance ratings (Murphy & Balzer, 1989; Murphy, Jako, & Anhalt, 1993). In any event, Landy and Farr (1980) concluded that no rating scale format was superior to the others in resistance to errors and called for a moratorium on research on rating formats.

Multisource ratings, or 360 degree assessments, became popular in the 1980s and 90s. The idea is to get performance ratings from peers, subordinates, supervisors, customers, and suppliers and combine them all into a set of appraisal documents (Balzer, Greguras, & Raymark, 2001). This sounds like a great idea, but it has large logistical problems. Contamination as described when the ratings are to be used for administrative versus developmental purposes is a problem when data are collected from peers and subordinates. In addition, peers may be in competition with each other, making the ratings suspect. Not often discussed in the literature, but discussed among raters, is the potential for political fallout; there is a fear that candid observations may be traced by the boss to the subordinate with consequent repercussions. In addition, peer and subordinate raters may not have all the information needed to make wise judgments. This is a common concern I have heard from many supervisors who are required by company needs, policy, or their own superiors to take unpopular actions without being able to provide adequate explanations to their subordinates. Today 360 degree appraisals are largely used for developmental purposes. If used for decision making, then the guidelines from Bracken and Timmrick (1999) apply and should be referenced.

Level   Level refers to the point at which we consider outcomes or behaviors as representing success, what is considered failure, and what is in-between. This is completely open to judgment, but judgment tempered by experience and business necessity. Frequently the level changes over time.

What was considered adequate in the past is no longer satisfactory. Thus, the level changes, and workers and management must change with it. In some organizations this is seen as performance creep or "raising the bar" and can be met with opposition, both overt and covert in nature.

Sometimes new performance levels in part of an organization result in unexpected problems in another part. For example, in one company production was limited by the machinery in the factory. The sales force could achieve satisfactory performance by selling enough work to maximize the production of the factory. However, new equipment and new procedures greatly increased the productive capacity of the factory. The sales force needed to climb to far higher levels of performance to keep the factory busy and to meet company goals. Although this level of sales was possible given the market, the sales people had a difficult time adapting to the new requirements because marketing systems and techniques were not up to the increased demands.

User Acceptability   When raters and the rated do not believe criterion measures to be appropriate it will not take them long to derail the system. Forced choice and mixed standard scales were devised to eliminate halo and manipulation of the system by raters. It did not work (King, Hunter, & Schmidt (1980). Viswesvaren (2001) reviewed the research on this issue and concluded that if people know about the standards, if there is a hearing process perceived as being fair, if standards are consistently applied across individuals, and if raters are involved in the development process there may be better acceptance. Achieving all this is not a panacea; it is hard to see how to make this work in many organizations in which people are hired based on differing types of expertise, and jobs become molded to the capacity of the individual.

Reliability   Reliability is important for all types of criteria, and rating scales present their own challenges. Viswesvaren (2001) reviewed the issues related to reliability of criteria in general. Unfortunately, he places more value on internal consistency than is warranted given the nature of most rating systems. Interrater reliability is often seen as the most critical form for ratings, but it is subject to inflation due to various forms of rater error (cf. Thomas & Meeke, 2010). Training of raters can help alleviate some of this problem. In addition, there is the problem of finding multiple raters who are roughly equally informed of an employee's performance. Even the best rater training cannot compensate for differential opportunities to observe and discuss performance such as exists between different levels of administrators.

Construct Validity | Viswesvaren's (2001) review indicated that attempts to demonstrate the construct validity of criterion measures through convergent validity procedures have not yielded particularly impressive results. A lack of discriminant validity across rating scales is usually blamed on rater errors or judgmental errors. Unfortunately, psychologists have a tendency to declare that when others behave in a manner that is not in accord with our expectations it is due to errors on the part of the actors. Seen from another perspective, the behavior may be completely reasonable and rational. So, the lack of discriminant validity may be due to a lack of distinction between constructs, not the failures of those who provide the data.

Thorndike (1949) identified three aspects of the construct validity of criterion measures: criterion deficiency, criterion contamination, and criterion relevance. Criterion deficiency is the extent to which the conceptual criterion contains aspects of job performance that are somehow missing from the measured, actual criterion. For example, an important part of a sales manager's job might be developing the skills of sales people. If we use a measure of sales volume in the manager's region we will probably miss this aspect of performance unless the measure is taken over a very long time and there is not much turnover in sales people during that time. Criterion contamination is the extent to which the actual criterion includes facets that are not supposed to be measured. For example, if the actual performance measure consists of ratings by supervisors (the most common type) and the ratings are influenced by sexual or racial bias, then the criterion is contaminated. Criterion relevance is simply the extent to which the conceptual and actual criteria match. We never know the exact degree of relevance, but it is usually estimated through the judgment of SMEs. When a criterion measure is brought into play it is necessary to describe how each of these is controlled, or not controlled when it is not possible to corral sources of invalidity.

All criterion measures should be as free as possible from contamination and deficiency; they should be as reliable and valid as possible. Different forms of contamination may impact criterion data collected for different reasons. Jawahar and Williams (1997), among others, found that performance ratings collected for administrative purposes, such as determining salary or promotion, tend to be more lenient than ratings collected for developmental or research purposes. It is important for the OBC psychologist to recognize how situational and political pressures can impact performance ratings (Kozlowski, Chao, & Morrison, 1998).

One common source of criterion deficiency is the failure to include contextual performance (Borman & Motowidlo, 1993), or what some call organizational citizenship behavior (OCB). OCB includes productive behaviors such as filling in for an ill colleague, cleaning up the lunch room, restocking shelves, and arriving early or staying late to serve a customer's special needs. OCB also includes counterproductive behaviors such as back-stabbing, taking needed resources away from a co-worker, spreading gossip and rumors, and retaliating against real or imagined slights. Many of the "dark side" behaviors discussed in chapter 8 come under this heading. Kaufman and Borman (2004) described the issues regarding the dimensionality of OCB and how it can be effectively and practically measured. Since behavior that is recognized and rewarded tends to predominate and unrecognized efforts tend to extinguish, if positive OCB is important for an organization's success it must be included in any performance assessment system. Similarly, if counterproductive behaviors harm the organization, which seems obvious, they too should be included the measurement and reward systems, albeit in a negative manner.

SIX

Assessment for Employee Selection, Promotion, and Termination Programs

Psychologists have been involved with employee selection for well over 100 years. Even at the earliest stages, psychologists expected that the use of scientific methodologies would enhance productivity. Since science demands systematic methods, the early industrial psychologists insisted that any tests or other instruments developed by psychologists for use in hiring have demonstrated empirical relationships with job success. Thus, the standard models for validation were developed in a form recognizable to current psychologists by the mid-1920s. As recently as 1998, Guion (1998) attributed his basic approach and methods in personnel selection as coming from Freyd (1923). Today's workplace would astound Freyd and others of his era. Through technological change, economic advance to a service and information economy, changes in demographics and social roles, civil rights, and immense changes in the science of psychology, the basic pattern in many ways remains much as it was so many decades ago. The psychologist is expected to provide evidence that the methods employed in selection, promotion, and classification procedures are helpful in making better decisions. The methods may be statistical/empirical (criterion-related validation, validity generalization), judgmental (content validation), or empirical/theoretical (construct validation). They are all forms of evidence under one validity umbrella, although there is some controversy over the status of the content strategy as providing validity evidence versus being a method of test construction (Murphy, 2009). Today's OBC psychologist must have many competencies far beyond those expected of our forebears. In addition to knowledge of validation and assessment techniques, today's psychologist must be knowledgeable about social trends, demographics, culture, and, most important, the laws, regulations, and court decisions that constrain personnel actions.

Although the focus is on selection, much of the following also applies to other personnel decisions including classification, promotion, and termination. Of course slightly different technologies are employed for these, and the competent psychologist working in those areas is cognizant of the difference. Professional and legal standards were covered in chapter 3. They permeate all aspects of personnel decision making and could be cited every other sentence. The fact that they are not cited at every opportunity in this chapter is only a consequence of trying to keep the chapter as readable as possible.

Criterion-Related Validation Strategies

The basic approach to criterion-related validation was described by Guion (1998): Analyze jobs and organizational needs, choose a criterion, form predictive hypotheses, select methods of measurement, design the research, collect data, evaluate results, and justify the use of the selection procedure. These methods have been augmented over the decades as many more sophisticated methods of establishing validation evidence have been developed and the meaning of validation itself has evolved (cf. McPhail, 2007). But the basic ideas remain. When using an empirical approach to validation, small sample studies do not suffice for generating empirical validity evidence. Conditions often preclude predictive studies, leaving only concurrent approaches as practical options in spite of controversy over the meaning of the results (Barrett, Phillips, & Alexander, 1981; Guion, 1998). Faced with small or inappropriate samples, the psychologist must use more creative methods of demonstrating empirical relationships between predictors and criteria. The volume edited by McPhail (2007) provides current information on the use of job component validity, synthetic validity, and validity generalization for utilizing existing validity information in new situations. Some of these concepts have been around for decades, but it has taken years to develop the technology allowing for their common use. McPhail's book also presents recent methods for developing new evidence for validity, such as consortium studies. Because there are highly technical aspects of each of these methods, it is not feasible that all OBC psychologists have operational competencies in all these methods. Another newly developed method is the use of neuronetwork analysis (Scarborough & Somers, 2006). This method moves away from the traditional reliance on correlational methods and substitutes a nonlinear pattern recognition model. It is controversial in that the model may make predictions that are difficult to understand, and, perhaps hard to replicate. An OBC psychologist who is involved with test validation and usage should be aware of these methods and competent in the ones employed in the projects in which the psychologist participates. The psychologist should, of course, be able to justify the methods used in light of the project goals and resources.

Content Validation Strategies

For many years content validation was perceived to be a method that lacked scientific rigor and so was referred to with some embarrassment by I/O psychologists. Like Cinderella, content validity was hidden away, doing the dirty work, while criterion-related validation got all the attention. This changed in the 1970s as princes such as Guion (1974) placed the glass slipper on content validity and elevated it to royal status.

The content validation procedure depends heavily on the job analysis. The job analysis establishes the KSAOs, defines the content domain to be covered, and indicates the relative importance of each KSAO, task, or outcome. If SMEs are used, a procedure for identifying those who are sufficiently knowledgeable to contribute to the project must be established. Once a content domain is clearly defined, it is necessary to determine the selection procedure (SIOP, 2003). The possibilities may include a broad range of methods including written or oral tests (often specially developed for the particular use), simulations and job samples, evaluations of prior experience and education, and interviews. There can be unexpected difficulties for the unwary in this process. SMEs and consequent job analysis results may refer to KSAOs developed as a consequence of training or experience after hire. These would be off-limits to a test or other selection procedure. For example, R. S. Barrett (1992) gives the example of a school principal job in a district where only the principal deals with the teacher's union. Barrett stated it would be inappropriate to test an applicant for promotion on dealing with the union. The competent OBC psychologist would recognize that even though specifics of dealing with the union would not be appropriate for a test, the job analysis might reveal that skill in negotiating, conferring with experts such as attorneys or human resource professionals, or similar skills could be developed in earlier positions and contribute to success in dealing with the union. Similarly, it is sometimes thought necessary to test on material that is easily looked up or rarely actually done on the job. R. S. Barrett gave an example of police officers needing to refer to lists of other states with reciprocity agreements with the home state on traffic violations. The list might seem like a good candidate for a content valid promotion test, but most officers simply kept a copy of the list in their pocket and referred to it as necessary. The requisite knowledge is to know the information is important and where to find it, not what is on the list. Knowledge of the rules of engagement with an armed and dangerous suspect could be testable since there likely would be little chance to reference the information. It is important that the test measure what is actually used. Barrett gave the example of a firefighter setting the pressure on a pumper based on experience and feedback from the person wielding the nozzle rather than using an extensive knowledge of theoretical hydraulics. Testing on material that is rarely actually used on the job is a common trap when SMEs choose to show off. The psychologist is not in a position to second guess the technical aspects of the job, but he or she should be asking, "Does anyone ever actually do that in that manner?"

Subject matter experts will be needed in the development or adaptation of tests, simulations, and job samples. They may help generate items, scenarios, and similar components and will be very important in the development of scoring rubrics. The SMEs will typically judge the relevance of each component and the correct mode(s) of response. Items and such that cannot be shown to be important or for which there is little agreement on scoring need to be eliminated or modified. Obviously, interrater reliabilities of these judgments need to be calculated and be sufficiently high to allow the process to be defended. Many psychologists ask SMEs who are members of protected groups to evaluate the components to identify any unintentional bias built into the test. Even if there are no incumbent SMEs from these groups to serve, it is still desirable to conduct this sort of screening with non-SMEs if necessary.

Once the test, simulation, or interview is developed, pilot testing should be done to ensure that it operates as planned. This may include training of observers or interviewers. Ideally, indications of potential adverse impact can be detected at this phase and changes to the instrument made if possible. Once the test is operational these checks need to continue to protect the client organization against claims of illegal discrimination.

CUTOFF SCORES

Without empirical data showing the relationship between scores and job performance, any cutoff scores will have to be determined through a judgmental process. Frequently these cutoffs are the target of discrimination complaints. Cascio, Alexander, and Barrett (1988) reviewed the legal and professional issues related to the setting of cutoff scores. They concluded that there is no single "best" method for setting cutoff scores in all situations. Once the validity of the measure is established based on job analysis and the development process, it is important to set cutoff scores high enough that they will capture minimal performance standards. Cascio et al. also recommend that the cutoff scores be "consistent with normal expectations of acceptable proficiency within the workforce" (p. 22). A later review by Kehoe and Olson (2005) examined cutoff scores with regard to legal and regulatory requirements, case law, professional standards, and a variety of methods; some have developed or have come on line in the two decades since the Cascio et al. review. The conclusions were about the same as in the earlier review, although Kehoe and Olson gave more emphasis to the determination of the threshold level of work behavior and how the test score corresponds to that threshold. They also noted that cutoff scores may be adjusted to reflect various trade-offs between job performance and other organizational interests such as the labor market. However, they recommended against lowering cutoff scores solely to reduce adverse impact, stating that such actions were unlikely to be supported by the courts.

Tests used for certification or licensure purposes are typically developed using content validation procedures. This process has its own chapter in the *Standards,* and psychologists who work in the area of certification and licensing should be aware of the differences between professional standards for these tests and others. It is clear that the same issues exist for setting cutoff scores, and Kehoe and Olson (2005) recommend close attention to the relationship between setting a threshold for behavior in the profession and setting an appropriate test cutoff. Since most candidates who fail a test are permitted to try again, alternate forms are typically developed over time. Developing equivalent alternate forms is a science in itself. A complete presentation of the methods and problems in this process is given in Dorans, Pommerich, and Holland (2007). A recent study of certification examinations for radiology technicians found that scores on retest tend to increase scores about the same amount regardless of whether the applicants took the same test or a parallel form (Raymond, Neustel, & Anderson, 2007). One possible result of these findings is that low-volume credentialing bodies may be able to avoid the cost of developing parallel forms. However, before this decision is made, some replication of the Raymond et al. study is desirable.

MINIMAL QUALIFICATIONS (MQs)

Setting minimal qualifications (MQs) for a job is similar to the problem of setting cutoff scores in a content valid selection system. Levine, Maye, Ulm, and Gordon (1997) presented a procedure based on the content validation process for setting minimal experience, training, and education standards for jobs in a large state hospital. They were able to demonstrate satisfactory levels of content validity for MQs for several jobs. A similar process was followed by Buster, Roth, and Bobko (2005) in another state. The results of this project were challenged in federal court and upheld, giving added incentive to follow this procedure. We can expect that a competent OBC psychologist will describe and defend the method of setting cutoff scores for any minimal qualification, test, simulation or job sample, or interview regardless of the method of validation.

Construct Validation

Construct validity is evaluated through the entire research corpus on a test; the issue is whether scores represent the construct of interest or are contaminated or deficient in some way (Cronbach & Meehl, 1955). Although construct validity is considered synonymous with validity in the *Standards*, demonstrating this in an unequivocal manner is not easy. The Uniform Guidelines include construct validation as a possible source of validity evidence, but the wording is confusing and inconsistent with professional standards (Guion, 1998; Jeanneret, 2005). The type of evidence required includes demonstrations that characteristics (constructs) important for job success identified through job analysis have been related to performance and other constructs in other studies. Thus, this becomes an issue of validity generalization, synthetic validity, job component validity, or transportability of validity evidence. Since each of these has clearer procedures and practical theory associated with it, it generally makes sense to concentrate justification for test usage on one or more of them than it does to rely on a case for construct validity. An exception to this lies in individual assessments, as described in the next section.

Individual Assessment

Psychologists have performed individual assessments on job candidates and people being considered for promotion for generations. Although many I/O psychologists engaged in this practice, it was not widely discussed until relatively recently because it was seen as somewhat questionable since none of the validity models current at the time could be applied. In addition, it seemed that many psychologists doing these assessments were using unstructured interviews or clinical instruments and did not bother with a job analysis (Ryan & Sackett, 1987). Up to that point a technology acceptable to the mainstream had not been developed even though there were nationally known consulting firms that regularly developed their proprietary instruments and methods.

There are three key problems in the process of individual assessment. The first is that with only a few candidates, it is not possible to perform any sort of empirical work beyond the job analysis and job modeling. Deductive methods of job analysis and information from sources such as the O*NET can provide guidance on personal characteristics believed important for success. The psychologist who chooses to measure the characteristics in those being assessed still must justify the use of particular instruments or techniques. Recently Prien, Schippmann, and Prien (2003) have presented a workable and practice method of designing an individual assessment based on job and competency modeling methodology. Their book provides templates for job analysis, likely competencies, and some direction in how to match assessment instruments to the competencies. It is an invaluable resource for OBC psychologists engaged in individual assessment.

The second key problem in individual assessment is more difficult to resolve. It is the breadth of the criterion. Although the job analysis will indicate the types of performance that are expected, in the high-level positions for which individual assessments are commonly performed, criteria are necessarily diffuse. The type of high performance that was originally expected may not be possible once a person is in office and external conditions change. Abraham Lincoln provides a good example; had the American people hired a psychologist to assess Lincoln prior to his presidency, the report probably would have concentrated on Lincoln's ability to build infrastructure such as canals, manage Congress, build foreign trade, and, perhaps, constrain the growth of slavery. The assessor would have missed completely Lincoln's ability to deal with insurrection and rebellion; choosing and evaluating military leaders, including one who eventually ran against him; rallying the Union during its darkest days; and using the elimination of slavery in rebelling states as an economic incentive to end the rebellion. On the other side, referring to recent political scandals involving state governors, an assessor might have tried to examine Illinois's Rod Blagojevich's propensity for corruption. It is doubtful that an assessor would have examined Eliot Spitzer's moral turpitude that led to the end of his governorship of New York. For better or worse, OBC psychologists do not assess political figures, but similar problems plague them in industry. The number of ways of failing as a corporate leader are infinite and there are only so many factors that can be evaluated even in the most extensive and expensive assessment. For obvious reasons, cases of individual assessment are not published, and even if they were, the hiring board's tolerance for false negative versus false positive errors could make the difference in who gets hired. Thus, we can't learn from others' past experiences at the highest levels. A very interesting ethical dilemma is what to do with assessment information that is damaging to the candidate but concerns potential behavior not established by the job analysis.

The third problem lies with the psychologist. According to Somerville (1998), the skills of interpreting results from proper assessment instruments are learned relatively quickly by doctoral-level psychologists, although learning to use the data wisely can take years. Interviewing skills take longer to learn and "it is a significant blunder to take them for granted" (Somerville, 1998, p. 238). For psychologists originally trained as clinicians there is a significant tendency to rely on models of pathology, "thereby doing the individual and the company grievous damage" (Somerville, 1998, p. 238). The psychologist must learn about the job, organization, industry, and about his or her own tendencies in interpreting others' behavior. According to Somerville (1998), it takes 2 to 3 years and 50 to 100 assessments under the supervision of an accomplished practitioner to become a capable assessor.

Common Assessment Instruments and Methods for Employee Selection

There are literally hundreds, perhaps thousands, of tests and other methods of assessing potential employees. The volume edited by Thomas (2004) contains descriptions of the most common tests and methods used in selection. That section of the volume runs over 300 pages with chapters provided by a number of authors with special expertise, so it obviously is not feasible to cover all instruments and methods in this chapter. Many of the methods may be employed in large-scale employee selection programs and in individual assessment. As a practical matter only one or a few paragraphs on selected methods are possible in this book.[1] Of course, the

---

[1] In order to keep this book to a reasonable size (and given the number of possible citations for this section, which could run into the thousands), I will rely heavily on

competent OBC psychologist will be able to evaluate, choose, and justify the use of whatever measures were employed.

COGNITIVE ABILITY

The testing of cognitive ability and intelligence has a long history in psychology. Tests of general mental ability (GMA) on average have the highest correlations with job performance of any type of measure (Grubb, Whetzel, & McDaniel, 2004). Unlike clinically oriented intelligence tests, tests of GMA are relatively easy to administer and score with relatively inexpensive paper and pencil and computer/Internet versions available. GMA tests may measure a general intelligence factor (*g*) or multiple factors. All else being equal, their use could be widespread in virtually all organizations. Unfortunately, GMA tests have a serious limitation that prevents this widespread usage. There is a very large score difference between racial groups; an overall effect size, *d*, of about 1.0 can be found in meta-analyses of Black-White differences. This difference is somewhat moderated by type of job or industry, but it remains high nonetheless (Roth, Beviev, Bobko, Switzer, & Tyler, 2001). There is a somewhat smaller difference between "Hispanic" test takers and White test takers.[2] There is not a corresponding difference in the prediction of job performance, indicating that the tests may be used for predictive purposes equally well across groups. The costs of doing so are potentially serious. It reduces the opportunity to hire a diverse workforce and, second, exposes the organization to probably expensive claims of discrimination. These claims, even when disproven, are expensive both in legal fees and in poor publicity, so many organizations shy away from using tests that may bring them on. Grubb et al. (2004) write that this is due to a bias in the law, not the tests. Unfortunately, that may be the worse situation since the law is less amenable to change than are the tests.

An alternative is to use cognitive ability tests that are more targeted to specific aspects of selected jobs. Mechanical ability tests and spatial ability tests used to predict performance in engineering, technical, or mechanically

---

the information in Thomas (2004) and cite the information in chapters in it whenever possible. In general, I will refrain from citing particular tests or instruments to avoid replicating the earlier book.

[2] There are many separate cultural groups who unwittingly and unwillingly are lumped together into the general category "Hispanic" or, sometimes, "Latino." Although they share a common language of Spanish (sometimes as a second language), they are culturally distinct. It is not clear that studies that engage in this combining of cultures are particularly informative, although it is often a reaction to small sample sizes from any one culture.

involved jobs are examples (Muchinsky, 2004). As expected, meta-analyses have found these to be less valid for jobs in general, but more valid for the jobs for which they are intended. Mechanical aptitude tests are basically tests of applied physical principles such as leverage, pulleys, and gears. Spatial ability tests assess the extent to which the test taker can envision the components of figures or see how a three-dimensional object may be depicted in two dimensions. As with tests of GMA there are problems with adverse impact, but in this case the differences in scores lie across genders rather than race or ethnicity. This is not difficult to explain given the traditional differential opportunities and tendencies for boys and girls to engage in mechanical pursuits. A potential contributor to the difference is the drawings used in the figures in many mechanical aptitude tests; they tend to be outdated with old cars and out of fashion garments that Muchinsky suggests may differentially affect test takers depending on gender. In the past, some organizations used separate scoring procedures for men and women. That was outlawed in the Civil Rights Act (CRA) of 1991, so test users are faced with the dilemma of choosing between "high validity" and "high adverse impact" (Muchinsky, 2004, p. 25). The OBC psychologists must be aware of these decision points and make sure the client organization is informed of potential consequences of the use of these tests.

Consistent with the use of specialty cognitive tests such as mechanical aptitude and spatial ability, there are entire sets of tests of several specific abilities known as multi-aptitude test batteries (Doverspike, Cober, & Arthur, 2004). The aptitudes measured by these batteries vary somewhat but are typically comparable to those reported by the U.S. Department of Labor's (DOL) General Aptitude Test Battery (GATB). According to Doverspike et al. (2004, p. 38), the nine factors reported by the GATB are

1. General Learning Ability (Vocabulary, Arithmetic\Reasoning, Three-Dimensional Space)

2. Verbal Aptitude (Vocabulary)

3. Numerical Aptitude (Computation, Arithmetic Reasoning)

4. Spatial Aptitude (Three-Dimensional Space)

5. Form Perception (Tool Matching, Form Matching)

6. Clerical Perception (Name Comparison)

7. Motor Coordination (Mark Making)

8. Finger Dexterity (Assemble, Disassemble)

9. Manual Dexterity (Place, Turn)

In the 1980s, the DOL began encouraging states through state employment agencies to use the GATB in the selection of employees for all jobs. Because the GATB had racially adverse impact common to cognitive ability tests used in industry, the DOL used separate norms by race. This ran into legal challenges and eventually the GATB program was discontinued. However, by then employers had a need for multi-aptitude test batteries, so several batteries were developed or updated. In addition, the U.S. military has used its own multi-aptitude batteries for many years and continues to do so. Because targeting specific tests to components of jobs identified in job analysis provides both a modicum of face validity and easier to understand justifications for test use, while maintaining reasonable validity effect sizes, it is likely that multi-aptitude batteries will continue to be used in many work settings.

BASIC SKILLS

At times a job analysis may reveal the importance of the basic academic skills that are supposedly possessed by high school graduates or even drop-outs who completed more than elementary school. Unfortunately, some people who have educational credentials do not have the skills in reading, writing, mathematics or arithmetic, speaking, listening, or learning that the diploma implies. Fortunately, some people without the diploma do have skills at an adequate level to achieve success in certain positions. In such cases the psychologist may choose to validate and rely on tests designed to measure these basic skills. A number of basic skills batteries (Cornwell, 2004) are available with sufficient psychometric properties and validity evidence to permit their consideration as possible predictors, particularly for lower level jobs. Because the basic skills batteries have been developed or updated relatively recently, efforts have been made to reduce adverse impact. Still, the OBC psychologist needs to evaluate the battery for the situation for appropriateness, validity, fairness, and the possibility of adverse impact.

PERSONALITY AND INTERESTS

To many laypeople, psychology is the study of personality, both abnormal and normal. Although virtually all psychologists would disagree with this concept, it is sufficiently widespread that many requests for consultation are to help select the employees with the "right personality" for the job and to keep out those with the "wrong personality." Early conceptualizations of personality concentrated on traits or needs without much consideration of situations. An exception was Allport (1937), who distinguished between *cardinal, central,* and *secondary traits.* Cardinal traits are always in play in influencing the individual's behavior, central traits are normally active, and secondary traits come into play only when the situation allows or calls for them. There is a lot to be said for Allport's taxonomy, but because whether a trait is cardinal, central, or secondary is idiosyncratic to each individual, it was not very useful in traditional selection paradigms. Simply correlating trait scores of a number of people against job performance without regard to situation or person factors was not particularly successful, and by the mid-1960s the prevailing view was that the evidence indicated personality tests were not apt to be valid for personnel decisions (Ghiselli, 1966; Guion & Gottier, 1965). Interest revived in the 1970s with the development of the Big 5 model of personality (also known as the Five Factor Model) and with validity generalization results indicating the situation was not as dire as it had appeared a few years before. The Big 5 came about after numerous investigations around the world tended to find the same five (or four or six, depending on whom you read) personality factors. The factors have different names depending on a particular author; this book will use the terms employed by Kroeck and Brown (2004): conscientiousness, extraversion, emotional stability (opposite of "neuroticism"), agreeableness, and openness to experience. Across all jobs, conscientiousness appears to be the strongest predictor of performance; thus science seems to have confirmed what parents, grandparents, and kindergarten teachers have said for eons. Even for this factor, the validity generalization coefficients are not high, ranging up to the mid .20s at the highest. The other factors do not fare quite so well in general. Barrett (2008) maintained the validity generalization evidence for Big 5 and other personality traits is tenuous at best (I'm not sure he would agree with the "at best" qualifier). He describes several situations in which U.S. Department of Justice attorneys and experts attempted to cause a replacement of cognitive ability tests with personality tests based on flawed analyses of the validity of personality testing studies. It would be surprising if one or a few traits predicted success in all occupations. Environments differ, and, just like the case for abilities, we would expect different traits to be influential in different environments.

There is some controversy over whether the Big 5 traits are too broad to be useful in many situations (Hough, 1992; Hough & Oswald, 2008), known as the bandwidth-fidelity problem. Levy, Cober, and Norris-Watts (2004) reviewed the controversy and several personality inventories that concentrate on more specific traits. Trait measures with narrow bandwidth often predict performance measures as well as, or better than, even tests of ability in some, but not all, instances. So long as the instruments measure theoretically meaningful constructs, it makes sense to continue to use these measures when job modeling suggests their potential and validity evidence can be obtained.

Hough and Oswald (2008) discussed the bandwidth match between personality trait measures and performance criteria. Although broad, complex criteria should be best predicted by broad, complex predictors, that is true only if the complexity matches. That is, a broad trait, such as a Big 5 trait, may include a good deal of construct variability that is not related to all aspects of the criterion.

A fundamental assumption of psychology is that the situation influences behavior and that individual characteristics, such as personality traits, generally operate within the constraints of the situation. Indeed, even psychopathological traits can be seen as behavior that is inappropriate for the situation. For example, it is reasonable for all people to feel anxiety in certain situations. It is not reasonable to feel anxiety in all situations as a person with generalized anxiety disorder does. Part of the role of job analysis and job modeling is to identify the particular traits or characteristics that may be important in specified situations. One aspect of situations that appears to impact the ability of personality to exert itself is the extent to which the situation is "strong" or "weak" (Mischel, 1977). A strong situation is one that limits the type of behavior that can be expressed, or in Mischel's terms, has limited outcome expectancies. A weak situation exerts little influence. At a funeral almost everyone is somber, quiet, subdued. There is little difference in behavior and not much impact from personality differences. The only exceptions might be a person with severe problems such as dementia or a child who hasn't yet learned to read situations. A resort or gambling mecca may be a weak situation, witness the advertising campaign slogan "What happens in Vegas stays in Vegas." Whether or not the happenings stay there, and I doubt they do, it does seem that personality has a greater influence there than it would at home. Thus, we would expect personality to have greater influence when an element of choice of behavior is involved (Hough & Oswald, 2008). So personality may predict behaviors such as absenteeism or turnover since there is some discretion in whether to come to work when an illness or injury is mild. Pro-organizational citizenship behavior is largely voluntary and it can be predicted by personality (Hough & Oswald, 2008). Identifying the degree of strong versus weak in situations is a challenge for job analysis and modeling.

There is considerable controversy over whether personality measures are susceptible to faking and whether any faking that does occur is important enough to reduce validity. In their reviews, Levy et al. (2004) and

Hough and Oswald (2008) concluded that faking was not such a problem and noted that some researchers believe the ability to manipulate how one presents oneself may be an advantage in some jobs. Much of the faking data came from laboratory studies with effects that were not replicated in the field. They did agree that people can fake or distort responses when instructed to do so, but that social desirability response in real life was not as large as found in lab studies (Hough & Oswald, 2008). This conclusion was challenged by White, Young, Hunter, and Rumsey (2008) in their commentary on the Hough and Oswald paper. Their longitudinal analysis of the Army's Project A data indicated that social desirability attenuated the predictions of performance by personality measures to a much greater extent than the concurrent study had indicated. On yet another hand, Griffith and Peterson (2008) disputed that social desirability measures had been shown to be reliable and valid measures of faking. At this point the issue is unresolved. The OBC psychologist should be able to defend his or her use of personality tests through some validity evidence and be able to deflect criticisms of faking potential through some reasonable set of arguments.

The adverse impact of personality tests tends to be low for race and gender (Hough & Oswald, 2008; Kroeck & Brown, 2004). Indeed this may make the use of such tests inappropriately attractive (Barrett, 2008), since the constructs they measure are limited to nonabilities and because the evidence may be misinterpreted by advocates. Care must be taken, however, to make sure that the test is using the same norms for both men and women; otherwise the requirements of the CRA of 1991 will not be met (Jones & Arnold, 2008). These same authors warn that some measures of Big 5, and presumably other traits, include questions that may be related to psychological disorders such as depression, anxiety, or even bipolar disorder. If used in preemployment screening, this would violate the Americans with Disabilities (ADA) act.

INTERESTS

Psychologists began their attempts to measure interests soon after Parsons established the field of vocational counseling (Parsons, 1909/2005). Parson's collection of information from a counselee mixed together what would be considered abilities, interests, and personality. Strong published the Strong Vocational Interest Blank (SVIB), now the Strong Interest Inventory, in 1927 (cf. Donnay, Morris, Schaubhut, & Thompson, 2005; Hansen & Dik, 2004). Ever since the SVIB there has been controversy over whether interests are separate from, or a form of, personality. Current thinking has not resolved the issue. A major theorist (Holland, 1997) sees interests as integral to personality. However, Low and Rounds (2006) described many differences as well as similarities between interests and personality traits. Interests seem to be somewhat more stable and relate to somewhat different outcomes. Interests predict occupational membership fairly well; personality traits generally do not. On the other hand, personality traits, particularly conscientiousness and emotional stability from the Big 5, tend to have at least moderate correlations with performance across a wide range of jobs. Hansen and Dik (2004) point out that interests correlate well with measures of job satisfaction, adding fuel to the notion that interests are important in determining the types of work environments that are most appealing to an individual. Personality may be more important in explaining the type of behavior emitted once on the job. In general, interest inventories are probably more apt to be useful in classification rather than selection. They also have a clear and important role in career planning.

SPECIAL CONCERNS IN PERSONALITY AND INTEREST TESTING: IPSATIVE VERSUS NORMATIVE MEASUREMENT

Psychometricians distinguish between *ipsative measurements*, those that are based on individual (within person) norms, and *normative measurements,* based on distributions of scores in groups (Broverman, 1962). Most psychological instruments are normative, at least in intent. Some personality and interest inventories are ipsative, relying on comparisons within the person such as forced-choice formats. For example, if you ask a person whether he or she prefers chocolate or vanilla ice cream, the answer does not indicate how well the person likes either flavor or ice cream in general. The consequence of this type of measurement is noteworthy resulting in changes in statistical and psychometric characteristics of the instrument, including correlations with outside criteria, factor structure, and reliability (Baron, 1996; Broverman, 1962). Some instruments combine ipsative measurement with other questionable practices such as dichotomization of continuous variables resulting in an uninterpretable mishmash (cf. Pittenger, 2005). Should an OBC psychologist use such an instrument, a demonstration of competence would include being able to justify its use given these limitations.

INTEGRITY TESTS

Not too many employers, at least of those who hire psychologists, wish to hire dishonest employees. There are two types of test that attempt to predict honesty by employees. Overt integrity tests directly ask about attitudes toward theft and the history of dishonest or illegal acts by the test taker (Cullen & Sackett, 2004). Others are personality-based measures that attempt to infer a "propensity for dishonesty" (Cullen & Sackett, 2004, p. 150) from personality attributes. Both appear to be valid, although how valid and why remains an issue. More recent research may give the edge to personality-based tests, at least for predicting absenteeism (Berry, Sackett, & Weimann, 2007). A recent study by Oliver, Shafiro, Bullard, and Thomas (in press) found that the use of an overt personality test reduced worker's compensation claims and associated costs in four organizations: a state automobile club, a nursing home chain, a food processing company, and a multimedia company. There are two interesting issues with regard to these tests. One is fakability. Studies indicate that it is possible to fake scores, but there is little evidence that this happens (Berry et al., 2007). A second issue is the legality in some states of "honesty testing." Two states, Massachusetts and Rhode Island, forbid the use of written honesty tests. This appears to cover both covert and personality based measures (Jones & Arnold, 2008). Psychologists and test users are cautioned not to position other tests as measuring honesty to avoid legal problems in these states (Jones & Arnold, 2008).

JOB-RELATED EXPERIENCE, TRAINING, AND EDUCATION

A client once told me he wanted to hire someone with 30 years' experience, not one year's experience repeated 30 times. Experience counts, but only if the person has taken advantage of the opportunity to learn and change his or her ways in accord with what has worked and not worked. Most people intuitively accept this notion and it has been borne out in numerous studies (Levine, Ash, & Levine, 2004). Experience and time on the job does correlate with performance. Presumably there is both job knowledge and world of work knowledge (Osborne, Brown, Niles, & Miner, 1997); that is, socialization into what is expected in a workplace, and some supervisory or mentoring capacity. Education is also necessary for many jobs. At times it will compensate for lack of experience; good examples of this are given in Buster et al. (2005) of how various forms of experience and education can combine for minimum qualifications as a pharmacy technician. Levine, Ash, and Levine describe several methods for establishing the amount of credit to award for education, training, and experience. These tend to parallel the methods used to establish the content validity of MQs. An interesting problem is how to deal with online resumes and applications. Review of these materials may be either scientific or nonscientific (Handler, 2001, cited in Levine et al., 2004). The difference, as you might expect, is whether the screening method is based on doing one's homework and a job analysis. Depending on the technology used, the screening can be relatively cumbersome or mechanized by searching for a small subset of characteristics. I am not aware of any applications of data-mining techniques to do this, but if it hasn't been done already it is only a matter of time before someone begins using it. Online screening and recruiting do have associated equal employment opportunity issues. Some of the differences in web usage between groups that were cited by Levine et al. (2004) may have changed; it is probably a moving target. However, using the World Wide Web to search for candidates may change the definition of the labor market, and consequently change adverse impact statistics. Since these trends continually change, the OBC psychologist should be aware of the possibility and take steps necessary to allow the client organization to make informed judgments about how to proceed.

BIODATA

Systematically scored biographical data have been used in personnel selection for well over 100 years (Stokes & Cooper, 2004). Once called the weighted application blank, biodata came into its own in the 1970s as Owens (1976) moved the field from a strictly empirical foundation to a more construct-theoretical position. Today the use of biodata rests on multiple theoretical foundations. Biodata forms have been shown to have predictive validity and incremental validity over cognitive and personality factors in a number of studies (Stokes & Cooper, 2004).

Several ways of developing biodata scales are described by Stokes and Cooper (2004). They provide extensive references to detailed accounts of how to use each method. All methods begin with job analysis; worker-oriented or attribute-oriented methods tend to be more successful and the critical incident technique is a proven performer. Once the job analysis is complete, potential items are identified and written to a set of specifications. Stokes and Cooper join with Owens (1976) in concluding that potential biodata items that are theoretically aimed at particular types of performance are more apt to prove valid than items that have no theoretical expectation of validity. The items are prescreened: first, rationally to make sure there are not multiple interpretations, and second, frequently to identify items that may generate negative reactions of applicants. Ideally, it probably makes sense to have members of a variety of minority groups participate in this prescreening to catch any inadvertent discriminatory or aversive content. Next, some data must be collected and the items scaled. Scaling may be done through empirical keying (i.e., relationship of items to criteria), following some theoretical approach, methods intended to maximize internal consistency, and a content or rational approach. Although Stokes and Cooper say the research does not identify a consistent best approach, they clearly have been disappointed by the methods intended to maximize internal consistency. Finally, Stokes and Cooper review some legal and ethical concerns about the use of biodata, including issues related to potential discrimination against people with disabilities. Obviously the psychologist developing or using biodata scales must be aware of these issues and be able to address them.

SIMULATIONS AND WORK SAMPLES

The director of a large symphony is less concerned with what school an aspiring violinist graduated from than whether and how well the candidate can play the violin. The candidate auditions, playing music he or she has selected (probably indicating maximal performance) and sight-reading material chosen by the director. No qualified director would attempt to build a world-class orchestra without auditions.

The audition is a work sample. Work samples, or job samples, have been critical methods of personnel selection, qualification, and promotion systems as long as psychologists have worked on these problems (Vinchur & Koppes, 2007). They may be very elaborate, multiple-day affairs such as many assessment centers or simple tasks designed to elicit specific information. As an example of the latter, for a time an assistant and I performed assessments of the potential of lumber experts to represent a wood products association. Part of the job was to explain lumber grading standards at mills. From a trip to the lumber yard we obtained boards of varying condition and type that the experts could grade and describe how each one fit or didn't fit standards. In this case we were assessing the candidate's ability to explain the standards; a more elaborate work sample would have been required to assess knowledge and ability to apply the standards.

The literature distinguishes between the terms *work* or *job*, *sample* and *simulation*. However, the distinctions are not obvious. Truxillo, Donahue, and Kuang (2004) presented a continuum based on psychological fidelity. At the highest level of fidelity are assessments based on "authentic" job performance, such as job tryouts, probationary periods, or portfolios. Even these have an element of artificiality. As an example that is probably familiar to many readers, university faculty members are considered for tenure after a 6-year probationary period. Deans, personnel committees, and colleagues fear the person who performs well during this time, then settles into a life of mediocrity once tenure is granted. Work samples grade into simulations as fidelity to the actual job is reduced. As another example, it is not desirable or practical in real life to assess how a police officer will respond to a person who might or might not pull a gun. Instead multimedia-based or video simulations are used.

Several common forms of simulation are described by Thornton and Rupp (2004) and Thornton and Mueller-Hanson (2004): case studies, oral presentations, leaderless group discussions, one-on-one interactions, role-plays, in-baskets, oral fact finding, business games, and day-in-the-life—an integrated simulation that includes several components. Assessment centers may include several simulations as well as competency testing and even cognitive and personality assessment, along with interviews. Work samples and simulations have been shown to relate very well to later job performance (Truxillo et al., 2004) and surprisingly, the degree of fidelity does not make too much difference. Most of the time work samples and simulations are developed following content validation procedures. Because they involve degrees of judgment in scoring, training observers and scorers is especially important and is given special attention. Work samples and simulations generally have high levels of face validity, leading to ready acceptance by participants. Some reviews have found subgroup differences in scoring, but adverse impact is typically less than found with cognitive tests (cf. Truxillo et al., 2004). The primary area of controversy on these methods is the construct validity of dimensional scores from assessment centers. Lance (2008) holds that ratings obtained after exercises reflect the exercise more than the dimensions the raters are supposed to evaluate. Commentators on this paper are split, with some agreeing (e.g., Howard, 2008) and others disagreeing. Arthur, Day, and Woehr (2008), in particular, claim that Lance's findings are a consequence of misinterpretations of the nature of constructs and construct validity. At this point, no definitive answer is possible; a psychologist engaged in the development and use of assessment centers should be aware of the issue and be able to justify the actions taken in the project.

INTERVIEWS

The interview is probably the most widely used selection procedure. It is the rare manager who will employ an applicant without any personal contact with the person. The employment interview serves many functions. It is an opportunity for the interviewer to sell the applicant on the organization. Even if the applicant does not get the job it is important that he or she leave with a positive view of the organization and process (Bauer, Truxillo, & Paronto, 2004; see also Posthuma, Morgeson, & Campion, 2002). A second purpose of the interview is that it often marks the beginning of the new employee's socialization process into the organization and the development of working relationships with new co-workers and superiors. This aspect is not often commented on in the literature, but it is a common experience, as shown by discussions with and observations of many interviewers and interviewees. Although these aspects of interviewing may foreshadow the form and level of job performance that may be attained, they are not directly related to the prediction of job performance or determination of applicant qualifications. An interview that emphasizes either of these functions may drift and be unstructured—the interviewer's decision reached through "gut feeling" rather than considered judgment. However, psychologists have long known that unstructured interviews have essentially no ability to predict an applicant's future job performance. Interviews that are intended to do this or determine applicant qualifications should be designed so that the sales or negotiating portions are separate from the selection portion.

The third function of the interview is to evaluate applicants and collect information that will be useful for making personnel decisions. For this purpose a structured interview is based on a job analysis (preferably including critical incident analysis), and includes systematic scoring, and training for the interviewers on how to conduct and score the interview. OBC psychologists are involved with the development of interview systems and often serve as interviewers. The primary types of structured interviews, behavioral and situational, were reviewed and described by Dipboye, Wooten, and Halverson (2004). These authors presented a three-dimensional model of interview structure; the axes were job-relatedness, standardization of interview conduct, and structure of data use. The first axis includes job analysis and the extent to which KSAOs are specified. The second axis involves issues of question focus, flexibility, and note taking or other means of recording the interview. The third axis is concerned with how the data are used to evaluate the candidate; types of rating scales, how data are combined, whether the interviewer has the opportunity to access ancillary materials, and whether a decision model is used. There is a tendency to believe that the more an interview system falls on the highly structured end of the axes, the more valid the interview will be. However, there are some caveats to this. For example, Dipboye et al. (2004) reviewed opinions and studies about the extent to which interviewers can deviate from a set of questions that are asked the same way every time. Interrater reliability may be higher, and it may be possible to do this with interviews for entry or low-level positions, but it doesn't seem practical for higher level positions. Interviewing someone for a top executive post with an inflexible interview style would probably reduce the interviewer's credibility to near zero.

Two common structured interview methods are the *situational interview (SI)* and the *behavior description interview (BDI)*. Both are based on critical incidents based job analyses. The development of the situational interview parallels the development of a behaviorally anchored rating scale in many respects. The incidents are allocated by SMEs into categories (with reallocation by another group), then yet another group of SMEs rates each incident as to where it falls on a continuum of performance. Questions are developed from this. The questions are posed as hypothetical situations presented to the applicant. Responses are scored based on a set of benchmarks developed by experienced interviewers. Dipboye et al. (2004) include some example SI questions in their chapter.

The BDI follows a similar development process. In the BDI the applicant is asked to describe an incident in which the applicant was involved. To eliminate as much as possible the tendency of applicants to search memory for what seems like the "best" example, the question is worded in terms of specifics "Tell me about the most recent time (worst time, last time, most satisfying time, etc.)." As with SIs, responses to BDIs are evaluated using a predefined and pilot tested scoring system.

To illustrate the difference between an SI and a BDI, consider the following real incident (in developing both interviews a good many incidents are gathered and more than one is used to define a dimension, but this is an example).

> A man entered an auto parts store looking for an oil filter. The counter person offered to help him find the right one but the customer refused her help because he thought a young woman wouldn't be capable of knowing anything about auto parts. When it was obvious that he was unable to properly read the applications book, she was able to show him how to find the correct part listing. She sold him the correct oil filter.

An SI question might be "A customer comes into the store and seems unable to read the applications book to find the right part. He has already refused help from you once. What do you do?" Common answers are identified and scaled. For example, "since he already refused my help I would ignore him and assist another customer" might be scored low, while the response "I would ask him again if I could be of some help" might be scored higher. Of course, if this interview is for an entry position, care would have to be taken to not score according to store policies that an employee would be trained in after hire.

A BDI question based on the same incident might be, "Tell me about a recent time that a customer refused help but clearly was unable to identify the part needed." The interviewer would be supplied with follow-up questions such as, "How did you know the person needed help?" and "How did you approach the person to offer help the second time?" Responses would typically be evaluated against a scale similar to the one used in the SI.

In both the SI and BDI, but more so in the latter, the scoring of responses may be specific to the organization. For example, a candidate for a senior executive position might be asked, "Tell me about a recent decision you had to make in which you knew popular sentiment favored one course of action and your belief was another course was better for the organization." It is likely that the answer will provide an indication of the executive's decision-making style, political adeptness, and willingness to take responsibility. In one organization that favors consensus, one type of action may be preferred; in another organization that favors "doing the right thing," another action could be scored high; and in another organization in which executives are expected to "take the bull by the horns," yet another form of response would be seen as most positive. A psychologist performing the interview on behalf of a client organization, as in an individual assessment would have to know the culture of the organization and whether a change in culture is in store.

Both SI and BDI methods have been shown to result in valid interview systems using both content- and criterion-oriented approaches. The BDI approach is not always appropriate for entry level workers because they have few experiences to draw on. In that case the SI would be more appropriate. However, the BDI is more predictive of performance in higher level jobs (Huffcutt, Weekley, Wiesner, Degroot, & Jones (2001).

There are other exemplary structured interview systems available (cf. Dipboye et al., 2004). Those developed by firms for use in a variety of organizations are based on long-standing research programs and utilize extensive job analysis systems in their implementation.

Although interviews can be highly valid, they are susceptible to sources of bias. Some evidence suggests that the adverse impact can be small, but other researchers indicate that the effect sizes may be larger than previously believed once corrections for restriction of range are incorporated into the analysis (Roth, Van Iddekinge, Huffcutt, Eidson, & Bobko, 2002). Interviewer training is always important, and part of that training should be oriented toward avoiding improper discrimination. Interviewers are typically aware of an applicant's appearance, gender, stature, and approximate age.

The psychologist should be able to describe what measures were taken to minimize undesirable effects of this knowledge. In addition, there is some controversy over whether the standardization of interview questions can undercut efforts to treat members of different cultures in an appropriate manner (Spence & Petrick, 2000, cited in Dipboye et al., 2004). Organizational culture and past practices can also impact whether interviewers adhere to a structured interview and whether the interview will attract applicants who will most fit the organization in the long run (cf. Dipboye et al., 2004). As a consequence, the OBC psychologist must not only know how to design, develop, validate, and train interviewers, and implement the interview program, but he or she must also know how to fit the program to the culture of the organization and to the labor market.

PHYSICAL, SENSORY, AND PSYCHOMOTOR ABILITIES

With expertise in testing and validation, psychologists were drafted to develop selection procedures for physical abilities, sensory capability, and psychomotor abilities some decades ago. Guion (1998) commented that the civil rights acts and ADA "damped what little enthusiasm existed for physical and sensory competencies for personnel decisions" (p. 146). Though it is often assumed that size matters, old-fashioned height and weight requirements have become passé except in situations in which a clear relevance can be demonstrated. Danica Patrick in auto racing and Dustin Pedroia of the Boston Red Sox and 2008 American League Most Valuable Player (MVP) demonstrate that small size is not an impediment to success in physically demanding jobs. Guion noted that even in cases in which size can be demonstrated to be a valid selection criterion, the better move is often to redesign the position than select people to fit it.

Some jobs require a certain level of physical ability. Fleishman has been at the forefront of identifying those that are most useful for employment (cf. Fleishman & Reilly, 1992). The list of physical factors consisted of static strength, explosive strength, dynamic strength, trunk strength, extent flexibility, dynamic flexibility, gross body coordination, gross body equilibrium, and stamina. Hogan (1991a) identified three general factors that subsume these: muscular strength, aerobic capacity (cardiovascular endurance), and movement quality (coordination); she later combined strength and endurance into one factor (Hogan, 1991b). Guion (1998) provides a model illustrating the relationships between the Fleishman and Hogan factors. Unfortunately, the adverse impact on female applicants when using physical ability tests can be very pronounced. There can be fairness issues as well when it is noticed that current, longtime workers do not have the level of fitness expected of new hires. When a degree of physical ability is required to prevent injury to the worker or others, such tests may be necessary. In general, whenever possible it makes sense to try to redesign the job. For example, at one factory where I consulted, a relatively inexpensive piece of equipment was purchased as an accommodation for a disabled worker. It worked so well that the same equipment became standard for all workers, increasing productivity and reducing injuries at the same time. Military organizations cannot easily redesign jobs and there are obvious physical demands on soldiers, sailors, and aircrew. Rayson, Holliman, and Belyavin (2000) described how the British Army developed criterion measures and selection tests that were as bias free as possible from discrimination between the sexes. Similarly, firefighters and other public safety personnel necessarily need a level of strength and fitness to perform these very difficult and demanding jobs. Henderson, Berry, and Matic (2007) found that for several years of firefighter recruits, the recruits' pretraining strength and endurance measures predicted how well they performed on physically demanding work simulations at the end of training.

Sensory abilities have engaged the attention of psychologists working in personnel selection and human factors over several decades. There was a considerable amount of research on vision for selection done in the years following World War II (Guion, 1965), but not very much recently. That is probably because of the ADA and because vision testing has shifted to the ophthalmologic and optometric professions. Color vision is important in certain jobs, which makes it difficult to design the job without the need to be able to distinguish colors—for example, in quality control. Birch (2008) examined the pass rates on one color vision test, the Farnsworth D15 Colour Vision Test, and concluded that certain patterns of scored responses are most applicable. Examination of her article quickly reveals the need for specialist knowledge beyond that of the typical OBC psychologist. As with most things, it is possible to access simple tests of color vision on the Internet. Care must be taken, however, because even if the test as presented is appropriate, the video display may not accurately present the colors in the actual plates.

Although it seems as if auditory perception would be as important as visual perception in many jobs, Guion (1998) was unable to find many studies of the use of auditory tests in personnel selection. This trend, or lack of one, appears to continue. A search on May 2, 2009, of Psych INFO using keywords of *auditory acuity, auditory discrimination*, and *auditory perception* combined with *personnel selection* identified only eight papers, none of which were relevant for this chapter. Since auditory ability is known to decline with age, and with an aging population, it is likely that more attention will have to be devoted to auditory abilities on the job, job and equipment design may be more important than selection testing. If an OBC psychologist is using tests of sensory ability the best way to judge competence is to ask how the psychologist established the validity of the test and include a discussion of special competencies and how these were developed.

CLINICALLY ORIENTED MEASURES

For personnel selection, classification, promotion, or other decision-making purposes, with only a few exceptions it is generally unwise to use clinically oriented psychological instruments. Unless done as part of a medical evaluation after a job offer is made, the use of these instruments will be a violation of the ADA. The few exceptions for their use lies in the post-hire decision for assessing fitness for duty or return to work evaluations or psychological fitness for occupations such as police officer in which the public safety is paramount. In these cases the tests should be administered and interpreted by qualified psychologists (or under their supervision) trained in these instruments and purposes.

PART III

Other Functional
Competencies—
Development and Change

SEVEN

Training and Development

All organizations must engage in training and development. They train employees, customers, and suppliers. Training is necessary for learning job tasks, to develop skills for advancement, for the establishment of interpersonal skills, and to protect the organization against legal problems. Because the internal and external environments of organizations do not remain stable for long, members of the organization must undergo continual development to master new conditions, remedy deficiencies, and meet additional challenges. Organizational and business consulting psychologists have been involved in training and development since the field began. Their roles have been varied across the training program cycle and its critical steps: needs analysis, program design and development, pilot testing, implementation, transfer of training to the job, and evaluation. Aguinis and Kraiger (2009) concluded that attention to each of these steps is necessary to maximize the value of training and development activities. The six steps are not always followed; a large meta-analysis of training effects found that only about 6% of programs were preceded by a needs analysis (Arthur, Bennett, Edens, & Bell, 2003). Training is often an interdisciplinary enterprise; subject matter experts are requisite partners, experts in technology utilization may be necessary, and frequently professional trainers deliver the material. On the development side, OBC psychologists may work with individuals, groups, or teams to achieve improvement in job performance, teamwork, interpersonal functioning, and promotability. These activities should ideally be preceded by the same steps as followed for training programs, although for interventions directed at individuals or small groups the steps may be less elaborate. This chapter covers the steps in developing training programs and the competencies and ethics of development activities. It ends with a brief discussion of how OBC psychologists work with organizations on problems related to dysfunctional employee behavior.

Training Programs

NEEDS ANALYSIS

The basic methods of needs analysis were covered in chapter 4. Analyses for selection and training can share data and results, although those done for training purposes will be more detailed. A cognitive task analysis may be necessary to identify mental demands of a job including decision making, problem solving, pattern recognition, and situation assessment (Dubois, 2002). Commonly, a training needs analysis will differentiate between *needs* and *wants* (Barbazette, 2006); the wants have to be justified as part of a larger strategy moving the organization toward a new technology or culture. Barbazette's book is an excellent resource for ideas and methods on conducting needs analyses.

The needs analysis process must include considerations of timing such as determining when the training needs to happen, the duration of training needed, and whether it can be accomplished during the regular work schedule. For example, a large hospital planned to move to electronic record keeping. Management assumed all the nurses would have basic knowledge of how to work with computers so that instruction could be devoted to navigating the interface and be accomplished during a slow period a couple of months before the implementation. A fairly quick and inexpensive needs analysis using a simple survey and some interviews indicated that these assumptions were wrong. Many of the nurses had little experience with computers, so more in-depth instruction was necessary. This would take longer than initially planned. In addition, the needs analysis showed that the nurses were apprehensive that they would forget the new knowledge and skills if they learned them too long before the system was implemented. Experts may scoff, thinking this should have been obvious, but validating that judgment with the needs analysis input led to a change in plans. This example also illustrates how training needs analyses can be done at the task, job, personal, and organizational level. The nurses needed to learn how to access the record keeping system and enter and retrieve information (task). The record keeping system either needed to fit into their daily routines and procedures or these would have to change to accommodate it (job). Nurses had varying levels of familiarity and expertise with computers, necessitating some individualized training (personal). In spite of complaints that the new system was disruptive and a pain to have to deal with, the organization needed the system to increase overall efficiency as well as meet external forces—such as payers, accreditation, legal system, and so on (organizational). A meta-analysis of training outcomes found that effects of training tended to be higher when more of these levels were analyzed (Arthur et al., 2003).

Management often turns to training to fix performance problems. This often makes sense. During periods of low unemployment the organization may have to hire people with less experience and qualifications or lower aptitude than it would prefer. Training is necessary to make up for what the selection system cannot provide (and vice versa). However, sometimes training is seen as a solution for a problem that does not arise from a lack of know-how. A PROBE (short for "profiling behavior") analysis (Gilbert, 1994) should be conducted to determine the nature of a performance deficiency before committing to training. The PROBE analysis examines both the behavioral environment and the behavioral repertoires of the people who perform the work. The behavioral environment consists of directional cues (information or signals that a qualified person needs to perform well), confirmation (availability of task-relevant feedback), tools and equipment, procedures, resources, and incentives. Gilbert asserts that if the behavioral environment is lacking in any of these features, changing the environment makes more sense than putting resources into training. Behavioral repertoire questions focus on knowledge and training (including knowing good from poor performance, having basic skills needed to benefit from training), capacity (identifying the cognitive and emotional limitations that may interfere with learning the job), and motives.

PROGRAM DESIGN

Once present and future needs are identified, training can be developed or purchased based on specifications derived from these needs. One set of specifications that typically trumps the others is practicality (Rogers & Peterson, 2002). It is often necessary to forego optimally effective training for training that gets done on time and with a minimum of interference to the daily routine. Early career psychologists who are working in applied areas such as training often feel as if their work does not measure up to standards expected by an academically oriented field, not recognizing that the measure of competence is how trade-off decisions were made to achieve the desired results, not how well the application represents the state of the art.

A second critical set of specifications that influences the design of training is the organizational culture and the greater cultures from which organizational members are recruited. The use of training technologies such as computers and Internet versus personal contact by a trainer may be more influenced by what is acceptable within and without the organization than by which technology seems the best based on training research. One high-tech organization has training delivered only via electronic media without regard to the effectiveness of the medium. High tech is what the company is and what it sells; anything else is contrary to what the company stands for. Thus, competence of the psychologist may be revealed in how the training is tailored to fit the situation; a simple inspection of the product may not reveal, and could belie, the nature of expertise involved in its genesis.

TECHNOLOGY IN TRAINING

Technological choices are an important part of training design. "Technology" is often shorthand for the use of computers and other electronic media in training. Kraiger (2008) (see also the commentary which follows his article) suggests that web-based training offers an opportunity to develop a "third generation" of social constructivist learning models. A somewhat incompatible model of "evidence-based principles" for designing multimedia was presented by R. E. Mayer (2008). His view is less social, but it also seems constructionist at its core. There is not complete agreement on this at the time of writing this chapter, but an OBC psychologist working in the area should be familiar with the controversy and its implications.

Brown and Ford (2002) reviewed the literature on the use of computers and found four elements that influence results: information structure and presentation, the extent of learner control and guidance, learning activities and feedback, and meta-cognitive monitoring and control during training. They provide excellent guidelines for guiding design. Some are surprising— for example, intuitively one might think the more control learners have over the training, the better. This turns out to not be the case; there are times when people do a poor job of estimating the degree of practice they need to gain a skill and often overestimate their level of proficiency. Many of Brown and Ford's guidelines apply for other forms of training and are a worthy starting point in making decisions.

The term *technology* encompasses more than the employment of high-tech devices. It includes the use of traditional classroom and trainer-based methods or on-the-job training when these are directed at producing particular training solutions. The physical and social environments are also aspects of the training technology and can impact training outcomes. A simple example: I recently observed a 3-hour diversity training program held by an organization with about 75 people in attendance. It was presented in a large auditorium, the only large space available, with large round tables seating eight or so participants each. The members of the organization generally get along and have a record of being supportive of each other and the organization's diversity initiative. During the group discussions that are key components of this sort of training, I noticed that many of the senior members of the audience were not participating in an engaged manner. After the training concluded, a quick check confirmed that the nonparticipation was not due to disinterest or reaction to the content. The noise level of the room made it difficult for these participants to hear and comprehend what was being said. How much latitude the trainers had in modifying their program to fit the space is not known, but such problems are common and should be expected and anticipated by those developing and delivering the training.

TRANSFER OF TRAINING

Training doesn't accomplish anything if on-the-job behavior does not change. The problem of transfer has vexed training professionals and consultants for decades. Lack of support by supervisors or a poor "transfer climate" have been blamed for lack of transfer (Aguinis & Kraiger, 2009; Salas & Cannon-Bowers, 2001), although research support is spotty, at least for the latter. Unfortunately, research on transfer has been done primarily using surveys (Salas & Cannon-Bowers, 2001), not examining what actually happened, so the meaning of the results is questionable. One can expect that transfer will be limited if leadership practices, performance appraisal and compensation systems, team members, and a host of other factors do not encourage it. Tannenbaum (2002) described how training has to fit the strategic initiatives of the organization. The training department does not set the strategic agenda for the organization, and if the business strategies the training is based on are not disseminated and accepted, there will be little transfer. There are a number of within-training and post-training factors that have been identified at one time or another that impact transfer (Machin, 2002). Some have been known for generations, such as the identical elements approach, in which the same interfaces, tools, procedures, and such are used both in training and on the job. Another classic transfer element is the time between training and usage: the longer the delay, the less transfer is expected. Health professionals need to periodically requalify on life-saving procedures such as cardiopulmonary resuscitation (CPR) to ensure that transfer occurs when needed. If you have a heart attack you want someone who has at least practiced CPR within the past few months helping you, not someone who learned it several years ago. More recent additions to the transfer tool kit include goal setting and relapse prevention. Although these do not seem to have an effect in every environment, it seems sensible to ask training participants how they will use their new skills on the job. For example, in one hospital the staff received annual training on the effects of patients' cultures on their response to treatment. Not much transfer happened; perhaps the training was too general or too infrequent, and the staff did not know how to apply it. A team of organizational consulting psychologists recommended that the training be revised to include more specifics and to build in goals for specific and immediate applications such as "I will ask Jose who he considers to be his family. How do members of his family provide social, emotional, financial, and other forms of support to each other?"

PROGRAM EVALUATION

Because nobody is smart enough to consistently develop training programs that achieve all of the objectives on the first try, evaluation efforts are encouraged by all recognized experts in training. One classic distinction is between formative and summative evaluation. *Formative evaluation* information is intended to be used to refine or revise the training so that the program continues to improve. *Summative evaluation* is done to provide "bottom-line" information for decision making. A summative evaluation may derive figures on the proportion of trainees who met certain criteria after training and whether the training was worth the expense. Although many organizations claim they want the latter, it is not clear that the data are used once obtained, particularly for programs that necessarily recur often due to regulation or mandate (Patton, 2009).

The second classic taxonomy of forms of evaluation was developed by Kirkpatrick over half a century ago (Kirkpatrick, 1959a, 1959b, 1960a, 1960b). It is still the predominant taxonomy in the field (Salas & Cannon-Bowers, 2001). Kirkpatrick noted that training programs could be evaluated using four categories of criteria: reaction, learning, behavior, and results. Reaction refers to the initial emotional response of participants to the training. It is often measured using the brief surveys ubiquitously passed out after training sessions, often called "smile sheets." Reaction can be better measured by asking participants what appealed to them and what did not such as might be done in a usability study. Learning criteria assess whether the material, skills, attitudes, and other elements covered in the training were actually learned by the trainees. Behavior criteria are intended to assess whether the trained material is actually used back on the job: Did participants' change the way they work due to the training? Behavior criteria are concerned with whether training has transferred. Results criteria are used to determine whether the behavior change due to the training made an important difference in operations. Results can be measured financially (e.g., benefit-cost analysis) or in terms of productivity, quality, or similar hard criteria. Although Kirkpatrick originally expressed the four criteria as following a causal sequence, a meta-analysis by Alliger and Janak (1989) found that reaction criteria were not related to the others. The data supported two causal models for the other three criteria; one is the expected learning → behavior → results model; the other is a more complex model with learning and behavior independently contributing to results. It seems reasonable to believe that reaction data other than smile sheets of questionable validity might have led to different results for that criterion and for the other criteria the choice of actual measures may influence the form of the causal model. A more recent meta-analysis by Arthur et al. (2003) found effect sizes of roughly .60 (using d) from training evaluations for each of Kirkpatrick's criteria. The observed effect sizes varied a good deal; only reaction and results had confidence intervals not including zero. But it appears that training will generally produce improvement in performance as measured with well-validated criteria.

Development

For purposes of this chapter, development refers to activities directed at individuals to improve their performance or opportunities for advancement.

A primary method of development is mentoring by leaders and more experienced peers. Mentoring consists of a long-term relationship in which an older, established person guides a new, or at least, younger person to "learn the ropes" (McCauley & Hezlett, 2001). A mentor teaches norms and limits, encourages development, introduces the mentee to the "right" people, advises, and coaches. McCauley and Hezlett noted that there are two primary ways of establishing mentoring programs. One is by developing opportunities for senior and junior employees to interact, and the other is through formal mentoring programs. Research supports both, but informal programs appear somewhat more effective (Chao, Walz, & Gardner, 1992). Mentoring programs can be beneficial in furthering the business career of the mentee and can have long-term benefits outside of work. Westermeyer (1998) examined long-term outcomes of college students having a mentor and found that those with a mentor had both higher status positions and better health at midlife. OBC psychologists get involved with mentoring in helping design programs, training and coaching mentors, and convincing the organization to support mentoring over the long haul.

Performance appraisal feedback is also a common developmental strategy. Somehow, in spite of all common sense, the yearly performance review has become institutionalized throughout organizations. In the words of one observer: "Performance appraisal could be compared to a medication that doesn't work very well, has lots of terrible side effects, but which we continue to use because we have nothing better" (Gellerman, 1992, p. 166). There are methods for making performance appraisal feedback useful; it is a job of the OBC psychologist to introduce organizations to these methods and assist in their implementation.

Performance is assessed in organizations for three basic reasons: administrative, research, and development and motivation. The research purpose is rare, so for practicality, there are two reasons. The administrative purpose of appraisal is to ensure that all employees know where they stand and to allow decisions to be made about employees. In a large organization there needs to be some way to distinguish between levels of performance and potential across many locations and functions. In many cases, to successfully fire someone you have to be able to show that the person was told of his or her inadequate performance.[1] For all practical purposes, yearly performance appraisals are essentially required by the legal environment, not for increasing employee performance and development.

Gellerman (1992) makes the very strong point that an appraisal system designed for administrative purposes is almost never effective at increasing motivation, and typically it interferes with other motivation initiatives undertaken by a manager. Note that performance assessment is oriented toward the past; you measure what the person has already accomplished. Performance appraisal should be oriented toward the future—what the person should accomplish in the coming months. The developmental or motivational purpose makes sense only if the performance appraisal gives credible feedback that either

- Can be acted upon. For this you need feedback that is negative, but appropriate for the current development and goals of the individual. Negative feedback indicates how the person is off track. The appraisal meeting should concentrate on how to get back on track.

---

[1]   This can also hurt your case. Lots of appeals, mediation, and lawsuits are lost because the employee had a history of receiving "meets standard," "above average," or even "excellent" ratings.

- Can sustain present performance. For this you need positive feedback. It must be specific enough that the person knows what behavior to continue.

- Can increase future performance and opportunities. Both positive and negative feedback are needed as well as frank discussions of the relative strengths and weaknesses of the person's capabilities. It should include what needs to change to allow for opportunities of the foreseeable future.

Several manager-related factors can limit the value of continuing the process. Time, the number of appraisals to prepare, the ability to observe and recall important details and incidents, and similar items are going to limit the value of the information (Barnes-Farrell, 2001). It has become common to utilize data obtained from multiple sources in addition to supervisors including peers, subordinates, and sometimes customers and suppliers (London, 2003). Multisource data have some value for developmental purposes but should generally not be used for administrative purposes unless managers using the data have been trained in the use and limitations of the information and the instruments meet technical standards (Bracken & Timmreck, 1999). London (2003) reviews the uses and limitations of multisource feedback and provides some suggestions for improving its use.

Meyer (1991) summarizes many years of work at General Electric and other places on performance appraisal interviews. The following are among the discoveries made 40 or more years ago:

- Having the manager split roles of both (1) giving developmental feedback and (2) determining merit raises, results in role conflict and a confused message.

- Once the employee hears about the raise, he or she doesn't listen to much else.

- Once the employee hears any negatives, his or her defenses come up and the employee doesn't attend to much else.

Meyers's solution is a five-step process in which an employee and supervisor discuss

1. Overall progress toward objectives; analyze accomplishments and shortcomings

2. Problems encountered in meeting job requirements

3. Opportunities to improve job performance

4. Long-range plans, opportunities for the job and the individual's career

5. General discussion of possible plans and goals for the coming year

Meyer's (1991) suggestions are consistent with recommendations made by London (2003). London goes further in describing personal feedback skills managers can develop. These parallel those used in coaching improved performance. The OBC psychologist has a role in training these skills.

Managers need both "soft" or "people" skills and "hard" business knowledge and skills. Some of this can come from formal education such as business schools, some from internal training, and much from experience. The most effective high-level managers have a variety of experiences that allow them to see business problems and opportunities from multiple perspectives. A development plan intended to increase the possibility of promotion of a current or potential manager should include a method for gaining new experiences. Methods can range from task forces and special assignments to working as part of a multifunctional team to job rotation. In the last the person moves to a succession of jobs in different departments or functions in the organization. These methods have been in use for decades but are still effective. A survey of 878 senior managers in Finland by Suutari and Viitala (2007) found that most had engaged in these methods and found them helpful. International assignments are also used as a form of development and are helpful for those in multinational firms (Suutari & Viitala). There are several cross-cultural considerations that must be considered in making these assignments; these are discussed in chapter 12.

CAREER DEVELOPMENT AND PLANNING

Organizational and business consulting psychologists may be called upon to engage in career counseling. In general this will not be the sort of career planning that vocational counselors engage in with students and new graduates. The information and competencies for such counseling is covered in such texts as Amundson, Harris-Bowlsbey, and Niles (2010) and the review by Fouad (2007). Instead, the OBC psychologist is apt to engage in career development and planning in four other ways. First, the psychologist may build career planning into a broader organizational initiative such as succession planning, planning for future human resource needs, or a performance evaluation system. Second, the psychologist may help design and manage a career center within an organization. Third, an OBC psychologist may provide services in outplacement, helping laid-off employees find new careers. Fourth, career planning may be part of an ongoing individual development or coaching relationship. For each of these the

OBC psychologist needs familiarity with career assessment instruments (cf. Hansen & Dik, 2004) and theories of vocational choice. There is a surfeit of the latter, with the Holland theory (Holland, 1997); Super's developmental theory, as updated by his followers (e.g. Osborne et al., 1997; Savickas, 2000); social cognitive career theory (Lent, Brown, & Hackett, 1996); and career anchor theory (Schein, 1993) as probably the most used approaches. Recent entrants, such as narrative, personal construct, and biographical-hermeneutic (Savickas, 2000) theories, appeal to many psychologists who focus more on phenomenological experience. Generally working with people who have anywhere from some to extensive work experience, the OBC psychologist will need to spend little time on what Super termed "World of Work" experience (cf. Osborne et al., 1997); instead, his or her attention will be more toward trends within and without the organization (Doyle, 2000) and life events that have occurred or will occur to the person (Sterns & Subich, 2002) and the salience of these events to the person and that portion of the person devoted to the career (Savickas, 2000). Because of this, the OBC psychologist needs a good understanding of development from young adulthood, through midlife, and into old age. This requires an ability to go beyond standard assessments and learn from people what is particularly meaningful for them, their sense of efficacy to accomplish career goals and clear hurdles (Lent et al., 1996), and their priorities in life. This requires skill at interviewing, rapport building, and sufficient empathy to understand the client's attempts to explain what is meaningful and whether such experiences are consistent with the client's value system.

COACHING

An individual development phenomenon that has grown tremendously in the past couple of decades is coaching, reaching what Levinson (2002) termed "fad level proportions" (pp. 415–416). It is probably not a coincidence that the great growth in coaching corresponds with the development of new forms of organization that eliminate many middle managers. These were the natural mentors for developing managers, and with their loss a void opened. At its best, coaching is an outgrowth of the practice of consulting psychologists who met with managers and executives on a one-to-one basis to help improve performance, remove impediments, and expand capability. Experts disagree on the nature and purpose of coaching. Levinson (1996) held that most coaching focuses on maladaptive behaviors while Peterson (2002) claims it has become focused more on helping all managers deal with change, with no implied dysfunction. It is critically important that the OBC psychologist keep the consulting role separate from the role of being a therapist. Although many OBC psychologists have a background in clinical or counseling psychology, when functioning in a consulting mode they avoid the unethical mixing of roles.

Regardless of the models used, there is very little empirical evidence indicating that coaching has any positive benefits (Lowman, 2005; Peterson, 2002). Not only is there little outcome data but there is almost no indication that clients change as a consequence of the intervention. The OBC psychologist engages in coaching when it is an appropriate professional activity, but those who are competent practitioners have more than one service or intervention to offer their clients.

In contrast to using therapy-driven coaching models, OBC psychologists who work one-on-one with managers or executives follow a different tack. As in process consultation, once the person's situation and goals are clarified, the psychologists are at times much more directive; often nondirective models only frustrate the client and do not accomplish the goals the psychologist was assigned. Winum (2005) presented a case that illustrates a structured approach typical of that used by competent OBC psychologists. In this case a company promoted an African American manager, Tom, to a senior position based on his potential. Due to urgency to keep a highly marketable young executive and to meet diversity goals, Tom was promoted with less experience than usual for those at his current level and he was not succeeding. Winum describes his meetings with Tom's boss and the human resources manager and with Tom. However, Winum did not rely on just one-on-one discussions. He collected a considerable amount of information from Tom's co-workers, subordinates, superiors, and others and analyzed it within the context of the company and the people who work there. Although Winum's work in the meetings may have been influenced by his clinical experience from years ago, the critical ingredients included his fact finding, knowledge of business in general and the business in particular, his knowledge of leadership, organization, learning, and most other topics covered in this book.

DEALING WITH INEFFECTIVE PERFORMANCE

Sometimes an organization member's performance is seriously deficient in some way, yet he or she retains significant value to the company so there is a reluctance to dismiss the person. Take, for example, the production manager who is absolutely brilliant in implementing new processes, putting his plant at the forefront of innovation, but he is one of the worst managers of people on the planet. There is a very high proportion of the population who at one time or another can be expected to perform below standard due to behavioral problems (Thomas & Hite, 2002). Whether these are seen as personality or mental disorders, as dysfunction, or ineffective coping skills, solving the individual's problem is probably beyond the OBC psychologist's scope. The OBC psychologist may well be asked to help the organization as personified by supervisors, team members, and the individual in question adapt or manage the behavior in a fruitful manner. It is possible that success in the workplace will spill over into other areas of the person's life, but that is not the goal.

Frew (2004) differentiated between individual dysfunction and systemic dysfunction. The former was defined as "an impairment in the capacity to work that is related primarily to psychological distress which has nothing or very little to do with the workplace itself" (p. 294), while systemic dysfunction is "not solely the domain of the individual but is a product of the dynamic relationship between the individual and the environment" (p. 295). Examples of systemic dysfunction include disputes with a boss, transfer to an unchallenging job, or sexual harassment. Individual dysfunction probably falls into the domain of the ADA (see chapter 3). Accommodations may be necessary. Once the ADA requirements are met, Frew recommended four guidelines for managers. The OBC psychologist's job is to help management comprehend the situation, understand options, and be able to follow these guidelines:

1. Assessment and disclosure. The assessment consists of work-related metrics (attendance, productivity, etc.), not psychological. Once the data are identified the manager can arrange to meet with the employee.

2. Work or leave determination. If it is not possible to raise performance to requisite levels the employee may need to leave the job either through resignation, retirement, disability, or transfer.

3. Designated implementation and follow-up of a plan of action. If the employee stays, the action plan must be implemented and followed.

4. Motivation and leadership. Employees will not follow a leader they do not trust. In working with individual dysfunction, trust is an extremely important factor. Managers should try to find a means of developing trust between themselves and employees.

Frew assumes that in the case of systemic dysfunction the employee was once in a balanced situation which was thrown off kilter by some change. Systemic dysfunction is more complex to work with because there is no single feature such as a mental disorder as the central causative factor. The person, other people, and the organization may need to engage in difficult change efforts. Ultimately, the same guidelines as for individual dysfunction need to be followed. The demands on the OBC psychologist are greater because the increased complexity requires a broad view of organizational, business, and legal principles and flexibility in implementing change strategies. For managers, the methods described by Schein (2009) for helping may be useful.

EIGHT

Organizational Psychology

Organizations are complex systems. As a complex system, an organization melds the social, individual, technological, financial, and other components. To navigate such a system one must understand organizational culture, leadership, how decisions are made, and motivation. OBC psychologists must understand systems theory and how an organization has evolved to fit its environment if they are to devise interventions that will be accepted and will result in the client's meeting its objectives.

Modern organization theory was formed from the conjunction of open systems theory stemming from biology, specifically ecology, and information theory from mathematics and engineering. The former is generally explicitly recognized; the latter has had most of its direct influence through the development of cognitive theories and in engineering psychology. Information theory is, however, at least implicit in systems theory. Coming from ecology, open systems theory emphasizes the relationship between a system, such as an organization, and the environment. An organization that does not fit in its environment is doomed to eventual extinction. Organizations evolve and, unlike individual members of species, individual organizations can evolve or change with the times. That insight forms the foundation for this chapter and the next.

Systems Theory

The classic presentation of systems theory as it applies to organizations was that of Katz and Kahn (1966, 1978). They noted that the fundamental issue with a system is identifying its boundary. A system does not exist without a boundary between it and the rest of the universe. Boundaries may be more or less permeable. Employee selection systems are a good example of how organizations manage one aspect of permeability—who is and is not a member of the system. However, this illustrates a problem with defining boundaries. Many people who are associated with organizations are not "members," including temporary workers, contract workers, new hires on probation, vender personnel located on site, and so on. Church and Waclawski (1998) bemoaned the fact that even though they were highly qualified professionals, to their client organizations they were just vendors, people who are not worthy of full system membership. Just as people from different cultures may have different meanings for the word "family," organizations differ in who and what is considered inside the boundary. Regardless, once established, the system must take pains to maintain the boundary or risk disappearing. A second fundamental issue with systems is they strive to survive. That is typically the number one goal.

A third fundamental is the fact that there are subsystems—systems within systems. Just as our Earth is part of the solar system and we belong to systems on the Earth, one system can be embedded within another. As another example, companies hire law firms to represent them. The lawyers bring with them attorney-client privilege, meaning most, but not all, communications are protected and confidential. Thus, the lawyers cross into the organization's boundary, yet remain within their own firm. The subsystems have their own boundaries and these can be distinctly different from the boundary of the greater system. For example, an automobile manufacturing company has a marketing subsystem that makes arrangements with dealers who purchase cars from the company, sometimes on credit from the company or a subsidiary (i.e., subsystem) of it. The dealers are both separate entities and in a sense belong to the system. To add more weirdness to the soup, the dealers may sell more than one brand of car, thus being parts of competing systems. So, the nature of subsystems can confuse the boundaries. Katz and Kahn (1966, 1978) identified five types of subsystems that all systems must have: the managerial, supportive, production, maintenance, and adaptive subsystems. An important goal for the OBC psychologist when consulting with organizations is to identify these subsystems. Within a given organization the tasks of each may be split among multiple subsystems and a given subsystem may serve more than of these roles.

As a biological theory, open systems theory operates on the basis of energy exchange. An animal, for example, takes in energy in the form of food, converts the energy into a form the body can use, and the result is movement, nerve conduction, and by-products from digestion and respiration.

Katz and Kahn (1966, 1978) identified five common characteristics of all systems based on this energy transfer. The first is the importation of energy. For an organization, inputs include people, ideas, money, raw materials, customer needs, orders, and so on. The second characteristic is the through-put. Just as the body transforms food, the organization must transform these inputs into something usable. This transformation process itself takes energy, as when the organization provides training to new employees. Third is the output. Some outputs are desirable and expected, such as products and services. Other outputs are not desirable, but expected, such as emissions from a smokestack. Then there are unexpected outputs—for example employees who take a new idea out of the company to form their own firm. Fourth, systems are made up of cycles of events. A great symphony is made up of movements. Each movement is distinct, but themes may be carried from one movement to another. Some cycles are short, some long. It is important for the consultant to observe and identify the cycles within a system in order to create interventions that fit the system. The fifth characteristic is negative entropy. Since entropy as a law of physics says that all organized systems will eventually disorganize and disperse, the organization works to put that fate off as long as possible. That means that the organization must continually bring in more energy than it expends. It must either hoard resources against lean times or attempt to control the environment so that lean times do not occur. For example, a manufacturing company can either build up inventories or slack resources, or it can adopt a just-in-time delivery system. The latter requires careful control over the habits of suppliers, delivery systems, and other components.

Causality in systems is complex. There is often not a single cause of a problem, nor a single problem, nor a single solution at hand. If there were, there would be little need for consultants. There are multiple causes, some more tractable than others. There is also a phenomenon of equifinality; there is usually more than one route to a goal. There is also the fact that a change at one point in a system can result in unanticipated changes in other parts. Sometimes these are beneficial and sometimes they create new problems. Organizations and their consultants work hard to anticipate these changes, but there are always some that are not predicted.

Organizational systems are constructed from roles (Katz & Kahn, 1966, 1978). Each member of the organization has at least one role and may have more. Since people belong to multiple systems—some work and career related, others centered outside the workplace, such as family, friends, and clubs—Katz and Kahn observed the phenomenon of partial inclusion, meaning the entire person is not necessarily immersed in a given role.

Roles are socially defined and role expectations are sent by others, within and without the system. This can lead to role conflict—for example, role expectations sent by the organization that the person work late and the role expectation sent by the family that the person spend quality time at home. Role conflict can also arise just within organizational systems; the problem of multiple bosses is a classic example. OBC psychologists as both inside or outside consultants can take advantage of permeable system boundaries and of the psychologists' status as partial members of the organizational systems they consult with by (1) avoiding some role signals to bring new perspectives into the system and (2) to interject new role expectations. The process consultant (see chapter 9) is the quintessential example of this, but the psychologist can accomplish regardless of the type of project or most relationships with the client. Sent role expectations are a form of norm setting and norms are an aspect of organizational culture.

Organizational Culture

The first and, perhaps, most critical aspect of consulting with organizations is to understand the culture of the particular organization. The concept of organizational culture derives from anthropological notions of culture. There are several definitions of organizational culture; Schein (2004) lists 11, each with variations. Schein lists several basic elements of organizational culture: structural stability, depth, breadth, and patterning or integration. The last refers to the various components of a culture including rituals, climate, values, and behaviors that combine into a coherent whole, or Gestalt. From these considerations, Schein goes on to provide a formal definition of the culture of a group (and, hence, organization) as

> a pattern of shared basic assumptions that was learned by a group as it solved its problems of external adaptation and internal integration, that has worked well enough to be considered valid, and therefore, to be taught to new members as the correct way to perceive, think, and feel in relation to those problems. (Schein, 2004, p. 17)

Schein, however, is not the only one to provide a definition. Ashkanasy and Jackson (2001) note that there are at least three types of the definition stemming from different ontologies ranging from structural realist to social constructionist to a form of linguistic convenience. They also note that definitions depend on what epistemological approach is chosen by the definer. A deductive approach emphasizes the development of cultural dimensions, constructing measures of these, gathering evidence, and revising the dimensions as new results become available. An inductive approach, one favored by Schein in his writings, emphasizes tacit elements that may or may not be explicit. What Ashkanasy and Jackson term a "radical" approach has observers less interested in accuracy than "producing constructions that reflect their own interests and experiences" (p. 399). The choice of approach has resulted in considerable intellectual battles. Most prominently, those who create surveys are concerned with finding dimensions or factors that explain the common elements of organizational culture the world around, much as personality theorists have focused on the Big 5. Others, of whom Schein is the most prominent, seem more inductive or intuitive. They tend to eschew universal elements and concentrate on what aspects of the local culture differentiate the organization from others and how the culture will impact attempts to change. Such attempts are thought by some not to be "scientific," because there is little interest in generalizing from one study to another. The counterargument is that the Schein approach is more scientific because it relies on multiple sources and types of information rather than questionnaires. Both sides have their strong points. There is no general resolution because the solution depends on one's aims. There is a close analogy to personality theory, in which there is value both in studying common elements of personality and in studying the idiosyncrasies of the individual. For the psychologist interested in intervention, the former allows comparisons with others in a normative fashion or a comparison with desired state, while the latter is most helpful in understanding the specific person, especially when changing the individual is the focus. As discussed elsewhere in this volume, the development of rival perspectives in clinical and counseling psychology has been more harmful than helpful and in the treatment of organizational culture the beginnings of such rivalries can be seen in OBC psychology.

There are several survey-based measures of organizational culture (cf. Ashkanasy & Jackson, 2001; Svyantek & Bott, 2004). The question has been whether the various instruments are measuring the same constructs, particularly as one moves from one social culture to another. Results are inconsistent, with Askanasy and Jackson (2001) reporting that only two broad factors, instrumental and expressive, could be consistently replicated across organizations and societies. Recently, De Beuckelaer, and Lievens (2009) reported success in finding similar factor structures in samples from the same organization around the world (as well as measurement equivalence between Internet and paper-and-pencil surveys). However, it is clear that less broad cultural elements, such as communications or safety, are more apt to be replicable, at least across organizations. There are serious limitations to the use of survey-based measures across organizations and societies, the most obvious of which are problems in verifying that the same linguistic concepts are being expressed in the items across translations (Spector, 2001). In addition, because the data are collected at the individual level but applied at the group or organizational level, there are concerns about level of analysis issues. The most serious of these are the potential for misspecification, aggregation bias, the cross-level fallacy (i.e., assuming relationships found at one level hold at another level), and contextual fallacies (not taking context into account) (Ashkanasy & Jackson, 2001). These are serious enough that Ashkanasy and Jackson (2001, p. 403) concluded that, "Taken together, these four problems represent a central threat to the validity of survey-based measures of culture and climate." Thus, it could be expected that an OBC psychologist relying solely on survey measures to establish climate would address these concerns in the situation the psychologist is working in.

Perhaps the most informative informal definition that is of use to consultants who are entering an organization for the first time is Schein's (1968; cited in Schein, 2004, p. 13) earlier definition that culture is "the way we do things around here." A consultant who has worked with multiple organizations in the same industry or functions knows exactly what Schein means. At an extreme level, one organization may value only individual achievement. Another organization in the same industry may emphasize teamwork. Even functions vary in how organizations do things. Employees in the accounting department are likely to follow procedures strictly while those in sales may stress flexibility and doing "whatever it takes" to make the sale. Culture functions in much more subtle ways, of course; these examples are of the more obvious manifestations.

Schein (2004) describes culture as occurring at three levels (a reduction from five levels in earlier work): artifacts, espoused beliefs and values, and underlying assumptions. Artifacts refer to the visible products and accoutrements of the group. Office decorations and layout are common examples:The size of a desk or depth of carpet in the office are traditional markers of status. Behavior is also a type of artifact: Do people interrupt personal conversations to answer the phone? Schein points out that symbols can be ambiguous to the uninitiated, so it is risky to make inferences from artifacts alone. They can be helpful, though. One small company had a central office area in which all managers, regardless of level, were housed. On an early visit I noticed the head of customer service had boxing gloves hung on the outer doorknob of his office. I'm not sure what the intended impression was, but after I mentioned to the president that the impression this might generate in both customers and company employees who worked with customers might not be desirable, the gloves were removed. Still, the boxing gloves demonstrated an attitude that "the company is right, the customer is asking for something unreasonable," an attitude that proved difficult to change. In the same company I noticed a degree of resentment in the back, production area against the young President/owner. Although reasonably well paid under a union contract, the workers felt they were being exploited by the executives. Whether accurate or not, the perception needed to be recognized and dealt with. As I reported this I made what I thought was an exaggerated fantasy example that the president ought to not park his Ferrari in the front lot. He looked at me strangely and only then did I learn that over the weekend he had bought a Lamborghini and it was parked out in front. The symbolism to the workers in back was powerful.

The values and beliefs of an organization are fundamental to its culture. These include beliefs about the environment (e.g., are regulators on the company's side or opposed to it?), customers (do they have highly sophisticated tastes or can they be duped into accepting anything?), the nature of employees and management, and a myriad of others. The critical point is that in a cohesive organizational culture, members are socialized to accept the values and beliefs and those whose adherence is questioned may be "excommunicated" from the fold. One problem is that since organizational culture is in a sense a Gestalt, there must be some elements that are figural at any one time. This can create conflicts when the culture holds incompatible beliefs or values. University faculty, for example, may adhere to values of "academic freedom" simultaneously with values of a more ideological or strict paradigmatic nature. A faculty member whose pronouncements or writings defy the ideology or paradigm may be condemned by some while others applaud the inherent freedom to present divergent views. Only when the institution becomes aware of two incompatible values does the culture quake and a shift become necessary.

The basic underlying assumptions made by an organization's members represent the deepest level of organizational culture. Many of these assumptions are not easily identified. Schein (2004) gives examples of how a person at work who is apparently doing nothing at his or her desk can be seen as "loafing" or as "thinking out an important problem" (p. 33). A school system that assumes that students differ in innate ability, and hence, potential achievement, will have quite a different culture from one that assumes that all students can achieve the same level of success. Schein presents some persuasive examples of cross-cultural (societal level) organizational culture problems that stem from different underlying assumptions, as for instance between an American manager and a Chinese subordinate working in China. The competence to identify these underlying assumptions must be continually developed; it is doubtful that anyone achieves anything close to perfection in this. The development of such a competency comes from self-reflection, discussion and instruction with mentors, working with and asking people in various organizational cultures why they do many of the things they do. I find it helpful to study the history of different societies to learn how their underlying assumptions impacted social structure and allowed the culture to surmount environmental stressors or to collapse. I believe it is much easier to get the gist of this reading about, say, the trials and tribulations of the Han Dynasty in China, the Meiji Restoration in Japan, or the European Reformation than it is to begin with the examination of the assumptions underlying one's own organizations. Other OBC psychologists may have their own ways of accomplishing this.

Organizational Culture Versus Organizational Climate

At some point it is important to confront the debate over the relationship between organizational culture and organizational climate. The two concepts are frequently confused and there is some debate over whether they are independent from each other or from other concepts such as job satisfaction. Syvantek and Bott (2004) addressed the distinction. They see organizational culture as more oriented to the big picture; to long-term values and norms; and more integrative. Climate is said to correspond to management practices that are linked to specific behaviors thought to be important in the specific organization. Svyantek and Bott expect that climate will be more closely linked with specific aspects of organizational performance, while culture will not link with performance. The lack of relationship, or inconsistent relationships, between culture and performance was also noted by Ashkanasy and Jackson (2001) in their review of culture and climate. Culture is important because it limits what can and cannot be done in an organization. Presumably culture evolves to fit the internal and external environment, both of which it then influences as much as possible. Thus, culture will limit the effectiveness of the consultant's activities if the consultant has not adapted them to fit the organization. Culture will take a long time to change, while climate will change more quickly and have a more immediate impact on certain aspects of performance.

Leadership

Ask 20 people what leadership is and you will get 20 different answers. To illustrate the diffuse nature of the concept, in recent weeks the subject of leadership has come up in a number of encounters I've had with colleagues, administrators, consulting clients, friends, and family. A high school teacher told me of a student who was acting in an immature manner around his friends. The teacher said, "He was not showing good leadership." Is a manager who is avoiding taking sides in a controversial issue and pushing decision making down to subordinates engaging in "good" leadership as some say, or "demonstrating a lack of leadership" as claimed by others? Is a politician who is reneging on campaign promises showing poor leadership through a lack of character or great leadership by changing with the times? Is a basketball coach whose teams win games and championships but who engages in fits of temper on the court a great leader or such a poor role model he should be banned from competition? If a fictional man-of-action hero like the Lone Ranger is a leader, is there room in the concept for a quiet, unassuming soul like George Bailey, the central figure in *It's a Wonderful Life*? Is a Wall Street executive who pockets a multimillion-dollar bonus while laying off hundreds of employees a scam artist or a leader who keeps the best interests of the business and stockholders in focus? The last question leads to another: Who is the executive a leader of? Organizations have multiple stakeholders and the interests of these occasionally clash; whom each group sees as a leader and how they evaluate leadership can vary.

The examples in the previous paragraph suggest that leadership is many things and what it is depends on your vantage point. Part of the problem in understanding *leadership* is that the term encompasses many separate concepts. A leader may be the person at the top of the administrative pyramid of a large organization. Leadership may be seen as being a role model, a mentor, an efficient factotum, a dispenser of wisdom and justice, a decision maker, a builder of climate and culture, a money maker, a planner and strategic thinker, and so much more. OBC psychologists are frequently asked to evaluate potential hires for leadership qualities, to work with someone who needs to "learn leadership," to design leadership training, to infuse the organization with a culture of leadership, and similar leadership assignments. As psychologists we have a huge theoretical and empirical base to call on in meeting these assignments. But, psychology is not the only discipline that has examined the concept and the OBC psychologist needs to know these areas as well.

LEADERSHIP FROM HISTORY AND POLITICS

One of the most famous paintings in the country is Emanuel Leutze's *George Washington Crossing the Delaware*, which hangs in the Metropolitan Museum of Art in New York. The painting depicts the attack by the American Revolutionary Army on December 26, 1776, on the English and Hessian forces in the Battle of Trenton (see http://www.metmuseum.org/explore/gw/el_gw.htm for a photo and more information on the painting). Washington stands in the bow of the boat, in clearly bitterly cold weather. He is in the forefront of the troops, not commanding from behind. Washington is not asking the troops to do what he will not do. This quintessential image of leadership gets at the heart of what historically has been recognized as a sign of great leadership (Keegan, 1978, 1988). Teddy Roosevelt leaving his position as Secretary of the Navy to join the troops in the Spanish American War, ultimately leading the charge up San Juan Hill, is an example of this form of leadership (Brands, 1997). This is not culture specific. Keegan cites historical examples from around the world of respected leaders leading from the front. A tragic example is Japan's Saigō Takamori, "the Last Samurai" (Ravina, 2004), who devoted his life to living the ideals of the samurai and died leading his troops into a battle they could not win. Fortunately, most leaders do not have to lead their forces into battle to lead from the front. Nobody represented the Victorian era or epitomized her society more than Queen Victoria herself (Strachey, 1921).

Many cultures expect leaders to be humble, not self-aggrandizing. While the leader may profit from his or her endeavors, leadership in both the American and Confucian traditions requires humility and character. Shortly after the Revolutionary War was concluded, former Army officers met to form a new American government, one based on a new king: George Washington. They held what Flexner (1974) termed "the most important single gathering ever held in the United States" (p. 174) on March 15, 1783. Clearly this was a great personal opportunity for Washington, but he was opposed to a new king, even if he was to be the king. He originally announced he would not attend the meeting but then unexpectedly appeared. He spoke to the assembly, yet failed to move the crowd's opinion. Finally, at his wit's end, he pulled a letter from his pocket and could not see well enough to read it. Few had ever seen Washington rely on glasses, a possible sign of weakness in those days. He pulled them from his pocket: "Gentlemen, 'he said,' you will permit me to put on my spectacles, for I have not only grown gray but almost blind in the service of my country" (Flexnor, 1974, p. 174). In Flexnor's words, "this homey and simple statement did all that Washington's arguments failed to do. The hardened solders wept. Washington had saved the United States from tyranny and civil discord" (pp. 174–175).

George Washington's policies were not all successful; no leader's are. He is remembered as much for his character as for his victories. In the 20th century two presidents faced impeachment—Richard Nixon and Bill Clinton—not because of their policies (it is expected that presidents will pursue policies that will be criticized by others) but because of their moral failings. Klann (2007), a former Army officer and leadership trainer who is not a psychologist, placed character at the forefront of leadership qualities. His argument is historical and philosophical, not empirical, but it is one that should be studied by those who would build leaders.

PSYCHOLOGICAL AND SOCIAL SCIENCE-BASED THEORIES OF LEADERSHIP

Psychologists and other social scientists have studied leadership since their fields developed. Trends have followed the evolution of the disciplines. Early leadership studies concentrated on the "Great Man" phenomenon, examining what made historical or contemporary figures so important. The earlier examples of George Washington, Saigō Takamori, and Queen Victoria are typical of this school. Such studies are fascinating, thought provoking, and a mainstay of leader training. People do look to such figures as role models. Such role modeling can be important for guiding the behavior of followers and the next generation of leaders. Theories of transformational (Burns, 1978) and charismatic (House, 1976) leadership continue this tradition. Aditya (2006) reviewed the literature on transformational leadership and its relationship to personality. Although some aspects of transformational leadership can be predicted from combinations of personality variables, with explained variances running as high as .67, it is difficult to reduce transformational leadership to either personality or strict behavioral factors. One reason for this is that charismatic, and by extension, transformational leadership results from the dynamic interactions between leaders and followers. Transformational leadership has positive effects around the world. For example, in a study of bank branches in China, Thailand, and Kenya, Wang and Walumba (2007) found that transformational leadership moderated the relationship between the presence of family-friendly policies and organizationally relevant outcomes such as withdrawal and commitment. When transformational leadership was present the relationships were stronger.

Trait theories have been around almost as long as the Great Man theory. Inspired by that legacy, trait theorists believed there must be some trait or set of traits that predicted successful leadership. After years of study there are some traits that seem to be related to leadership (Bass, 1981; Northouse, 2007). Although findings are inconsistent across studies, Northouse determined that there seems to be support for intelligence, self-confidence, determination, integrity, and sociability as correlates of leadership success. Aditya (2004) reviewed trait theories and measures in the context of other leadership theories and concluded that there are at least some universal (i.e., cross-cultural, worldwide) traits that contribute to leadership in business settings. Citing the GLOBE studies, a series of large scale international surveys, Aditya concluded that charismatic/value-based leader behaviors are seen around the world as contributing to effective leadership. Participative leadership was almost universal in its endorsement while self-protective behaviors were globally seen as inhibiting the effectiveness of leaders. Aditya also pointed out that certain leadership measures were developed and validated in studies within single organizations over as many as 30 years.

One problem that trait theories, as well as other leadership theories, encounter is defining the criterion. Relatively few studies examine the effects of leader behavior on organizational outcomes; most concentrate on defining good leadership through follower perceptions. Emotional intelligence has been ballyhooed of late as a critical leadership trait. According to Frost (2004), the currently accepted definition is from Mayer and Salovey (1997) that emotional intelligence has four components: emotional perception and identification, emotional facilitation, emotional understanding, and emotion management. Zaccaro (2007) reviewed trait theories and concluded that relationships are, at best, complex and moderated by situational factors. The OBC psychologist is most apt to rely on traits during the selection or assessment process. In such a case a job analysis or competency model should indicate which traits are most apt to be successful in the position and environment, somewhat simplifying the theoretical issues. Aditya (2004) provides descriptive and evaluative definitions of several measures related to leadership.

An interesting development over the past few years is the recognition that leadership traits may have a "dark side." Robert Hogan and his colleagues have suggested that flawed leadership is common; perhaps as many as 50% of corporate leaders are, in Hogan's view, ineffective (Hogan, 1994). Some incompetence can result from nonpersonality factors, but severe disruptions can occur because people in leadership positions have seriously flawed personalities. Hogan cites arrogance, insensitivity, vindictiveness, selfishness, and dishonesty as representing the dark side of personality. These become a problem when they are paired with excellent social skills. Presumably a person with lousy social skills would not be placed in these leadership positions in the first place. Perhaps it is no coincidence that the popular media typically portray hard-hearted business executives with exactly these qualities. Hogan's firm has gone so far as to develop a personality inventory that assesses personality traits analogous to the personality disorders described in the *Diagnostic and Statistical Manual-III-R* (American Psychiatric Association, 1987). Hogan and Hogan (2001) report relations between these scales and other personality traits as well as ratings from spouses and coaches. Moscoso and Salgado (2004) validated a similar non-clinical personality instrument developed in Spain to match the *DSM-IV* personality disorder criteria and found the predicted relationships between personality scales and task, contextual, and overall performance ratings.

It is generally agreed that the most perilous hires are people who fit the mode of a "subclinical psychopath"; that is, a person who has the requisite personality traits associated with psychopathy but (so far at least) has not engaged in the criminal lifestyle that people with a full diagnosis must engage in to be accorded that label. A good deal of attention was directed at these people following the excesses of Wall Street and businesses such as Global Crossing and Enron in the 1990s. One can be assured that following the conviction of con-man Bernard Madoff and other exposés of financial frauds in 2008–09 the interest will skyrocket. The subclinical psychopath—or as they are often called, aberrant self-promoter (ASP)—worms his or her way into positions of leadership and power through such devices as having excellent social skills, forming allegiances with people who can help advance them, dropping allies once they are no longer of value, taking credit for others' work, spreading tales and "badmouthing" superiors to higher bosses in an attempt to undermine the supervisor, and similar behavior. Babiak (1995) presents an excellent case study of an ASP who successfully snaked his way up the corporate ladder sowing discord and broken dreams along the way. LeBreton, Binning, and Adorno (2006) reviewed the literature on subclinical psychopaths and presented a theory of how the personality develops. The most recent conceptualization has three factors that predominate in the personality. First is an arrogant and deceitful interpersonal style characterized by grandiosity and a narcissistic sense of self-worth. Such a person will engage in personal self-promotion and grandstanding. They will criticize anyone who is a potential rival or a threat. They might claim to have specialized knowledge in some field, although this is easily detected by true experts. In addition, they are well practiced in deceit. Second, like full psychopaths they have deficient affective experience. They lack empathy in the sense that they have no regard for the effects of their actions on others. They do, however, have skill at reading and playing on the emotions of others. They tend not to have strong emotional attachments to others and their relationships tend to be one-sided. They have a general failure to feel fear and anxiety in situations that others would find arousing. The latter is consistent with Lykken's (1995) theory of psychopaths, which holds that they are born with a higher fear threshold than other people due to an inability to connect feedback to their actions. There is, however, a tendency to project malevolent feelings onto others; they feel others are out to get them. The third factor is an impulsive and irresponsible behavioral style. There is a narcissistic quality to this in that they describe their lifestyle as spontaneous, unstructured, free-spirited. Others see them as "hasty, reckless, and triggered by whims with purpose of immediate egocentric gratification" (LeBreton et al., 2006, p. 393). To avoid boredom, they may move from job to job or turn to drugs or promiscuous relationships. They often fail to honor commitments. They have great expectations for the future, but no way of making effective plans to reach these goals. They consequently often must use parasitic relationships to achieve a degree of success. Remember, however, all this is coupled with excellent social skills that allow them to sell themselves to unsuspecting others.

Base rates of subclinical psychopathy are not known, but it is widely believed that people possessing these traits will migrate toward industries that are fast moving, have the opportunity for big financial gains, and are relatively free from standard operating procedures. Thus, it is expected that they will appear more often in financial industries than, say, an electrical utility. However, Enron was originally based in utilities, so the general rule is not foolproof.

This material on ASPs could have been located in the sections of the book dealing with employee selection, motivation, teams, or organizational citizenship behavior. It appears here because the ASP is rightly regarded as the most toxic possible leader. It is quite likely that the OBC psychologist will encounter such individuals during assessment or coaching assignments. Care must be taken to not fall under their spell and, as always, the psychologist needs to rely on multiple sources of data in making judgments.

Behavioral theories of leadership have been popular for 60 years. The famous Ohio State studies of Initiating Structure and Consideration more or less paralleled work on employee versus production orientation at the University of Michigan of roughly the same era (see Bass, 1981, for a detailed discussion and history). The theories culminated in the Grid models of Blake and Mouton (1964) and Blake and McCanse (1991). Given a traditional production organization, the behavioral theories may be useful in training leaders.

The last couple of decades have seen a number of leadership theories presented and subjected to some level of research. These are fully reviewed by Avolio, Walumbwa, and Weber (2009). One set of theories is exemplified by leader-member exchange (LMX) theory in which the relationship between the leader and follower is a critical consideration. More recent thought on LMX emphasizes consistency between leader and follower goals. There appear to be some relationships with performance and organizational citizenship behaviors, although there has been criticism of the type of performance measures used. In general LMX gets criticized for a number of reasons (see Avolio et al., 2009). There are also cognitive theories that emphasize self-concept, meta-cognitions, and implicit leadership. Other theories seem to be more trendy, servant leadership being a good example. I'd like to make a comment about the competent OBC psychologist having mastered all these theories, but to be honest, few of the practitioners I encounter have either heard of them or, if they have, take them seriously. I have had the chance to observe a number of leaders at various levels in different types of organizations and at no time did their behavior bring any of these theories to mind.

Leadership can thus be seen as a set of traits, charisma and visionary qualities, behavioral patterns, or an exchange between leaders and followers. But what happens when the leader is leading? Leadership is often seen as being rooted in power. An alternative way to envision leadership is as an influence process. Indeed, in his undergraduate text, Northouse (2007) defines leadership as "a process whereby an individual influences a group of individuals to reach a common goal" (p. 3). Instead of asking where power devolves from, it is more profitable to ask how a person gains influence. French and Raven (1959) presented the classic taxonomy of sources of social power as forms of influence. They identified five sources: legitimate, reward, coercive, referent, and expert power. If a person's boss makes a request, the person may comply for any of these five reasons; the boss's job is to make assignments, the boss can proffer rewards now or in the future for compliance, the boss can institute punishment, the boss may be a friend so compliance comes from mutual regard, or the person may believe the boss knows what is best and complies due to the boss's greater expertise. Reversing the situation, a person may request an action from the boss. Why would the boss comply when the person has no authority?

Perhaps the boss wants to ensure getting greater cooperation in the future (reward power), the person may quit if he or she doesn't get the boss's compliance (punishment), the two may be friends, or the person may know something the boss does not. In the latter situation the boss must acknowledge the greater expertise of the subordinate; perhaps that results in an equalization of power in some sense. Viewing power, influence, and leadership through lenses such as these promotes an optimistic view among both leaders and subordinates. For example, one organization I worked with recently held one of its periodic diversity trainings for the staff. The facilitator assigned various groups to discuss which groups held power in the organization, which, of course meant that some groups did not. Unfortunately, the use of the term "power" can lead to a variety of mental images. Perhaps the powerful groups consist of benevolent tyrants, but tyrants nonetheless, or they could be misusing their power to oppress the others. These mental images dictate how the session will proceed and whether anything useful may come of it. Another approach would be to ask which groups have influence and through what means that influence has been accrued. This leads to strategies through which the other groups can learn to exert influence and gain power, an outcome more likely to benefit the organization.

Decision Making

Individuals, groups, and teams make decisions—some big, some small; some important, some less so. There are extensive literatures in psychology, management, operations research, consumer behavior, and economics, and SIOP considers that an understanding and ability to apply decision-making theory is a competence an I/O psychologist, and by extension an OBC psychologist, should have. The literature on decision making can be roughly divided into two types. The first is prescriptive and deals with how decisions should be made. The second is descriptive and is concerned with how people actually make decisions. As in human affairs generally, how people should do something and how they actually do something are quite different things. Gigerenzer (2008) summarizes the main themes and findings in the decision-making literature as it applies to individuals, and his summary will be relied upon here. The prescriptive decision-making literature is largely concerned with optimization: how to make the best possible decision given a known and defined set of criteria, constraints, and probabilities of future events. Given a team of highly competent mathematicians and operations researchers, a good deal of time and resources, and the most powerful computers, optimized solutions can be determined only for problems containing a few variables. Optimization models tend to not generalize and can lead to seriously bad decisions when their assumptions are not met (Taleb, 2005, 2007). Even when the assumptions of optimization models can be met the computing requirements are beyond human capacity, to the point that many observers believe they should not even be considered as suitable comparison models to the way humans actually behave (Gigerenzer, 2008; Klein, 1998, 2009; Reason, 2008). The shortcomings of optimization models have been recognized for many decades; Simon (1955, 1956) proposed the alternative satisficing model over a half-century ago. In this model constraints are established prior to the decision making and the decision maker examines each alternative in turn and accepts the first one that meets the constraints. Satisficing models represent a more practical description of how one should make decisions and have been supported in several instances (cf. Gigerenzer, 2008). They are not workable in every circumstance; constraints sometimes prove to be modifiable or redefined. They can even shift at the last minute, as for example happens in the auto show room when a customer who has come prepared with a set of constraints regarding price, safety, comfort, and mileage suddenly shifts to purchasing a model based on styling.

The cognitive constraints on decision making led researchers to identify some heuristic strategies that people employ. Originally these were characterized as leading to characteristic errors because the resulting decisions varied from those specified by the researchers' version of optimization (cf. Tversky & Kahneman, 1974). More recently, heuristics have come to be viewed as effective adaptations that often lead to decisions superior to those that would be arrived at even if optimization models could be employed (cf. Gigerenzer & Selton, 2001; Klein, 2009). The opportunity for the OBC psychologist is to work with clients to identify when particular heuristics are apt to be effective and when not and to develop training or decision-making systems that encourage adaptive heuristics. For example, Klein (1998) both observed and interviewed decision makers in high-stakes, fast-paced situations such as fire fighting and military situations and found that effective decision makers utilized certain identifiable and replicable decision procedures. For instance, a fire crew captain may draw upon past experiences to understand an unusual feature of a fire, establish a few constraints, and generate solutions one at a time to be compared to the constraints. The first solution that meets the constraints is implemented. Klein's Recognition Primed Decision Making has been shown to be effective in a number of situations. It is similar to Simon's (1955) satisficing model but incorporates the use of experience and setting of constraints. Klein's model has the advantage of being amenable to post-event reviews and root cause analyses leading to improvement in the decision-making system. Klein's work demonstrates how the OBC psychologist can benefit from collaboration with human factors or engineering psychologists and from creative use of alternative research methodologies.

Decision making at the organizational level is influenced by individual limitations and strategies but has characteristics of its own. These were reviewed by Koopman, Broekhuijsen, and Wierdsma (1998). Understanding and working with an organization on decision-making processes requires an understanding of the organization's culture, history, context, power relationships, and other fa2ctors (Koopman et al., 1998; Schein, 2004). It is also necessary that the goal structure of the organization be understood. For example, the classical, rational decision-making model applied to organizations requires that there be only one, clearly specified goal. A satisficing model requires broad goals, limited information regarding risks, the impossibility of knowing all alternatives, and a short-term orientation (Koopman et al., 1998). A "garbage can" model was identified by Cohen, March, and Olsen (1972) based on the workings of universities. In this model there are inconsistent and unclear goals, an obscure and little understood technology, and very variable member participation. In this model problems, solutions, participants, and choice opportunities in which a problem and solution can be joined are jumbled together much as trash in a garbage can. Since there is little prioritizing and, often, little concerted effort to tackle certain problems, the combinations resulting from the choice opportunities are largely unpredictable. Having worked in an academic setting, I would have to say this model has some appeal in its descriptions. However, a form of recycling has been developed in which innovations or "best practices" at one institution are adopted by others in the classic "solution in search of a problem" paradigm. This recycling depletes the garbage can of needed components and distracts from true decision making. Last, but not least, is a political model. It is based on the assumption that the participants have divergent and perhaps contrasting goals. In this model of decision making the key element is how conflict is handled. The criterion for a decision is whether it is acceptable to as many players and coalitions as possible. In this model, the use of, and nature of, power is critical. In addition to identifying which of these or other models are being followed in the organization, the OBC psychologist must also be aware of the phases of decision making, how context and environment are considered and conceptualized, how solutions are generated, how problems are identified, and a myriad of other details. Consultants are frequently asked to help an organization improve its decision making. To do so competently requires a high degree of expertise in understanding and working in the culture and context of the organization, yet being able to bring in an outsider's informed view.

Motivation

Motivation in the workplace has been of interest to psychologists for many decades, both as a scholarly pursuit and because the consultant who solves the riddle of how to consistently motivate employees is going to be very successful. Pinder's definition is this:

> Work motivation is a set of energetic forces that originate both within and as well as beyond an individual's being, to initiate work-related behavior and to determine its form, direction, intensity, and duration. (Pinder, 1998, cited in Latham & Pinder, 2005, p. 486)

As with leadership there have been a number of theories that can generally be divided into need based, trait based, values, context, person-context fit, cognition based, and affect and emotion based (Latham & Pinder, 2005). This section is based largely on the review by Latham and Pinder, 2005.

NEED BASED THEORIES

The most widely cited need theory is Maslow's need hierarchy theory, the theory that would not die. As every introduction to psychology student learns, Maslow posited five levels of needs: physiological, safety, social or relationship, esteem, and self-actualization. He included a notion of prepotency, that needs at a lower level must be satisfied before the next level becomes prepotent. Maslow's theory is periodically chased from the domain of OBC psychology, only to reappear a few years later. Latham and Pinder (2005) cite recent research by I/O psychologists supporting the theory, and Warr (2007) presents a large amount of cross-cultural research that is consistent with Maslow's. Other need-based theories include Alderfer's (1969) existence-relatedness-growth (ERG) theory and the socioanalytic theory of Hogan (cf. Hogan & Warrenfeltz, 2003). As Latham and Pinder point out, need-based theories account for action but not specific actions, and they do not allow for individual differences among people with similar levels of need fulfillment.

TRAIT-BASED THEORIES

Latham and Pinder (2005) review several meta-analytic studies indicating that some traits are able to predict job search, choice of job, performance, and satisfaction. The list of traits includes extraversion, conscientiousness, self-regulatory and self-monitoring strategies, tenacity, core self-evaluations, and goal orientation. There appear to be important person-situation effects and job characteristic effects that moderate these relationships.

VALUES

Values are seen as functioning midway between needs and action. They are not conscious but can be easily accessed, and they are acquired through cognition and experience (Latham & Pinder, 2005). Values play a major role in vocational theory (Osborne et al., 1997) in the choice of occupation and role. According to Latham and Pinder (2005), there has not been much research on values as motivators since at least 1977.

CONTEXT

Two aspects of context have been examined in terms of motivational effect (Latham & Pinder, 2005). One is national culture. There is no question that the culture a person identifies with has a major influence on values and needs. There are some constants across cultures, such as self-efficacy, but it goes without saying that to understand motivation, one must take culture into account. The second context feature discussed by Latham and Pinder is job design characteristics. There has been a considerable amount of theorizing about the effects of job design, ranging from socio-technical systems theory (see chapter 9) to its effects on job satisfaction and happiness as discussed later on in this chapter. According to Latham and Pinder there is some conflict between designing jobs for efficiency and designing them for satisfaction. One wonders if the expertise of engineering psychologists were utilized whether this would continue to be the case.

PERSON-CONTEXT FIT

Since Parsons (2005/1909), vocational counselors and psychologists have assumed that people will be happier in jobs that match their interests, values, and abilities. This has not been easy to test and some say the research offers only small effects (e.g., Fouad, 2007). However, if people largely sort themselves over time into positions that more or less fit them, or adapt themselves to fit the position, there will not be much variance that fit can account for. Latham and Pinder (2005) review some recent studies

which indicate that person-context fit is a viable concept, although sometimes what is being fit is preferences for hours of work rather than factors
related to the work itself. The role theory of Miner (1993, 2006) states that
people have role repertoires and that they move into environments most
suitable for the roles they are most comfortable in. Miner does not attempt
to specify levels of success once in these environments and roles other than
asserting that attrition will be lower for those whose role preferences fit the
environment.

COGNITIVE THEORIES

Cognitive theories of motivation have been the most fashionable for the
past two or three decades. One of these is goal-setting theory. Goal setting
was well established as one of the most powerful motivational techniques
as early as the 1960s, but only in 1990 did the first full theoretical treatment
appear (Locke & Latham, 1990). Research on the theory was reviewed by
Latham and Pinder (2005) and they reported positive results for several
studies, but it is not clear if the results are due to the technique or the theory.
There are some interesting theory-based results on contextual moderators
and feedback conditions that can have practical implications.

Expectancy theory was all the rage from the late 1960s through the
1980s. Interest cooled by the 1990s as psychologists realized the theory
made impossible demands on human cognitive capacities. There has been
little research since the early 1990s and Latham and Pinder (2005) cite
Ambrose and Kulik (1999) as concluding that there are "few theoretical or
applied reasons for additional research on the application of this theory to
organizational behavior" (Latham & Pinder, 2005, p. 502). In other words,
the theory is dead. There have been attempts to resuscitate it—for example, Lord, Hanges, and Godfrey's (2003) attempt to reduce the cognitive
load using neuronetwork theory. It would seem just as easy to create a new
theory as to burden the dead with additional complexity.

Social cognitive theory is an outgrowth of what was originally known
as social modeling theory (Bandura, 1977). It was elevated to the status of
a cognitive theory by its originator Bandura (2001). Social learning theory
originally was concerned with learning that occurred without direct
contingencies—for example, a younger sibling could learn to avoid "bad"
behavior by observing an older brother get in trouble for various offenses.
With the shift to a cognitive focus came the introduction of self-efficacy
and goal setting. This theory has had enormous theoretical impact and has
some good support in the work setting (Latham & Pinder, 2005).

AFFECT/EMOTION

One cognitively based theory of motivation is founded on social exchange, the idea that people seek to maintain a balance in their relations with others. Adams (1965) proposed that workers seek to maintain a ratio of their inputs to the workplace and outputs from work that is comparable to the ratios of relevant others. Inconsistencies between ratios result in predictable outcomes depending on the situation. In an underpayment situation, if wages are fixed or hourly, quantity of output is expected to drop. If work is done on a piece rate, so it is impractical for the worker to reduce output, quality will go down. An overpayment situation will result in corresponding increases in productivity or quality. Most likely in that case, the person will simply eventually recalibrate the inputs to bring the ratio in line with others. Alternatively, he or she could redefine who the relevant comparison people are. In recent years the theory has been extended to include the concepts of procedural and distributive justice, as well as a more controversial concept of interactional justice (Latham & Pinder, 2005) and taken on overtones of affect and emotional reaction to the situation. Social exchange theory intuitively seems to be a theory that would not cross cultural boundaries very well. However, Chinese scholars at least appear comfortable with the concept. Zhang (2009) presented a theoretical analysis of the social exchange implications of the value of money and self-esteem that seems consistent with equity theory. In addition, Zhou and Martocchio (2001) compared Chinese and American managers making compensation and recognition decisions. It would appear that the major cultural difference lies in how various inputs and outputs are valued and weighed rather than on the relations between them.

Industrial/organizational psychologists have historically left emotions out of their theories, with values, satisfaction, and valence of outcomes being about as close as they get to affective reactions. That has begun to change, for which the recent volume edited by Ashkanasy, Zerbe, and Härtel (2002) is evidence. It is too early to tell whether emotions and affect will have a major impact on motivational theories, but anecdotally, it is common for the OBC psychologist to be asked how to deal with emotionally charged issues or employee emotional reactions to change.

Behavioral approaches to motivation have not been fashionable in OBC psychology for the past 25 years or so (Latham & Budworth, 2007), despite evidence indicating they can have powerful effects within organizations (Nord, 1969; Stajkovic & Luthans, 1997) as well as other areas of application within psychology. Latham and Budworth (2007) attribute this decline in interest to a desire to utilize cognitive approaches in theory and discomfort with deterministic philosophy. The absurdity of assuming that a cognitive approach obviates a behavioral one would be obvious to anyone who has ever attended a meeting of the Association for Behavioral and Cognitive Therapies and demonstrates the problem of an insular I/O psychology that is not open to studying other applications of psychology. Consistent with Harrison's (1974/1968) depth of intervention approach presented in Chapter 11, a good psychologist should begin at the simplest explanation and intervention, then move to more complicated and deeper theories and methods when needed.

EXTRINSIC REWARD SYSTEMS

Compensation systems are clearly motivational devices, even though they were not discussed in the Latham and Pinder (2005) review. It is generally believed that few people would show up for work at most jobs if they were not being paid.[1] Pay, then, at least motivates showing up for work. Because the compensation has such a large impact in recruiting, retaining, and motivating personnel, organizations often use pay systems as a strategic device to achieve their objectives (Heneman, Fay, & Wang, 2001). Designing compensation systems is often an interdisciplinary effort because there are economic and labor market analyses involved besides the human resource and psychological analyses to perform (Gerhart & Milkovich, 1992; Rock & Berger, 1991). Market surveys and job evaluation surveys are still commonly used methods to determine appropriate pay levels and ranges for job families, and a psychologist working in employee compensation would be expected to know how to conduct them. These methods are not without their problems; different methods of job evaluation surveying may lead to different results (cf. Heneman et al., 2001). In addition, such a psychologist would be aware of compensation issues relating to Equal Employment Opportunity and comparable worth as well as state, federal, and local laws regarding compensation systems in general. Compensation traditions, systems, and laws vary around the world and a psychologist working with international or multinational organizations will need to know these in each venue in which the organization operates.

---

[1] There are obvious exceptions to this rule. Many retired people volunteer at hospitals or charitable organizations, often doing work they might have considered beneath them during their employed years. Members of some religious groups may donate the pay they earn if circumstance dictates that they work on their Sabbath. Professors often work for less than the going rate for their profession.

The use of pay systems for encouraging high levels of productivity is common, although the issue has been largely ignored in the psychological literature for the past several decades (Rynes et al., 2005). According to Rynes et al., this lack of attention is at least partly the product of an emphasis on theories relating to need fulfillment, intrinsic motivation, or negative effects of performance feedback. Rynes et al. discuss several pay plans that can serve to reward performance at the individual or collective (i.e., team, department, or corporate) levels and conclude that there is good empirical support for the use of such plans. There are, of course, possible negative effects of tying pay too closely to limited forms of behavior. This can result in a single-minded concentration on doing only what pays, meaning noncompensated tasks go begging. This can disrupt teamwork. As this is being written the nation is focused on the bonuses paid to executives and other high-level workers in the financial services industry. Without more information, the bonuses seem remarkably high and clearly out of proportion to the poor financial results the companies posted in the previous year. At this point (Spring, 2010) it seems a distinct possibility that the recession of 2008–09 was in part brought on by pay-for-performance plans that led executives to ignore standard risk-management practices because their pay was determined by bringing in business, not avoiding risk.

Recognition programs are another form of extrinsic motivation system. Informal systems can be used by any manager and can be very inexpensive; a common example is giving an employee a gift card to a popular coffee shop. Such gifts are often in recognition of an employee's going beyond the expected demands of the job and used to encourage good organizational citizenship behavior. Formal systems are also popular. In these systems employees are given certificates, public recognition, or small gifts in token of performing at a desired level. Although used in all sizes of organizations, small companies, government agencies, and nonprofits find these systems especially useful. For example, Saunderson (2005) received survey responses from over 300 U.S. and Canadian managers of public service organizations. He found that over 90% of the respondents believed that recognition improves morale, belonging, commitment, and satisfaction.

Impact of Organizational Structure and Job Design on Efficiency, Satisfaction, Happiness, and Stress

Organizational structure and job design are not usually paired together although they have a good deal in common. Both have been said to impact efficiency, effectiveness, employee satisfaction and commitment, and motivation. Organization design is often thought of solving the problem of how the boxes on the organization chart are arranged and connected. Viewing organization design this way leads to the traditional issues of "tall" versus "flat" organization and whether the boxes should be organized by product, function, work flow, or in a matrix. The choice of structure depends on several factors that have been recognized for several decades (Üsdiken & Leblebici, 2001). These include the degree of uncertainty in the environment and the need for stability (Burns & Stalker, 1961) as well as the predominant technology employed by the organization (Lawrence & Lorsch, 1967). Government agencies often opt for the traditional bureaucratic structure because it ensures a consistent, though often inefficient, delivery of services. The bureaucratic structure comes at a price—slowness to respond to changes and an inability to innovate—but that is what governments want to ensure; equal treatment to the citizens and compliance with laws and regulations. The same is true of organizations such as public utilities. Some organizations have chosen to organize by process, such as those that adopt "six sigma" systems or their predecessor, Total Quality Management (TQM). Process-oriented organizational designs attempt to bring a high degree of certainty by strict adherence to the processes and attention to details. In this way they are today's new bureaucracy. Many businesses have found they need a design that allows faster response to environmental change and eschew bureaucracy in favor of less formal or confining designs. Even in those organizations some elements of bureaucracy are retained—for example, in the accounting department. Accountants are expected to meet certain standards and, to safeguard the money, have strict procedures in place designed to track where the money comes from and where it goes. Thus, differing demands from the environment require differing structures. In addition, internal expectations and a long- versus short-term outlook within the organization can create mixed messages and strain when not consistent with the structure and culture.

Designing an organization necessarily involves assumptions about authority and decision making. Sometimes this is explicit, sometimes implicit. The OBC psychologist can be of great assistance in bringing these assumptions to the fore because they do not always represent the foundational principles that the organization needs to survive and prosper. At this point we may see a conjunction with leadership theory, motivation theory, and team practices as organization design creates constraints on the form of leadership and motivational initiatives that may be applicable and successful in the organization. The OBC psychologist, having expertise in each of these areas, can provide valuable expertise in alerting the client organization to the issues and assisting with the design process.

Job design has been a matter of interest to both I/O and human factors psychologists for decades. On the one hand, the design of a job or work is believed to have a motivational effect on the worker, permitting the satisfaction of higher order needs or similar outcome (e.g., Hackman & Lawler, 1971; Hackman & Oldham, 1976; Herzberg, 1966; Herzberg, Mausner, Peterson, & Capwell, 1957). When the job is designed with a compensation system at the core, as in piece-rate or commission selling jobs, the design directs attention to what is considered by management to matter most. Jobs can be designed so they can be performed efficiently and easily, with reduced risk of discomfort or injury. The human factors, or applied experimental, or engineering psychologist has expertise in this aspect of job design. For some reason there is not much interaction between those who would design jobs for motivational purposes and the human factors professionals. You would think there would be a powerful combination and an excellent market niche for a firm of consultants.

For generations of psychologists there has been a controversy over the relationship between job satisfaction and job performance. A recent, comprehensive meta-analysis was published by Judge, Thoresen, Bono, and Patton (2001). Combining all facets of performance and satisfaction, they found that the overall correlation is best estimated as .30, but with a wide confidence range of .03 to .57. An examination of moderators revealed some influence of methodology (e.g., cross-sectional designs had higher correlations than longitudinal designs). The only job design characteristic they were able to study as a moderator was complexity, which had confusing results. Unfortunately, the critical moderator, the extent to which performance depends on discretionary actions (Herman, 1973), was not investigated. In some jobs, the assembly line being the classic example, productivity is not dependent on the worker, the worker's pace, intentions, or attitude. A toll taker at a bridge cannot bring in more tolls than there are cars. Attitudes do seem to impact behavior that is under the control of the worker—for example, absenteeism (Johns, 2002).

The concept of job satisfaction in all its manifestations was thoroughly explored by Warr (2007), including its relationship with job design, leadership, and organizational factors. In a move worthy of Blackstone the Magician, the chess master Bobby Fischer, and Brett Favre, Warr began by dethroning the concept of job satisfaction from its haughty position as a lead construct in psychology with the argument that what people are really interested in is happiness. Centuries of thought have been devoted to understanding happiness. Two general perspectives have developed, each of which had enormous influence on the world's civilizations.

One view, generally associated with Western culture, emphasizes accomplishment. Warr presents Aristotle's vision as the defining example; happiness comes from achieving that which is *worth* desiring, not to be confused with merely gaining what is desired. Thus, happiness can be derived from future-directed activities such as striving for goals. It does not derive from the accumulation of wealth for its own sake a la Scrooge. As much as we would all like to win a big lottery, studies of lottery winners indicate their newfound wealth has not increased their happiness (Brickman, Coates, & Janoff-Bulman, 1978). The other view, generally seen as Eastern or Buddhist in origin, sees happiness as a sense of personal meaning and inner peace. "By training oneself to emphasize tolerance, compassion, and harmony with one's context, a person may experience positive states or inner peace that are independent of pleasure in a hedonic sense" (Warr, 2007, p. 11). Contrary to the habit of societies over the millennia of proving which perspective on happiness is the truth by going to war with one another, Warr offers a compromise: Both forms of happiness are legitimate and to understand happiness in the broadest extent one must take both into account. Following Warr, we need to recognize that happiness is an internal qualitative state that may be influenced by the workplace. You cannot make someone happy; you can, perhaps, set the stage so that people have the opportunity to attain happiness in one or both forms.

Given this insight into job satisfaction as being a subset of happiness and that happiness represents two distinct, yet interrelated forms, Warr was able to reconceptualize the research and theory on job satisfaction and make sense of it. Warr finds that the effects of some job design elements can be best described through a vitamin analogy; up to a point more is better, but levels beyond that point can become toxic. Variety is a good example. A job that requires a person to do the same thing over and over again elicits anathema in most people, but a job that is always changing such that it must be remastered with every new task could have the same effect. Other job characteristics with vitamin-like effects include opportunity for personal control, opportunity for skill use, externally generated goals, environmental clarity, and contact with others. Given the curvilinear relationships, the fact that people attempt to sort themselves into jobs that fit them best, and achieve some degree of adaptation, it is no wonder the research has returned rather low relationships. There are some job characteristics that do not follow the same path; if more is not always better, at least it doesn't hurt. These constant effect (CE) factors include availability of money, physical security, and valued social position. Warr's theory has some similarities with the Herzberg motivator-hygiene factor theory from the 1950s and 1960s (Herzberg et al., 1957; Herzberg, 1966) and is even compatible with Maslow's (1943) need theory. It is not possible to summarize Warr's book here. It is too soon since its publication to state that all competent OBC psychologists should be familiar with the contents, but it is highly recommended that they read it.

STRESS, STRESSORS, AND WORK FAMILY INTEGRATION

Stress has become one of the major variables of interest in psychology over the past few decades, and OBC psychology is no exception. Few factors have the clear origins in physiological, social, personal, and physical environmental influences as does stress. A useful background in the biological responses to stress and associated disease and mental health relationships associated with the workplace is provided in the volumes edited by Quick and Tetrick (2003) and by Antoniou and Cooper (2005). A briefer version is provided by Smith, Sulsky, and Uggerslev (2002). The most readable general introduction to the biology of stress is by Sapolsky (2004). Interest in the effects of job stress, as well as safety conditions, was partly responsible for the spawning of a new subdiscipline, occupational health psychology, with its own journal and several books on the topic. The OBC psychologist should have a basic understanding of the underlying biology and an acquaintance with its relationships with health and mental health, but only needs a command of the details if working specifically in this area.

There are a number of theories regarding the nature and origin of job stress, some emphasizing the response basis, others the stimulus, the interaction between stimulus and response, and others person-environment fit (Sutherland & Cooper, 2002). Sutherland and Cooper identified six sources of job stress defined as the following:

1. Stress in the job itself—includes workload conditions, the physical work environment, hours of working, decision-making latitude, and so on.

2. Role-based stress—includes stressors such as role conflict, role ambiguity, and job responsibility.

3. Stress due to the changing nature of relationships with other people at work—includes relationships with managers, supervisors, subordinates, and coworkers.

4. Career stress—associated with the lack of opportunity for career development and promotion, as well as job insecurity.

5. Stress associated with the organizational structure and

climate—includes the stressful nature of culture and politics of the organization, the restrictions imposed on behavior, and no sense of belonging. Essentially, it is about "simply being in the organization."

6. Stressors associated with the home and work interface—includes conflicts of loyalty, the spillover demands from one environment to another, life events, and life crises. (Sutherland & Cooper, 2002, p. 53)

The sixth source was added to an earlier list prepared by Cooper and Marshall (1978) because of increasing emphasis on the home and work interface of the employee and how it impacts work and life stress. Although work and family conflict and its relation with job and life satisfaction has been studied for decades, there has been increasing interest in the topic over the past several years (Hammer, Colton, Caubet, & Brockwood, 2002). Organizations have been struggling to adapt to changing conditions and the willingness of employees with family obligations to invest as much time and energy in the workplace as previous generations are thought to have done. This has opened new opportunities for consultation for the OBC psychologist.

NINE

Organizational Change and Development

Organizational and business consulting psychologists frequently work with organizations in creating, planning, implementing, and evaluating organization-wide changes. Large scale organizational change was defined as "a lasting change in the character of an organization that significantly alters its performance" by Ledford, Mohrman, Mohrman, and Lawler (1989, p. 2). Admittedly this definition does not include some forms of change efforts included in this chapter because they are "too micro" (p. 9), but the present chapter includes procedures and methods intended to change the character of an organization and improve its performance. Change efforts may be directed at selected groups, such as executive teams, certain units, locations, or the entire organization. Projects involving organizational change vary greatly in the nature of planning. Specifically, Who does the planning with regard to the degree of participation by rank and file? Is the change effort is seen as an evolutionary progress without preset objectives and building on the culture and values of the organization? Or is the change an imported vision, structure, or objectives that may or may not conform with the values and past culture of the organization? At one end of this spectrum lie traditional organizational development and process consultation. At the other end are externally driven efforts such as those targeting process change and dealing with mergers and acquisitions. The requisite competencies are similar but change in emphasis depending on where in the spectrum the psychologist is operating. In all cases the psychologist must be able to analyze the organization's structure, culture, functions, and goals. Managing organizational change requires the use of extensive communication and influence networks. The consultant does not directly create or disseminate the change. Instead, information is gathered from, and disseminated to, opinion leaders within the organization who have a major role in diffusing innovations (Rogers, 2003). This was recognized as soon as action research strategies were developed; Lewin's (1947) writing on the subject is remarkably prescient in his recognition of what evolved into modern theory and practice. Thus, an important area of competence lies in the understanding and ability to utilize information networks and influence channels within the organization.

Organizational Development

Organizational development (OD) refers to endeavors intended to create changes in organizations with the intent of increasing organizational productivity, efficiency, and livability. The term is broadly inclusive, taking in activities, processes, and methods that are aimed at entire organizations down to subsystems and even small groups. The time scale of an OD project can range from a few days to many years in duration, with a bias toward long-term undertakings. There may be a single consultant or an entire team. The goals of OD projects are equally broad, so much so it is not possible to portray a useful logic model for the field as a whole. The purposes—and there may well be more than one—of an OD intervention may be to change management styles, organizational climate or culture, ways in which organizational members perceive and interact with each other; to modify the organizational structure and the functions of the people who populate it; to infuse new strategies and organizational missions and visions into organizational life, and several other possible goals.

A related approach, socio-technical systems design (STSD) originated in the early 1950s as psychologists studied the relationship between technological and social systems in workplaces (cf. van Eijnatten, 1998). Early STSD studies demonstrated that organizational structures need to be fitted to the technology used in performing work; later it was recognized that the opposite could also be true: Technology could be designed to fit with desired social systems. Superficially this seems to have much in common with a human factors/engineering psychology approach, but the latter focuses on the individual while STSD concentrates on large-scale systems. For example, in a large factory the human factors psychologist may attempt to optimize operator-machine interfaces while the STSD practitioner would be concerned with participation of workers in the design and governance of the greater technical and social systems. STSD has been studied and used around the world, with its largest impact in Europe and Australia. At present it appears that STSD principles have been incorporated into both mainstream OD and literature dealing with job design, employee satisfaction, and commitment. In addition, the influence of technical systems and worker participation has had a large impact on process change efforts as discussed later in the chapter.

Beckhard (1969) listed eight characteristics of OD that generally continue to hold. He noted that OD efforts are planned and involve the whole system. A caveat to this is that many times an organization has begun what appears to be a small change and is unsuccessful and brings in the consultant only after it becomes apparent the change is not working. Thus, the planning may not take place at the beginning; it may be part of a repair effort by the consultant. In addition, the members of the client organization may not fully comprehend the nature of possible changes or their desirability at the beginning; hence, planning may proceed in phases. Beckhard noted that the effort is supported by the top management of the organization. This is generally true, but there have been many successful change efforts within subcomponents of the organization. The third characteristic he listed is that the OD effort is directly related to the organization's mission. There are, of course, occasions when part of the effort is either to determine or to change the organization's mission. Fourth, the effort is long term. There are times when the consultant is involved for only a limited time, but the intent is typically to set the stage for long-range changes. Beckhard wrote that the fifth characteristic is an action orientation for all activities. The activities are engaged in to achieve some later objective; they are not done for their intrinsic value. This point is frequently missed by clients who desire an intervention. Someone hears of an OD activity, say, team building, done in another organization and asks the consultant to conduct a similar activity in the person's organization. When the consultant agrees to this, without doing further assessment, doing the work pays the bills for the consultant, but it is not a hallmark of ethical, effective, or competent practice. Admittedly, it may serve as an entre for such a practice to develop with the client. Sixth, Beckhard noted that OD has a focus on changing attitudes and/or behavior. The relationship between attitudes and behavior are controversial and certainly complex, but the practitioner works with what is available, changing attitudes when necessary and behavior when possible. A weakness of the field is that evaluations often focus on attitude change and consequent behavior change is assumed. Beckhard's seventh characteristic is that OD typically relies on a form of experienced-based learning. Consultants may present educative material, but they rely on experiences that their clients engage in to create change. Finally, Beckhard observed that the efforts are commonly directed at groups. The competent OD consultant has a high level of knowledge of group dynamics and the skill needed to guide groups through change experiences.

Mirvis (2006) provided a history of OD thought and distinguished between evolutionary OD and revolutionary OD. Evolutionary OD was "developed from a system's existing base" (p. 47). Change was built on prior knowledge and practice; many elements of the organization were left intact. Revolutionary OD is based in "death and rebirth" (p. 47); old norms and practices are discarded in favor of new ones imported by the consultant. This is not necessarily a positive development; revolutionary OD is founded on a set of ideological principles that may be shared by many psychologists and social theorists but are not necessarily accepted by organization members. The needs analysis exists in the head of the practitioners, not the needs of the system. As Kendler (1993) noted, psychologists may effectively inform social systems of the probable or actual consequences of social change, but they cannot dictate morality. Harrison (1974/1968) established a guideline that the psychologist should intervene only as deeply as necessary to achieve the goals of the intervention. Thus, revolutionary OD activities imposed on organization members without informed consent would be unethical, incompetent, and antithetical to the original values of OD. It is the client, not the consultant, who should own the problem and the solution (Schein, 1999).

This chapter does not attempt to cover all forms of OD exhaustively but discusses competencies required for common forms directed at various degrees of organizational levels and inclusion. OD efforts follow the same general pattern of most interventions by psychologists. They begin with assessment, move to diagnosis, then go to the design of the OD effort, implementation, and evaluation. Ideally, the process begins anew with reassessment, and so on in an action research paradigm until the envisioned change is achieved. The importance of beginning and renewing with assessment and diagnosis cannot be understated. It is generally recognized that failed organizational interventions often result from inadequate assessment and diagnostic activities (Kurpius, 1985). Organizational change theorists vary in the nature and timing of these efforts, but regardless of which form of change effort is employed, the competent psychologist working in organizations spends a good deal of time and effort in assessing the organization's situation, culture, needs, and other factors. Indeed, all organizations, and the people within them, are parts of larger systems. This is sometimes illustrated with the metaphor of Russian dolls, each one fits inside the next. However, the various systems are intertwined, and no one doll encapsulates another. The psychologist must remember at all times that the organizations and people the psychologist is working with are influenced, perhaps pressured is a better word, by many forces in the environment including the social, technical, political, financial, physical, cultural, legal, moral, and, often, spiritual. Given that each member of the organization has roles outside that system (e.g., family), the number of influences can increase exponentially. Notice that we haven't even mentioned individual differences in personality, education, family background, gender, ethnicity, and so on. This is why no single perspective can be used by a psychologist who aspires to competence. Such an approach is naïve at best and apt to lead to poor decision making at worst.

Although some theorists such as Schein (1999) state that one goal of OD is to have the client learn to identify the need for changes and to successfully implement these, continuing relationships are common. Organizations change, the people change, processes and technology change, and so on, and it is likely that consultation will continue to be necessary.

Process Consultation

Process Consultation (PC) is the most commonly used OD technique, if for no other reason than almost all consultants use it at one time or another (Schein, 1999). In Schein's words, "it is a philosophy of 'helping,' and a technology or methodology of how to be helpful" (p. xi). Explicit in PC, the consultant is helping the client to make improvements. Again, in Schein's words:

> Process Consultation is the creation of a relationship with the client that permits the client to perceive, understand, and act on the process events that occur in the client's internal and external environment in order to improve the situation as defined by the client. (1999, p. 20)

Note that neither the client nor consultant may have specific outcomes in mind in creating the relationship other than making things in some sense better. The emphasis on relationship as the method for creating change makes PC more like psychotherapy than other organizational change efforts. It is, however, quite different. Typically the consultant observes the group as it conducts business. Contrary to the OD characteristics listed by Beckhard (1969), the PC consultant necessarily cannot plan activities long in advance. Often the consultant is changing roles between process consultant and expert (i.e., one who knows where the group should head and what it should accomplish) rapidly during the consultation in response to the actions of the client group (Schein, 1999). Early in the PC effort the group is typically more task focused and the consultant attends to how group members relate to each other, group norms, culture, often the unstated issues that impede group effectiveness. The consultant may or may not point out group task process issues; it depends on the consultant's knowledge. Schein (1999) takes care to point out that the consultant works from a state of ignorance and attempts to use that ignorance to ask questions for which the answers may inform both the client group and the consultant. As the relationship with the group progresses and the group develops a degree of trust with the consultant, the group meetings may begin to concentrate more on process: how dialogue is conducted, the emotional connections between members, and similar issues.

Teams and Team Building

Team building is one of the most common interventions for achieving organizational change. A myriad of activities fall under the rubric of team building. They range from the silly, such as the "fall backward and your team member will catch you" satirized in television commercials to consulting actions based on reasonably well-developed theory and empirical evidence. Although there is empirical support for team building (Armenakis & Bedeian, 1999), the support for these atheoretical activities is scant (Kozlowski & Ilgen, 2006). Consulting actions that actually improve team performance are based on empirically validated models of teams. The consultant recognizes that the team is embedded in a larger system, which itself is embedded in other systems. In addition, the consultant recognizes that team members' roles are, at best, partially included in the team; team members often have other roles at work and certainly have other roles outside of work. Team members have areas of individual expertise that enhance their contribution to the team effort, yet they also need skills related to working effectively in a team (Salas, Burke, Fowlkes, & Priest, 2004). Today many organizations are structured around teams but have human resource systems based on individual efforts. The reward system, in particular, must reinforce team-based actions and accomplishments, but most organizations still focus on rewarding the individual's achievements (Kozlowski & Ilgen, 2006). Expert consultants recognize this and either work with the organization to change these systems if teamwork is really desired, or propose a reduction in emphasis on teams. Building reward and recognition systems for teams requires attention to stages of team development in creating performance assessment measures (McIntyre & Tedrow, 2004). It should also be noted that basing rewards solely on team performance can be problematic, resulting in social loafing (Rynes et al., 2005).

Teams that work together over long periods of time go through developmental sequences that inspired the notion of team building. An early, simple, but still useful model was proposed by Tuckman (1965) of having the stages of forming, storming, norming, and performing. During the forming stage team members get to know one another, and through storming, learn to manage conflict. Norms eventually develop allowing team members to predict and expect the actions of others. While these are particular to the individual group, organizations with a history of having teams will sometimes develop shared group climates that allow some movement between teams. A shared set of norms or climate is associated with better team performance (Kozlowski & Ilgen, 2006). Only after conflict resolution methods are established and norms recognized by team members can high performance result. Schein (1999, 2009) points out that teams will often focus on task issues prematurely before process issues have been worked out. It is an evolving process, with task and process issues coming to the fore at various points. Schein also states that the consultant who seeks to work with a team must get to know the team norms before working on process issues. Thus, the process consultant in team-building mode may confine his or her activities to task-relevant problems until familiarity with the team permits process work.

It is not surprising that teams that train together are more effective than those that do not (Edmondson, Bohmer, & Pisano, 2001; Kozlowski & Ilgen, 2006). This is easily seen in sports leagues in which all-star teams consist of athletes who are experts in their positions, but the team does not achieve at the level of even an average or even below average team from the same league. For many task teams it is possible to separate the training phase from the doing phase. The psychologist should be involved in both to be maximally effective. For other teams, such as top management teams, training in task execution is not feasible—hence, the role of process consultant. There are, however, teams that may not exist in an intact form for very long periods of time. Team members must be trained in their roles, and those of everyone else, so that the team can form and perform on short notice. In the Navy, for example, firefighting or gunnery teams may need to form unpredictably and consist of whoever is available. Commercial flight crews are brought together for the flight and may have never worked together before. For these teams it is necessary to employ special training models that develop shared mental models of how to perform the task and how to communicate, make decisions, and get along (Cannon-Bowers & Salas, 1998; Kozlowski & Ilgen, 2006). The shared mental models approach may not be useful for other teams for which performance requires diverse viewpoints and means of negotiating or otherwise managing conflict. Obviously, the role of the consultant in these teams will involve more process than task expertise.

One of the earliest forms of OD concentrated on the development of teams through nonstructured groups termed T-groups, sensitivity training, or laboratory training (Burke, 2006). Such groups had only the behavior of the participants as learning material. The idea was that participants would eventually come to grips with their "authentic" selves and learn about group behavior, norms, and how they are seen by others. Although widely hailed as a social breakthrough (Rogers, 1968, cited in Burke, 2006), problems were soon identified. Marrow, Bowers, and Seashore (1967) recounted a near disaster when a CEO unexpectedly visited a group and was shocked to learn what his subordinates had discovered about him. By the end of the 1960s considerable research had been conducted on T-groups with the finding that some behavior change may occur, but there was no convincing evidence that performance on the job was improved (Campbell & Dunnette, 1968) and that attitudes were lightly impacted (Neuman, Edwards, & Raju, 1989). One would expect that in a science-based psychology, sensitivity training would have died out decades ago. Similar interventions are still employed, sometimes under their original guise, other times as diversity training, cultural awareness, and similar endeavors. Without being able to specify logical linkages between the group activity and some set of desirable outcomes as well as some reasonable degree of empirical evidence, a psychologist employing these techniques would have a difficult time defending a claim of competence.

Survey Feedback and Action Research

There once was a time when it was an uncommon occurrence to complete a survey. You would go to a restaurant, eat, and pay your bill without being asked to evaluate the server and food. You would take your dog to the vet, get the car filled up with gas, buy groceries, and play golf and never complete a survey form. All that has changed. Back then, completing a survey was a big deal, a rare event to be savored and done with plenty of thought. Back then you could survey employees regarding their boss, the company climate, communications, and all manner of other potentially important factors and it was an event to remember. You could work with an organization, design an appropriate survey, pass it out, and later, work with the sponsors to analyze the results. If a work team was involved from beginning to end, they "owned" the results and were apt to make changes based on them. At least that was the theory behind survey feedback as described by Mann (1951) and enlarged on by Likert (1961). For some decades the method of survey feedback was one of the most important OD techniques. The idea of surveying employees, then feeding the results back to managers has caught on and been extended beyond anything its originators ever imagined—to the point that it is so ubiquitous that survey feedback as a distinct method has disappeared.[1] Although the method originally centered on written surveys, today the consultant is likely to use written or Internet surveys, focus groups, interviews, or a combination of techniques to collect and assemble data. The competencies listed in chapter 1 (Table 1.1) indicate that the OCB psychologist needs to have expertise in this process and in action research in general. The specific competencies include being able to write high-quality survey questions, sample the work groups, probably using Internet-based survey software, analyze the data, and prepare useful reports.[2] For focus groups and interviews the consultant must know how to design the group, write questions, collate and analyze the data, and prepare the report. For both, the consultant competency that is critical and most difficult to learn is the feedback process. For that reason it makes sense to devote extra attention to that issue. Not every consultant would necessarily handle feedback the way my team does, but the following procedure taken from the team's informal procedure manual has worked well for us.

FEEDING BACK THE RESULTS OF SURVEYS AND FOCUS GROUPS

The results of surveys and focus groups are rarely entirely positive. If they were, there would be little problem in feeding back results to the sponsors of the project, organization staff, and other interested parties. So, based on experience and a little bit of psychology, here are some observations on how to feed back results.

First, remember the program is a political system and exists within a larger political system (which is embedded in a larger political system, etc.).

---

[1] A search using PsychINFO in March 2009 found 71 references to the term "survey feedback"; only two of the papers were published within the last decade.

[2] Patton (2009) points out that writing a report on a project may take up to a third of the budget. Noting that many reports remain on the shelf unread, he suggests that it may often pay to not prepare a final report, but rather present the information to the client, engage in action planning, and move on. This is consistent with an action research model used by many consultants.

The client may want as scientific an evaluation as possible, but science is secondary to politics 99% of the time.

Before you design your feedback, remind yourself of the following:

- Who are the stakeholders?
- What are the relationships between stakeholders?
- What was the purpose of the project? Was it the same for all stakeholders?
- Who benefits from positive findings?
- Who would benefit from negative findings?
- How does the culture of the program impact the way feedback is utilized?
- What kind of pressure are stakeholders under?

Related to the preceding, Schein (1999, 2009) presents a case of a colleague he called Jim. Jim was consistently getting fired from consulting jobs. Upon investigation, Jim and Schein determined that on at least one occasion Jim provided negative feedback on the organization's culture to the CEO of an organization. The problems with the culture could be seen as reflecting poorly on the CEO. Jim then presented the same information to a management team with the CEO present. Although the CEO was able to take the results in private, presenting them in public was more than he could handle. One lesson from this is to know that you are sure of the context in which you are presenting data and results and try to determine whether there are any hidden agendas before going on.

Second, you have an ethical and professional obligation to present the results as objectively as you can. But keeping in mind the purpose of the project may assist you in presenting the results in a manner that is most likely to lead to positive use of the results. Ask and answer these questions before your presentation:

- What is your relationship to the organization?
- Do you care what happens to the people who run or work in the organization? (Have you unearthed evidence of misconduct or unethical behavior? Have they made a good-faith effort to run the organization as well as they can?)
- Put yourself in the place of the various types of stakeholders. How would you react to the data?

Third, the results are rarely wholly negative. Make sure you understand the results before you pass them on. This means thinking about what is working as well as what may not be working.

- What actions would you recommend to make the organization work better? Even if this was not in the scope of your work, somebody will ask you. You should try to identify two or more options (Schein, 2009). If you can't think of options, give guidance on constraints or on goals.

- Are there some parts of the organization that are working well or are otherwise worth saving?

- Can you quantify or otherwise express your confidence in the results?

Fourth, attend to how you structure the feedback. If you present negative results you can assume that one or more of the following will occur:

- Defense mechanisms of various types will be raised (leading with denial). Nobody will listen to you (except those who are hoping for negative results) if you jump right in with the bad news.

- People will be thinking of why the results came out as they did. They will attribute the poor results to almost anything, but most likely

    ○ You, your biases, your competence, your political agenda

    ○ Unusual circumstances that occurred when the data were collected

    ○ An inability (on your part) to understand the true nature of the program

    ○ Invalidity of the outcome measures

    ○ Invalidity of the analyses

    ○ Invalidity of the design

    ○ Biased informants or other sampling issues

    ○ Something that was wrong with the database

- Some people will react with aggression, others passively. Neither response is especially useful for figuring out how to take constructive action.

- Strangely, some people will read more negativity into the results than there is in the report, even when it is not in their own best interests. Make sure that they do not overinterpret the results. Often I suspect they had an overly optimistic notion of what the results would show. Failing to achieve perfection leaves them only with negatives. Relatedly, there is often a tendency toward escalation and catastrophizing; "This program is worthless. It should be shut down immediately." This isn't therapy, but you need to stop this and redirect the thoughts. Also, you may have these same tendencies, so do some introspection and keep yourself under control.

- In an oral presentation, be aware of group dynamics. No one person may get out of control, but put several people together and it can happen. You encourage this in a focus group, as long as they stay on task. In a feedback session you encourage it only if they are heading toward resolution and action.

Therefore, structure the feedback as follows:

1. State the reasons for the project as agreed upon when it began.

2. Note how the project was conducted and the scope of your work.

3. Restate the goals of the program as defined early in the project process.

4. If the project scope, method, or goals shifted, comment on that now.

5. If the situation dictates that the negative results be presented first, give some encouragement that positive results will be presented later.

6. Unlike a scientific paper, in giving feedback to the client you usually don't divide the results and conclusions.

7. The emphasis should be kept on the system or program at all times, not individuals. If somebody is screwing up it will become apparent without fixating on it during the feedback session.

8. Highest priorities are for action based on the results. You may or may not be the person(s) to decide on action. You can keep the client focused on determining actions. Don't let them rush into a series of ill-considered actions. Sometimes you need to slow down decision making.

Externally Imposed Change

Organizational development as it was originally construed involved the organization finding its values or vision and learning to make changes to reach that vision or to live its values. Just as evolutionary OD gave way to revolutionary OD, in which the consultants imposed their values on the organization, much organizational change has become externally directed. Early examples would be court-directed school desegregation from the 1970s, the introduction of total quality management in the 1980s (Druckman, Singer, & Van Cott, 1997), reengineering in the 1990s (Druckman et al., 1997), accrediting and credentialing requirements in hospitals (current), and the development of new accreditation requirements that change the way universities are run (current). In these situations the consultant is not concerned with questions of identifying the values or visions of the organization's members and creating new ways of doing things. Instead, the issue may be "how do we adapt our values, visions, and accepted norms to fit this new environment?" Much as in the case of mergers and acquisitions (discussed in the next section), there may be a period of grieving for the old ways before acceptance takes hold. It seems likely that in these cases it will be somewhat easier to find internal champions for the new order than in the case of a merger.

To illustrate the complexities of externally imposed change, my consulting team has been working with a large, public, multisite medical facility that serves a restricted clientele. The buildings at the main site are well over a century old and have been condemned for two decades. They are still in use because there is no option except continuing to use them. Under federal pressure, new buildings are on the drawing board and should be built soon. Another site has a building that was built for a hospital but for a very different form of medical specialty. In both sites the architecture limits the form of the organization and how it can most efficiently deliver services. In addition, both sites are having to change treatment methods and who engages in treatment, again due to federal requirements. This, in turn, changes social relationships that have built up over the past century. People are confused about status, roles, and competence. A third external force involves accreditation standards and a simultaneous need to upgrade information technology and medical record keeping. Units may go from having no computer or one old enough to have a green-font-on-black-screen monitor to state of the art computers and interfaces. Our surveys indicate the staff members are frightened of the technology change and they require much more training than had been planned and budgeted for. Fourth, as the demographics of the region change so does the clientele. Traditionally clients have been White Americans, with the occasional Native American or African American. It is clear that in the not-too-distant future the facilities will need to serve clients from a variety of cultural backgrounds. Focus groups indicate the need for more and better interpreters and, equally important, better access to training or other resources on cultural differences. In these circumstances, no one is asking the staff whether they want to change buildings, whether the new treatment regimens fit their values, if a new record keeping system makes sense to them, or the desirability of treating people from other cultures. These things will happen. The consultants' role is to help management and staff adapt as effectively, and in this case, as quickly, as possible to the new world that has already arrived. In this project we have two senior psychologists who supervise the project, two relatively advanced consultants who both coordinate activities and do survey and focus group work, and several beginning consultants on their first project. Competencies not listed in Table 1.1 (see chapter 1) that are involved include maintaining good relations between the consultants, and between the consultants and managers and staff.

Mergers and Acquisitions

Those who follow the business news are aware that one indication of the state of the economy is the level of activity in mergers and acquisitions (M&A). The successful combination of two organizations is a problematic business involving corporate history and culture, product or service lines, individual and team identities, the integration of differing methods and procedures, and numerous other facets of organizational life—indeed, all other facets of organizational life. In an acquisition, one company takes over another and the latter firm ceases to exist. In a merger two companies decide to go forth as a single entity. At times it is difficult to tell the functional difference from the perspective of an insider, customer, or supplier because even in mergers of equals one partner often tends to dominate; consequently the two are treated as a single subject of M&A. A readable, short, but useful discussion of the business side of M&A is provided by the Investopedia website (http://www.investopedia.com/university/mergers/).

M&As are typically developed by specialist bankers or brokers. Their business is to bring together candidate companies. The M&A specialists are concerned with "the numbers"; that is, the economic advantages of the deal. Their rewards, and the rewards of the executives involved, are based on closing the deal and are not dependent on the ultimate success of the M&A (Marks, 2002). Deals are kept as secret as possible and only the minimum number of people are in the know. Unfortunately, that means psychologists are unlikely to be involved, so issues involving loss of key personnel and incompatibility of cultures are unlikely to be considered. The expected financial advantages of many M&As accrue from reductions in personnel and other cost-saving measures—practices sure to increase rumors, job stress, feelings of insecurity, and inevitable turnover. Turnover is not limited to lower levels in the organization; Walsh (1988) found it was higher in merged companies than other firms at the highest executive levels. Although over 20 years old, this finding seems to still be relevant. For example, Krug and Hegarty (1998) compared U.S. companies taken over by foreign firms, U.S. companies taken over by domestic companies, and those that were not taken over. Walsh's top management turnover effect was replicated and even higher in firms taken over by foreign companies.

The cost cutting associated with M&As leads to what Mirvis and Marks (see Marks, 2002) termed "merger syndrome." The psychologist can help with managing merger syndrome through informing employees in workshops, collecting data on employee response to organizational changes, and working to develop leadership practices that encourage constructive engagement between management and employees. Thus, the competencies are consistent with those in Table 1.1 but require contextual understanding of the situation to be helpful. Not listed in Table 1.1 are competencies in the area of outplacement. These are the individual-level competencies for career-related problems and career counseling. Many business organizations operate internationally. Dealing with the different cultures within the company itself can be a challenge. M&A activity is often international in scope and this can complicate matters exponentially. A psychologist working in this area may need additional cultural competence covering specific cultures or in melding many different cultures.

Planning and Managing Change

"Change Happens" reads a popular statement. It is true. But change that is managed and planned is much more likely to achieve goals. This requires two distinct sets of skills; one psychological, the other business oriented. The psychological skills include understanding resistance to change or, alternatively, how people cope with demands for change. The psychologist must also be able to see the change within a larger context. In planning and implementing change efforts it has been shown that the organizational context is a critical concern (Armenakis & Bedeian, 1999). Contextual variables include what might be termed organizational demographics (e.g., age of the organization, size), recent experience with change, stability of the environment (technological, regulatory, competitive, and other factors), and past effectiveness of the organization in responding to environmental change. Some commentators note that resistance to change or cynicism of organization members regarding the potential value of change efforts is more common than support for change measures. Probably most

OBC psychologists have had the experience of entering a client organization to assist with some change or another and being told by jaded employees that whatever they, the consultants, did, would not make much difference because management keeps trying to make changes and nothing ever works. Herold, Fedor, and Caldwell (2007) studied over 500 employees in 25 organizations undergoing various types of change. They found that regardless of the type of change, commitment was clearly related to an interaction of personal self-efficacy and turbulence, the extent to which there were other changes going on in the organization (context). In a highly turbulent organization with multiple changes, there should be a strong sense of being able to accomplish any given change among employees to have much commitment to carrying the change out to a successful conclusion. Thus, important competencies are to both assess and work with the organizational context and commitment to change by its members.

A lack of commitment to change is sometimes thought of as comparable to the clinical concept of resistance to change. In this conceptualization, the client resists changing due to some internal conflicts that prevent movement. Three alternative views are helpful in understanding the failure to commit to change that could inform consulting practice. Prochaska and DiClemente (cf. Prochaska, 1999) identified five stages (actually phases) that people go through as they change or don't change. The first of these, precontemplation, describes the state of people who either never seriously considered changing or are planning to do so at some indeterminate time in the future. An example would be a smoker who says he or she may stop next year. A person planning a change in the next 6 months would be in contemplation. Such a person is aware of the advantages of changing, but also the disadvantages (quitting smoking would be uncomfortable). Once the time for the change the person is planning draws near, within a month, he or she is said to be in the preparation stage. Such people have a plan for action and can be persuaded to change with action-oriented interventions. Those who are actually implementing changes are in the action stage and those who have completed a change and are vigilant about backsliding are in the maintenance stage. This taxonomy works reasonably well with people who are making personal changes. In organizations, the need for change may be imposed from outside and may not have been apparent to many organizational members. Stayer (1990) recounts a decade-long change process in the sausage company he ran. He determined that changes were necessary, announced this to his top managers out of the blue, and was dismayed that they did not buy into the change and failed to accomplish his objectives—to the point that he ultimately replaced them. They were in the precontemplation stage and had never imagined the need for or the nature of the change that was foisted upon them. It is fair to say that this is common in organizations, and the clever consultant recognizes this and works with the client organization to help members see and adapt to the necessity of change, thus reducing apparent resistance.

Another clinician who has tackled resistance or lack of commitment to change in a manner useful in organizations is Leahy (2003). A cognitive therapist, he wondered why many clients would recognize the need for change (i.e., be in the contemplation, preparation, or even early action stages) but never carry through with implementing it. Borrowing an idea from economics, portfolio theory, he analyzed several forms of psychological disorders using financial concepts as metaphors including available assets, future earning potential, functional utility of gains, replications of investment, duration of investments, and portfolio diversification. It is well known that people place different valuations on the components of portfolios (the risk tolerance of someone 60 years old is probably lower than that of someone who is 30 since there is less time for the 60-year-old to make up for losses). Basically, Leahy found that failure to change could be predicted when potential losses exceeded potential gains, but that the valuation and probabilities associated with gains and losses are characteristically skewed by various disorders. There is an old question that underlies willingness to change: "What is in it for me?" To answer that involves understanding the costs and benefits of change as seen by the individual, work group or team, department, and so on. Leahy's work can be easily adapted to fit the business setting and can be understood by managers.

A method of accomplishing Leahy's portfolio analysis that is effective with less financially sophisticated organization members is to lead them in an examination of the rewards and punishments of changing and not changing for the organization (department, team) and the individual. An example is shown in Figure 9.1. The consultant works with the client or team to complete the squares following these directions:

1. Identify the change that has been proposed or implemented.

2. Identify a specific individual or set of individuals of special interest. If there is more than one individual or set of individuals, create more columns. Many stakeholders could result in many columns. Stop before it gets too complicated. You can come back and do the exercise again to include more stakeholders.

3. The next steps involve identifying rewards and punishments for making the change and for retaining the status quo. All may be

FIGURE 9.1 **Simple method for understanding forces for and against change in an organization and selected individual(s)**

	Organization	Individual
Rewards for changing		
Punishers for changing		
Rewards for status quo		
Punishers for status quo		

tangible or intangible. If something is listed in one cell, it can't appear in another (e.g., a punisher of change is the cost; a reward for not changing can not be not having the cost).

4. Identify rewards for the organization for making the change. These include tangible and intangible advantages. Include rewards that may accrue in the reasonable future.

5. Identify punishments for the organization for making the change. Again, these are tangible and intangible. Include those that may accrue in the reasonable future.

6. Identify the rewards for the organization for not making the change. These may be tangible or intangible. Some rewards that are always included are avoiding the costs and hassles of the change, and avoiding uncertainty.

7. Repeat the above steps for the individual. The rewards and punishments will be different (e.g., if the organization makes money, the

individual reward might be greater prestige, power, or security). This is the time to use your empathic powers to see the pressure to change and not change from the individual's point of view.

8. Finally, use the information in the cells to

- Identify levers for changing (or not changing)

- Identify obstacles for change

- Identify factors that must be mitigated if the change occurs (i.e., costs, loss of influence, stress from uncertainty).

Nevis (1987) presented a somewhat different approach that is not inconsistent with those based on stages of change and portfolio theory. Nevis does not see resistance as resistance. Rather, it is the attempt by employees to retain their integrity. As the crew of a boat crossing a river has to avoid being blown off course by stray breezes and shifting currents, organization members seek to maintain equilibrium by staying the course as much as possible. They creatively adjust to conditions but make major changes as they perceive the need, much as Katona (1953) observed that people establish routines and it takes "strong motivational forces" (p. 310) to get them to abandon these habits in favor of problem-solving behavior. Nevis invites naysayers to participate when they decide to do so. Probably Nevis, and certainly Katona, would suggest having those who appear resistant to redefine the situation such that problem solving begins. In such cases the psychologist and management are taking the risk that the end result may not be the same as planned from above.

Whether through these means or others, the competent OBC psychologist plans for and has a repertoire for reducing resistance or inducing commitment. Of course, it is not the psychologist who accomplishes these; that is up to the organization. The consultant works with sponsors within the organization to help them strategize and actualize change. A consultant should never expect to create a climate for and acceptance of change solely through personal action. In cases where this is attempted by some superhero consultant, the change is doomed to fail because the consultant cannot control the costs and benefits or rewards and punishments the organization and its environment can provide.

PART IV

Foundational
Competencies—
The OBC Psychologist
as a Professional

TEN

Business and Consulting Skills

A number of competencies needed for success in organizational and business consulting psychology are not specific to the field. Under Industrial and Organizational Psychologists (subsuming Consulting Psychologists), the O*NET describes the extent to which a large number of knowledges, skills, and abilities are required by the professional (O*NET On-Line, downloaded 10/10/2008). Obviously no single person's repertoire will match the list, but it is instructive to examine the top 10 of each. The knowledge list provides few surprises. Psychology is the most important item, followed closely by Personnel and Human Resources; Education and Training and Mathematics are fourth and fifth, just behind English Language. More salient for this chapter is the listing of Customer and Personal Service, Administration and Management, Communications and Media, and Clerical (i.e., knowing administrative and clerical procedures, knowing how to use word processing, and designing forms). These are the sorts of knowledge expected of anyone in middle to upper management in most organizations and in most professions. They illustrate that success will not flow just from competence in psychology; one must know how to operate in a businesslike manner to get the job done.

Table 10.1 lists the top 20 skills for I/O psychologists from the O*NET. Most require no elaboration; a few deserve special comment.

Writing is a skill that ought to be taught in high school or college; in graduate school psychologists are taught to write using the style dictated by the American Psychological Association (APA style; American Psychological Association, 2009b). While APA style is appropriate for writing scientific papers and technical reports, the OBC psychologist writes for

TABLE 10.1 **Top 20 Skills for the Industrial and Organizational Psychologist from the O*NET**

IMPORTANCE RATING	SKILL	O*NET DESCRIPTION
96	Critical thinking	Using logic and reasoning to identify the strengths and weaknesses of alternative solutions, conclusions, or approaches to problems.
92	Active listening	Giving full attention to what other people are saying, taking time to understand the points being made, asking questions as appropriate, and not interrupting at inappropriate times.
87	Speaking	Talking to others to convey information effectively.
85	Reading comprehension	Understanding written sentences and paragraphs in work-related documents.
84	Writing	Communicating effectively in writing as appropriate for the needs of the audience.
74	Coordination	Adjusting actions in relation to others' actions.
73	Judgment and decision making	Considering the relative costs and benefits of potential actions to choose the most appropriate one.
73	Science	Using scientific rules and methods to solve problems.
69	Time management	Managing one's own time and the time of others.
68	Learning strategies	Selecting and using training/instructional methods and procedures appropriate for the situation when learning or teaching new things.
67	Mathematics	Using mathematics to solve problems.
66	Monitoring	Monitoring/assessing performance of yourself, other individuals, or organizations to make improvements or take corrective action.
64	Instructing	Teaching others how to do something.
63	Complex problem solving	Identifying complex problems and reviewing related information to develop and evaluate options and implement solutions.
62	Social perceptiveness	Being aware of others' reactions and understanding why they react as they do.

IMPORTANCE RATING	SKILL	O*NET DESCRIPTION
61	Active learning	Understanding the implications of new information for both current and future problem solving and decision making.
56	Persuasion	Persuading others to change their minds or behavior.
53	Service orientation	Actively looking for ways to help people.
52	Systems evaluation	Identifying measures or indicators of system performance and the actions needed to improve or correct performance, relative to the goals of the system.
50	Management of personnel resources	Motivating, developing, and directing people as they work; identifying the best people for the job.

Source: O*NET On-Line (2009). Details report for 19-3032.00 – Industrial-Organizational Psychologists. Downloaded 10/10/2008 from http://online.onetcenter.org/link/details/19-3032.00.

a much broader and varied audience. Scientific writing calls for description of exact details and rationale for procedure, but a report prepared for a client may be confined to one or a few pages with just the most important points discussed. Technical details can be presented in a technical report that is rarely read by anyone unless there is litigation. Similarly, APA style calls for a standard outline: Abstract, Introduction, Method, Results, Discussion. A report for a client may have an Executive Summary containing a brief description of the project and action items followed by the report itself consisting of brief descriptions of method, results, and implications mixed as appropriate. Other types of writing include letters for reporting and marketing, material for popular publications, websites, or blogs intended to inform the public and make the psychologist's name or firm known, material for company newsletters, and many other forms. Thus, an aspiring OBC psychologist may need to relearn how to write after graduate school.

Speaking is a necessary skill for the professional seeking to make a living providing services to businesses and other organizations. Speaking may be one on one, to small groups, or to very large assemblies. It may be formal, as in a sales presentation to a potential client, or impromptu. Successful OBC psychologists learn to think quickly and to express their thoughts verbally in a manner suitable for the audience and occasion. Graduate training typically emphasizes learning how to make presentations such as those given in convention symposiums; this is only one form of the speaking skills that are needed.

The monitoring and instructing skills have obvious relationships to the work performed by OBC psychologists. These skills also come into play in the work arrangements of many OBC psychologists. Many, but by no means all, work as part of groups either as internal consultants or in consulting firms. These groups may range from a few people to firms with many hundreds of consultants. A common career path is to start with a group as an entry-level consultant who performs most of the detailed work (e.g., job analyses). With time and experience the consultant moves into practice management, which involves wooing the client and managing projects once they begin. The senior consultants may do relatively little directly billable work on the details but they supervise the junior consultants. This career progression may be required just to remain an associate with some firms.

The primary abilities listed by the O*NET deal with oral and written communications, followed by deductive reasoning, inductive reasoning, and problem sensitivity (noting there is or may be a problem, not necessarily solving it). Interestingly, given the emphasis on mathematical tasks and skills, the abilities of information ordering—"The ability to arrange things or actions in a certain order or pattern according to a specific rule or set of rules (e.g., patterns of numbers, letters, words, pictures, mathematical operations)"—category flexibility, and fluency of ideas (both rated 63 in importance) are rated as equal in importance to mathematical reasoning (rated 63).

Characteristics Needed for Forensic Work

Some OBC psychologists will serve as experts in court. Most often this would probably occur in association with discrimination cases. Borden and Sharf (2007) describe personal characteristics to look for in personnel for projects that may be subject to litigation. Given appropriate professional training and experience and technical skills, the person should possess three additional characteristics: attention to detail, a suitable temperament, and communication skills. These are important for competently presenting information in court. Missing some details, however minor, may make the witness appear sloppy or unprepared. Similarly, being easily rattled, becoming defensive, or otherwise tending to behave inappropriately can provide an opposing attorney with an opportunity to make the witness look "bad," in spite of technical prowess. In general, court appearances not withstanding, it is hard to deny the importance of these characteristics for success in most facets of professional work.

Personal Qualities in Demand by Consulting Firms

In an attempt to identify the competencies most in demand by consulting firms, my graduate assistant, Heidi Meeke (2009), examined employment ads for the second half of 2008 and first part of 2009 and directly contacted 16 firms. The firms ranged from locally based consulting firms to those with a global practice and one that specializes in providing services to the federal government. Meeke's findings can be summarized as follows:

Training. Most firms require a doctoral degree in I/O psychology, while firms specializing in change management will accept a doctorate in clinical psychology. Some hire staff with a master's degree and several will take on interns with the hope of keeping them on. One firm will accept personnel with a bachelor's degree. Some firms primarily perform contract research and they also look for PhDs in human factors, applied experimental psychology, and, in one instance, consumer psychology.

Specific areas of training mentioned include statistics beyond the basic levels, psychometrics, selection testing and assessment, performance appraisal and 360 degree methods, program evaluation, and general psychology background.

Experience. Firms vary in that some take on interns or entry-level professionals. Most require "extensive" or "good" business experience for anyone above entry level. Experience in coaching and developmental training, data interpretation, feedback, assessment, and test development were mentioned often.

Work Skills. Firms expect to hire people who can work independently and as members of teams; plan, track, and manage projects; engage effectively with clients or customers; make presentations to clients; write reports; and market and bring in new clients.

Personal Characteristics. One firm listed five necessary qualities that sum up what such companies are looking for: insight, intelligence, solidarity (with the organization's culture), resilience, and impact (being "assertive, precise, and on-the-spot" with observations with colleagues and clients). Other firms desire people who are willing to "pitch in" in whatever way is needed to make a project succeed. The ability to lead other professionals in projects is listed by several firms. None of the firms specified creativity or critical thinking ability, results that are hard to square with the demand for advanced degrees and high responsibility to meet the client's needs.

Murphy (2006) wrote that the foundation for professional success is judgment, but none of the firms examined mentioned it. In addition, despite continuing discussion about the need to work with an increasingly diverse workforce, not one of the companies professed an interest in applicants having the skills necessary to do this. As a rule, companies do not list qualities such as honesty, integrity, and ethical behavior, but that does not mean they are unimportant. In addition, and also unstated, a clear sense of boundaries is needed to maintain clear limits with clients.

Meeke also found resilience listed by one firm, and that is an interesting and instructive addition. Maddi (2006) wrote that one cannot be resilient without hardiness. Hardiness is "a pattern of attitudes that facilitates turning stressful circumstances from potential disasters into growth opportunities" (p. 306). Hardiness stems from the conjunction of three attitudes toward living; commitment, control, and challenge. Together, these form existential courage, and courage is what is needed to be hardy, and ultimately, resilient. The OBC psychologist in daily practice who seeks to maintain competence while utilizing a scientifically based technology requires courage. Chapter 1 included a discussion of psychology as a technology. As stated in the design text cited by Petroski (2003), solving today's problems requires solutions today; you can't wait for the science to catch up. In making recommendations to a client the psychologist often has to stretch the limits of what is known by the field and combine that with what is known about the client, the context, and the environment. This requires courage. Those who cannot do it are advised to seek a career in a nonapplied area of psychology.

Prior to the Meeke study I ran across a set of job ads by a large, global consulting firm. Each ad required "executive poise," which I interpret as the ability to remain cool and take positive actions in the midst of chaos. Related to the resilience cited earlier, a good OBC psychologist does not give in to anxiety, and when members of client organizations are wailing and catastrophizing, he or she does not add to the panic but rather assists the client to develop positive plans to deal with adversity.

Business Skills for Consulting

The consulting firms surveyed by Meeke (2009) want the OBC psychologists they hire to have at least a modicum of business knowledge and skills. Certain of these competencies will be more important in small firms because there are fewer people to take up the slack. The OBC psychologist in private practice will need all of these. Stroh and Johnson (2006) provide an excellent outline of the basic business skills of a consultant. The following sections describe the typical phases in obtaining, managing, and ending a large-scale project such as the development of an employee selection system, training program, or organization-wide change effort. Smaller scale assignments such as performing individual assessments or development activities will not require such elaborate proposals and tracking, and they will employ more targeted reports and feedback.

CONNECT WITH THE CLIENT

The first step in any consultation is making a connection with the potential client, so networking and marketing skills are extremely important. The connection can come from referrals by existing or past clients or a professional colleague, from advertising or a website, or a formal request for proposal (RFP). These are sent by organizations, often government or quasi-government agencies. The RFP specifies what services are to be provided, the schedule, important contacts, and methods of billing and payment (see later section). In follow-up telephone or other informal contacts, it is necessary to obtain the following information:

- Nature of the problem
- Services requested
- Nature of the organization
- Special concerns
- Time and scheduling constraints
- Name and title of contact

The would-be consultant must be able to impress a potential client. New graduates often generalize the behaviors that were reinforced in graduate school and show off their extensive knowledge of the latest theories, techniques, and findings. By and large, the potential clients don't care about these things. It is not that knowing the field is not important, but the client is more concerned with what the consultant has done and can do than with the consultant's knowledge of what others have done. Basic competence in the field is often assumed by the client, for better or worse. Potential clients are looking for someone they can work with, who appears and acts competent, and, frankly, who looks and acts like the other people they deal with at work. Well-known and established consultants can get away with idiosyncrasies in dress and manner; new and junior consultants cannot. They must learn to dress, speak, and move in a manner consistent with the culture of the client. A little etiquette goes a long way. Depending on the type of client one is pursuing, it may make sense to cultivate knowledge of literature, arts, sports, world affairs, and current events. Oftentimes, it pays to take up golf or tennis. These sports can be fun and provide networking opportunities. Clients want someone who can help them. Whenever possible, the consultant should find out as much as possible about the potential client company through the methods listed in Table 10.2. Be as knowledgeable as possible about the client organization and its industry.

Experienced consultants will be able to speak intelligently about the type of problems the client is experiencing and suggest possible courses of action. The ability to think on one's feet and without noticeable strain is invaluable.

TABLE 10.2 Organizational Information to Gather About a Client

Understanding the workplace environment requires knowing the organization. Since organizations are complex, that means you have to know many aspects of the organization, present and future. Much, but not all of the following comes from Schippmann (1999). Not all of this information can be obtained prior to starting a consultation and much of it may not be necessary for a given client.

1. **Basics**.
   1.1 *Organization Chart.* This is a snapshot of the organization at a moment in time. You can get an indication of several things from it, including
       1.1.1 How "tall" the organization is.
       1.1.2 Where the unit(s) you are working with fit into the whole.
       1.1.3 Whether the organization is designed according to function, product, a matrix, or a combination.
       1.1.4 Whether individuals or teams are the key building block (maybe).
   1.2 *Annual Report.* How is the organization doing as a business? What products/services are central to its strategy? What financial problems or opportunities does it face?
   1.3 *Analysts' Reports.* If you can, find out what stock analysts are saying about the company. You don't have to go through a brokerage for these. Often they are available on the Internet. Also check Dun's (Dun and Bradstreet), *Wall Street Journal,* CNBC, and similar information sources.
   1.4 *Competition.* Who does the organization compete with? What are the market shares? What are competitors doing?
   1.5 *Strategic Plan.* Where is the organization going in the next few years? Marketing strategy? Production/service delivery strategy? Financial strategy? What is the optimal product/service mix?
   1.6 *Technology.* What technology is the organization using for core tasks? How old is it? How much investment is required to keep up with changes? How much retraining or reformulating of business processes is required on a periodic basis?
   1.7 *Laws, Regulations, and Standards.* What are the key legal issues in this industry? Is the organization vulnerable? Is this a hot or sore topic?
   1.8 *Human Resources and Labor Market.* (see attached Due Diligence checklist).
   1.9 *Cycle Time and pace.* What are the cycles in the organization or unit? Is there a rapidly repeating cycle or a slow, drawn-out cycle? What is the pace of work, of effort, of schmoozing, of change?

2. **The Future**.
  2.1. *Predictable Changes.*
  2.2. *Product/service.*
  2.3. *Technology.*
  2.4. *Competition.*
  2.5. *Leadership and Key Personnel. Is there a succession plan?*
  2.6. *Legal, Regulatory, and Standards.*
  2.7. *Financial.*
  2.8. *Risk Management.*
  2.9. *Human Resources and Labor Market. Are demographics changing? Are wages going up? Will organization create a new labor market (e.g., move manufacturing overseas)?*
  2.10. *Intellectual.*
  2.11. *Supplies and Suppliers.*
  2.12. *Customers.*
  2.13. *Unpredictable Changes.*
    2.13.1. *What assumptions are made about environmental stability? What if they are wrong?*
    2.13.2. *What assumptions are made about internal stability? What if they are wrong?*
    2.13.3. *Does planning include "worst case scenarios"? Should it?*
    2.13.4. *What if key people are lost with no successors?*
    2.13.5. *What if key customers or suppliers are lost?*
    2.13.6. *What if intellectual property is lost?*

PREPARE A PROPOSAL

Following the initial meeting or meetings, the psychologist may be asked to prepare a proposal. The proposal can be verbal for small projects such as coaching, but most generally will be written. Proposals can vary from one page to detailed affairs that run to scores of pages, depending on the client and nature of the project. The type of response to the initial contact will vary depending upon the type of contact and the nature of the services requested. Responding to an RFP usually requires a detailed proposal that specifies exactly what is to be done, important personnel, schedule, payment schedule, and other components. It is important to remember that any written proposal, no matter how brief, constitutes a contract with clients if it is accepted and signed by them. Great care must be exercised because it is possible for a proposal and contract to take effect even when the people who sign them are not the responsible parties designated by their organizations to enter into contracts. Work on any project should not begin until a signed commitment is received from the client. This may be in the form of a signed proposal, a letter, or a purchase order. *If you start work before the client has accepted the contract you may not be paid for that work. This is certainly true of government contracts.*

In many cases it will be necessary to prepare a lengthy proposal. The proposal will be quite detailed in its description of the services to be performed, who is to perform them, the schedule for these services, and other contractual matters. In most cases the proposal will include all of the information of the work plan (see "Prepare a Work Plan" below), although the actual work plan may need to be updated following acceptance of the proposal by the client. For projects that result in a "product," such as selection procedures, training programs, and the like, a typical proposal outline would follow the outline shown here. Projects for organizational change, development efforts, coaching, and other activities with less well-defined outcomes and time schedules may use a different format. Following is a guide for a proposal outline.

PROPOSAL OUTLINE

1. Executive summary. Similar to an abstract, this is generally no more than one page.

2. Description of client's request. This will include the information gained from early discussions with the client.

3. Scope of work. This section describes the services to be provided. This is provided in detail. For large projects more than one phase may be needed.

4. Responsible parties. This section describes the organization structure (from the consulting firm) for this project. A single person may take on more than one role. Typical roles include these:

   • Project manager. This person has overall responsibility for the project, including budget and schedule.

   • Technical director. For large projects, the person in this role is responsible for ensuring that all technical aspects of the project are properly completed. The technical director is responsible for quality assurance.

   • Consultant(s).

   • Support staff.

   The proposal will typically identify the individuals who will serve in the most important of these roles (project manager, supervisor/consultant(s), technical director).

5. Responsible parties from the client organization. For purposes of the proposal, much of this information can be described and the client

asked to identify who these people are. This section specifies who the contact person is, who has the authority to approve services or products, whom to contact regarding contract/business issues; also, it specifies who the client is. This last information is critical and must be agreed upon in writing by all parties. The client is usually the organization. Do not confuse the client with the contact person or the person who originally contacted you for services.

6. Products. If any products, including reports, are to be generated, they should be identified and described.

7. Schedule. Specify dates. Alternatively, specify relative dates (e.g., "within 2 weeks after approval of this proposal"; "within 1 week of client approval of the final report").

8. Terms and conditions. This section sets forth the actual business arrangements to be agreed upon including price, payment schedule, responsibility for expenses incurred, how change orders will be handled, and limits of professional conduct.

   Confidentiality, implied consent, research, ownership of materials, and warranty will be covered in this section. The following statements should be included:

   Confidentiality. *As licensed psychologists and to be effective we must promise to keep information and sources of information confidential. This means that we will not divulge the information we obtain in a way in which the source can be directly identified. If a person asks that we not disclose information he or she provides, we will honor that request. It may be possible to identify a source of information indirectly—for example, when the information could only come from one person or a small set of people. We will make every attempt to reduce this possibility but cannot absolutely guarantee complete confidentiality. If asked to divulge information that has been obtained confidentially, we will refuse the request. In case of a dispute over the release of confidential information, our judgment will prevail. In the case of mandated reportable information we will follow the current procedures established in the state.*

   Informed consent. *We will ask each person from whom we seek information or to whom we provide services to sign an informed consent. Each one will know of our confidentiality agreement and that our client is the organization.*

   Research. *Research involving humans must be approved by an institutional review board (IRB). If we determine that a project requires review by an IRB, we will submit a proposal to an appropriate IRB or to another, mutually agreed upon IRB.*

PREPARE A WORK PLAN

If the client accepts the proposal, a work plan must always be prepared and maintained in the firm's files. It is an internal document and is not to leave the firm (although copies may be disseminated to members of the project team). The work plan contains all of the information contained in the proposal plus additional information. It will be more detailed than the proposal in allocating billable hours to each member of the project team. The work plan will include the project budget, including hours to be spent. The budget will specify how every dollar associated with the project is to be earned and spent. Typically a percentage of the revenue is dedicated to overhead, so not every cost is detailed. All hours spent on the project are to be tracked.

A billable hour consists of time spent performing project-relevant tasks as directed by the work plan. In consulting firms it is the basis for payment to professional staff or allocation of profits to partners. Some members of the project team may be compensated on the basis of billable hours contracted consultants). For government contracts, all hours actually spent on the project must be accounted for. For nongovernmental contracts, hours spent redoing mistakes are not required to be included (although they may be tracked for other purposes).

Each project will have estimates of the amount of time to be spent on each task by category of team member, the amount to be charged per hour for that category, and other costs incurred in performing the work—for example, preparing manuals or the cost of commercially available surveys or assessment instruments. Travel costs, including mileage, will be included whenever necessary.

The estimation process is facilitated through the use of a Gantt chart that shows the phases of the project as bars on a timeline. Some organizations may use a program evaluation and review technique (PERT) chart instead, but for even large-scale consulting projects, the added complexity is not worth the effort required for and the confusion that results from a more complex presentation. Gantt charts are available in most project management software programs. There are several software packages for project management. Many are rather cumbersome for our purposes, being better suited for large-scale engineering projects such as building a large bridge. There are other programs that fit the scale of psychological projects and have the additional advantage of being inexpensive and easy to use.

My team uses a program that costs less than $120 for one application and a few hundred for multiple computers. Of course, the psychologist should use these skills throughout the project to verify that resources are spent as planned and that the client is getting the service contracted for.

Occasionally a client asks for a change in procedure or schedule. Except for very minor changes, these can be accommodated only if the designated contact person in the client organization asks for them in writing. Change orders have implications for the amount charged to the client, payment dates, and other matters, and these must be reflected in the work plan.[1]

Preparing a proposal involves determining an estimated or actual price to be charged. Generally one of three possible methods, discussed next, will be used for this.

Time and Materials   This is the least risky method for the consultants. The firm is to be reimbursed for the amount of time spent on the project and any expenses incurred. This method is typically employed for very small projects or for established, ongoing relationships with clients.

Time and Materials, Not to Exceed a Set Amount   This is the least preferred form of payment arrangement from the consultant's perspective. If the time to perform was underestimated, consultants are paid less than anticipated; but if the time exceeds the estimate, they do not get paid for the extra work.

Fixed Price   The consultant bids a price and that is what the client pays. The incentive in the typical firm is to bid a fixed price but do the work in less time than specified (hence more fee per hour of work). The risk is that the project will require more time than anticipated, and the extra time is not paid for. Generally, in making a fixed-price bid, a good faith estimate of the costs is made and a company specific percentage, often 10%, is added. The exception to this occurs when there are multiple bidders, in which case a decision to bid should be made after careful consideration of the accuracy of the estimated time and materials as well as how much the firm wants or needs the work.

---

[1] Contractors of all types usually like change orders because such orders almost always increase the price of a project, whether in consulting, construction, or remodeling. Many contractors bid a project at a low price assuming that they can make up the money not in the original bid through change orders. No matter how a project is discounted, change orders are priced at the full rate. If you go to work for a consulting firm you may be expected to generate revenue through change orders.

In a small project it may be reasonable to wait until it is over before invoicing the client. In a larger project it is necessary to schedule periodic payments. These may be monthly or after important parts of the project have been completed.

Consulting firms sometimes reduce their price by a percentage in order to make sure they get the business or to reward long-term, faithful clients. Discounting is always done for some strategic reason, such as (1) the desire to move the firm into a new service, geographic region, or client industry or (2) the desire to acquire work during slow periods to keep everyone busy and employed. If the firm does discount, then it is important to remember to discount only the labor portion of a proposal, not the costs of materials, travel, and so on. Discounting would be done only for "production" type projects, not organizational change projects.

TRACK BUDGET

As a project proceeds the project manager will track actual hours and expenses, and compare these to the budget. So long as the project remains on track and on budget, this task is not too difficult. The situation changes if deviations are noted and the consultant must become a manager. Reasons for the deviations must be discovered and changes made to get back on track. At times the consulting team will be able to adjust to meet the budget; at other times the project manager may have to open new negotiations with the client. This is where keeping close track of contacts, schedules, and receipt of information is important because projects often go awry because the client organization is unable to respond as planned. My guess is that large-scale organizational change efforts almost always take longer to accomplish than anticipated, perhaps by a factor of two or more. The project manager for the consulting firm will have to be able to show results when asking the client for more time and money.

REPORT ON PROGRESS

As a project progresses, interim reports, verbal and written, are often required and a report is typically delivered at the end of the project. Interim reports may be brief updates on current progress and whether the schedule and budget are on track. Obstacles and opportunities may be included, depending on the circumstances. Reports at the end of major phases and at the conclusion of the project are more extensive. In projects such as test development and validation, the reports must carefully document what was done—the methods and results—in order to stand up to scrutiny should a discrimination claim or court action occur. In other types of projects, such as those in which the OBC psychologist has assessed the capacity of groups or teams, performed a program evaluation, or done a similar service in which evaluative information is provided, the verbal and written report must be carefully structured if the client organization is to obtain any benefit from the work. Chapter 9 provided some guidance on how to present negative information to a client organization for the highest probability of positive response.

ELEVEN

Ethical Behavior and Competencies

The people who engage psychologists for professional services expect that the services will be at least to some extent arcane, but delivered in an ethical manner; that is, proffered within accepted bounds of honesty and integrity. The American Psychological Association (APA) has promulgated ethical principles since 1953. The current version, *Ethical Principles of Psychologists and Code of Conduct*, has been in force since June 1, 2003 (APA, 2002). Licensed psychologists are generally required to adhere to the APA code or a code established by the Association of State and Provincial Psychology Boards (ASPPB; 2005). Although the code covered all areas of psychology, there was a common belief in earlier decades that the code was so heavily oriented toward clinical aspects of practice that it was irrelevant for the everyday practice of OBC psychology; the current code is clearly written to cover organizational consulting activities (Lowman, 2006).

Principles of the APA Code of Ethics

The APA ethics code is based on five general principles: Beneficence and Nonmalficence, Fidelity and Responsibility, Integrity, Justice, and Respect for People's Rights and Dignity.

BENEFICENCE AND NONMALFICENCE

The first of these principles states the aspiration that psychologists will "strive to benefit those with whom they work and take care to do no harm" (APA, 2002, p. 1062). This would be easy to do except that virtually all of the services performed by an OBC psychologist are apt to result in positive outcomes for some and negative outcomes for others. For example, in employee selection, the client organization benefits if people who are hired based on the assessment system are likely to perform better than those hired through some other process. The people who were not hired but who believe themselves capable of doing the job may see harm in the system. An organizational change effort may result in increased opportunities for some and a loss of advantage to others. Different people or groups of people may have different perspectives based on their priorities and philosophy of life and somebody will not be happy with any substantive change. The OBC psychologist will do well to identify clearly who the client is and the goals of the project. Identifying the client can be difficult; the person who hires the psychologist may not be a target in the intervention—for example, an executive asks for assistance for a unit of the organization (Newman, Robinson-Kurpius, & Fuqua, 2002; Stroh & Johnson, 2008). However difficult, articulating the client's and the consultant's reporting relationship is critical in achieving the goals of beneficence and nonmalfeasance and will also help in achieving the aspirations of the second principle.

FIDELITY AND RESPONSIBILITY

Psychologists perform their work and achieve their results based on relationships built on trust. In the case of the OBC psychologist the relationships include the primary client (the organization) and those the contact in the course of the consultation including employees. An ethical psychologist behaves in a manner worthy of the trust placed in him or her by the client. In addition, the principle of Fidelity and Responsibility states that psychologists "are concerned about the ethical compliance of their colleagues' scientific and professional conduct." Thus, the psychologist has a responsibility to the client that includes maintaining as is possible the ethical conduct of colleagues. For this principle, clearly identifying who the client is establishes the responsibility of the psychologist. In addition, the psychologist must recognize that the client is the one who determines the conditions of work, access to the workplace and workers, whether additional funds are forthcoming, and ultimately defines the objectives of the consultation (de Wolff, 1998; Thorndike, 1949).

INTEGRITY

The integrity principle indicates that psychologists aspire to "honesty, accuracy, and truthfulness" (APA, 2002, p. 1062). Reports should be accurate and not misleading. Given that the technical prowess of the typical OBC psychologist exceeds that of the client's, it is not difficult to obfuscate results or prepare an executive summary that meets the client's hopes but diverges from the truth. Lowman (2006) presents a case in which this was determined to occur.

JUSTICE

The justice principle requires that psychologists take steps to ensure that their biases do not intrude on their work, or at least that the client is aware of how the bias may impact the results. In working with multicultural organizations it is particularly important for psychologists to be aware of the values, beliefs, and attitudes that influence their relations with, and perceptions of, others. In any consulting arrangement the consultant's interests and the client's may conflict at some level or point in time (Newman et al., 2002). Competency requires that the psychologist be aware of such conflicts and work toward an ethical resolution. Perhaps the most difficult situation is when the person who authorizes payment or continued work for the consultant is not going to receive favorably a set of recommendations. Perhaps the recommendations work against that person's personal interests. The OBC psychologist has to be willing to sacrifice future opportunities with the organization and not back off from meeting the actual client's needs.

RESPECT FOR PEOPLE'S RIGHTS AND DIGNITY

Justice, combined with the final principle, respect for people's rights and dignity, implies that the psychologist not impose a value system on the client. As Kendler (1993) pointed out, the psychologist can inform society and others about the possible impact of changes or the empirical basis for an intervention, but he or she cannot determine morality for others. For the OBC psychologist this tenet has its most basic application in the choice of intervention. Harrison (1974/1968) laid out the fundamental ethical rule as being to intervene no deeper than needed. This rule was presented at, of all places, a convention on psychoanalysis and at a time when organizational development (OD) efforts concentrated on sensitivity training and "removing the executive mask." Harrison believed that the ethical OD consultant should begin with interventions that changed aspects of the workflow and workplace, then move deeper only if this was needed. Although he did not rule out attempts to alter the fundamental values and identities of individuals, such interventions are rarely effective in the organizational context. Harrison identified five levels of depth of intervention:

1. Roles and functions (e.g., operations research and operations analysis).
   This level focuses on what people are assigned to do and how they do it.

2. Evaluating and influencing performance (e.g., selection, performance appraisal). These are limited to what is public and observable.

3. Instrumental process analysis (e.g., work style or organization of work). The focus is to change work behavior and working relationships.

4. Interpersonal process analysis (e.g., quality of human relationships in the organization, warmth and coldness). The focus is on feelings, attitudes, and perceptions; trust; love and hate.

5. Intrapersonal analysis. The focus is on increasing the range of experiences that the individual can bring into awareness and cope with.

One possible reason for the problems that Harrison observed and that prompted his ethical stand is confusion on the part of practitioners about the consulting versus the clinical or counseling role. Although some experts (e.g., see Freedman & Bradt, 2009, for several papers on the topic by Levinson) would vociferously disagree, a critical competency is managing one's roles and boundaries and not mixing being a consultant with being a therapist. Apparently this confusion is common and the mix is encouraged in some quarters. I recently received an advertisement for some coaching training. The firm offers workshops on building empathy, working with anger, working with fear, and similar topics. The OBC psychologist should be able to recognize problems in these areas but in this situation should only make referrals. Even if the psychologist has the professional expertise to work with clients in a counseling or therapeutic setting, attempting to do so in a consulting or coaching capacity is an inappropriate mix of roles.

Standards of the APA Code of Ethics

The APA ethical code has 89 separate standards. These, unlike the principles, are enforceable and not aspirational. An argument could be made that a competent psychologist should be able to cite each one, chapter and verse. It is not a very convincing argument. The competent OBC psychologist should be aware of the topics covered. Some standards deal with everyday practice management issues, such as maintenance and disposal of records. The psychologist would design adherence to these into the practice and not need to refer to the specific standard very often thereafter. Other standards, such as terminating therapy, are probably not likely to come up in a consulting practice. There are standards that can come into play at any moment—for example, those dealing with assessments—with which the

OBC psychologist needs familiarity, and given faulty memories, the discipline to look up the actual standard when necessary.

Other Ethical Issues

A number of other ethical issues were discussed by Newman et al. (2002), including the principle of informed consent and the problem of confidentiality.

INFORMED CONSENT

Members of client organizations are often asked to meet with consultants, either personally or in focus groups, to participate in surveys, or similar information gathering procedures. They may also be asked, seemingly required, to attend training sessions and development activities, or to participate in interventions in some other manner. Although the OBC psychologist may attempt to make clear that participation is voluntary, in actuality, it very well may not be at all voluntary. A manager may have asked for, or required, participation. Sometimes there is peer pressure to cooperate or not to cooperate. In most people's eyes the consultant is there for a brief time. They have the rest of their careers to worry about. For some services, such as individual assessment, there are fairly standard methods of gaining informed consent. For many other consulting activities there is no easy or universally correct solution to this problem. The psychologist should at least explain the principle of informed consent and attempt to come to an understanding with the client about what that means in the instant situation.

CONFIDENTIALITY

Confidentiality is closely related to the problem of informed consent. There are times when the consultant needs to report the results of interviews and other interactions but is limited by the ability of management to recognize who said what. Sometimes managers even demand to know who made certain comments. There are also confidentiality issues around assessment results and documents and similar matters. Overall, the psychologist needs to clarify the limits of confidentiality as early as possible in the relationship with a client organization and its members.

The primary resource regarding ethics in OBC psychology is the text edited by Lowman (2006). The volume was updated from an earlier edition to account for changes in the code. Rather than presenting commentary on each standard, Lowman and his associates gathered critical incidents and subjected them to scrutiny and evaluation based on the APA ethics code. The incidents in the book are categorized into practice activities (personnel selection and organizational diagnosis and intervention), practice management (managing consulting relationships, billing and marketing, and professional behavior), professional training and certification, and research and academic issues. An OBC psychologist should be capable of discussing similar cases and applying ethical principles and standards, although, of course, not citing each standard verbatim as in the book.

IMPROPER PERSONAL RELATIONSHIPS

Some ethical issues concern other professional psychologists much more than OBC psychologists, but that does not imply that these issues are unimportant or can be ignored. Clinicians may not have sex with clients and they have ethical limits on such relationships even after a professional relationship ends. When the client is a large corporation or government agency, this seems irrelevant. However, we can't be so incredulous as to believe that there have not been instances of consulting work being awarded or offered on the basis of sexual favors. Whether or not this violates the letter of the ethics code, engaging in such behavior is clearly unethical. OBC psychologists do have human desires and occasionally fall in love. They are, however, bound by the same restrictions as everyone else in the workplace regarding improper relationships with co-workers, interns, and the like. Lowman (2006) presents an illustrative case and explains how such a situation should be viewed from the ethical perspective.

IMPAIRMENT

Psychologists are not supposed to offer services when they are incapable of properly providing them. Impairment receives a lot of attention among clinicians and licensing boards (Barnett, 2008). Often the impairment comes from alcohol, drugs, or family issues, although disease or physical condition can be involved. The safest course of action is not to drink on or before going to the job. This gets complicated for some consultants in that clients expect the consultant to join them at meals, often with drinks or wine being served. Depending on the culture of the organization and surrounding society, it may be difficult to resist joining in. If the psychologist chooses to indulge, there is a risk that he or she will do or say things that are unprofessional and to the detriment of members of the client organization and the relationship necessary to continue as an effective psychologist. It is stupid to misuse drugs in any venue, much less a professional one. Unfortunately, stating the fact in this book will not stop anyone intent on doing it. Such individuals should just expect to be expelled from professional organizations, shunned by peers, and lose their licenses.

DUTY TO WARN

Finally, a licensed psychologist is typically a mandated reporter; that is, should firsthand knowledge of certain situations come to his or her attention, the psychologist must break confidentiality and report it to designated authorities. This includes information about child abuse and, sometimes, depending on the state, elder abuse or abuse of the disabled. There are no data or even a collection of anecdotes on this, so we have to rely on informed speculation. Encountering an occasion for having to make such a report seems rare for OBC psychologists, except possibly for those consulting in schools, nursing homes, or similar institutions. Having the license brings with it some 24 hour a day responsibilities. I know of one OBC psychologist who learned of a potential child abuse situation involving a friend of the psychologist's child that would have been reportable; luckily the authorities were already aware of, and working on, the case.

In some, but not all, states, there is a duty to warn; that is, if a psychologist becomes aware of an intention by a client to harm another person, the psychologist has to undertake appropriate action to warn the target. Again, I don't think this happens very often in the consulting field, but all psychologists must know what their responsibilities are. I once interviewed a woman at a company and asked how she would respond if her boss took a certain managerial action. "Oh, I'd kill him," she replied. Even though I thought she was being funny, I immediately clarified that her reply was a figure of speech and not a real intention. Since then I have found it useful to explain to the people I interview that the bounds of confidentiality include these mandated reporting limits and use that example as an illustration. They seem to appreciate hearing it and always deny they have any such intent or are abusing anyone.

Ethics Training

It must be assumed that ethics training for many OBC psychologists takes place after graduate school. Although ethics are critically important, informal research by graduate students in I/O psychology found that at least 45% of master's and doctoral programs in I/O psychology do not offer or require courses on ethics (McGinnis et al., 2008). At a SIOP convention on ethical issues, McGinnis and colleagues asked a convenience sample of 50 students which issues concerned them; their responses indicated three topics of general concern: competence, managing relationships, and research. These are indeed critical issues. The students turned to Lowman and his book for guidance and received good information. However, knowledge of ethics requires considerable study, reflection, practice, and mentoring. It is unfortunate that so many I/O programs choose to neglect this aspect of the discipline, throwing the responsibility to supervisors, mentors, and the students themselves.

TWELVE

Individual and Cultural Diversity

Applying psychology is applying a technology. A technology is only accepted and useful if it fits the situation and resources available and matches the culture. Culture shapes the technology and technology shapes the culture. A competent psychologist must know how culture at the organizational and societal levels impacts the services and interventions the professional provides. In addition to culture, a number of other factors differentiate individuals and groups, and the psychologist must be aware of these and take them into account in providing services. These include race, ethnicity, gender, disability, and other factors often categorized together under the rubric of diversity. This set of factors is important for nearly all services. OBC psychologists often work with organizations that operate globally with a global workforce or, even if not international in scope, have employees from a variety of worldwide cultures. The purpose of this chapter is to present some of the critical issues and competencies related to diversity. As is the case throughout this book, the requisite competencies depend on the nature and scope of the psychologist's practice.

Diversity

Diversity concerns should be incorporated into all aspects of the psychologist's daily work and, thus, are incorporated into competencies throughout the assessment and intervention chapters. There are specific competencies that may also be necessary, depending on the psychologist's work setting and type of practice.

Students in clinical and counseling psychology are taught a useful mnemonic by Hays (2001) called the ADDRESSING model. It includes several

of the diversity factors the students need to better understand and concep-
tualize their clients.

A   Age and generational influences

D   Developmental or acquired disabilities

R   Religion and spiritual orientation

E   Ethnicity

S   Socioeconomic status

S   Sexual orientation

I   Indigenous heritage

N   National origin

G   Gender

The ADDRESSING model can be particularly helpful in reminding us that
a person is not "one thing"; what we are is a consequence of many parts of
our own and society's history, environment, technology, beliefs, values, and
so on. Unfortunately, in a business context, the use of most of these factors is restricted by antidiscrimination laws, so it is difficult to use them
for working with an employee of an organization in the same way a clinician would use them. Clinicians are often advised to speak with the client
about applicable factors early in their relations, and in the right situation
this seems to work in organizational settings. Winum (2005) was advised
to directly bring up the race of his coaching client, Tom, and found that
addressing race early on helped make the consultation a success. Yet he did
so at some risk to himself and the client organization; if Tom had not performed well and had been terminated, there would be a long record of discussion about his status as a member of a protected minority. Would this
have influenced the outcome of a discrimination complaint? It is hard to
say. Regardless, organizations seek to avoid such complaints for reasons
of both cost and reputation. Professionals, too, may wish to avoid being
named in a complaint; that alone may be at least perceived as something
that would derail a career. If possible the psychologist must find a way to
provide services while disentangling performance, personal, interpersonal,
discriminatory, ignorance, experience, and other factors in such a way as to
help resolve a situation. Frankly, this will not always be possible. In some
cases the battle lines have been drawn for a long time and are impermeable
to attempts to create change. We can hope that as time goes on the battle-
scarred veterans on all sides will retire from the battlefield and the trenches

can be filled in. Until then all concerned must tread warily to avoid the buried land mines.

It is impossible and undesirable to memorize all the sources of differences in people—different cultures, experiences, cohort influences, and such. Each psychologist should be aware of cultural and other issues such as those included in the ADDRESSING model. A useful and extensive bibliography on culture, race, and ethnicity issues as related to organizational consulting psychology was published by Leong, Cooper, and Huang (2008).

The American Psychological Association (APA) has established a set of guidelines on multicultural education, training, research, practice, and organizational change (American Psychological Association, 2003). Although all of the guidelines are important, a few are particularly germane to this chapter. The first two guidelines fall under the heading of Commitment to Cultural Awareness and Knowledge of Self and Others and read:

> *Guideline 1:* Psychologists are encouraged to recognize that, as cultural beings, they may hold attitudes and beliefs that can detrimentally influence their perceptions of and interactions with individuals who are ethnically and racially different from themselves. (APA, 2003, p. 382)

> *Guideline 2:* Psychologists are encouraged to recognize the importance of multicultural sensitivity/responsiveness to, knowledge of, and understanding racially different individuals. (APA, 2003, p. 385)

Under the heading of Practice, the guidelines state:

> *Guideline 5:* Psychologists are encouraged to apply culturally appropriate skills in clinical and other applied psychological practices. (APA, 2003, p. 390)

Under the heading of Organizational Change and Policy Development, the guidelines read:

> *Guideline 6:* Psychologists are encouraged to use organizational change processes to support culturally informed organizational (policy) development and practices. (APA, 2003, p. 392)

These guidelines call for awareness of differences. Oddly, they do not ask the psychologist to extend the same form of respect for people who are at least superficially like themselves. Effective and competent practice involves adjusting to the person, group, or organization with which the psychologist is working. For historical and sociological reasons some groups are protected, but the fundamental ethical standards involve respect for persons, fidelity and responsibility, integrity, justice, and respect for people's rights and dignity (APA, 2002). Multicultural guidelines are a means to the end, but the spirit of the guidelines should extend beyond racial and ethnic origins. The psychologist should attempt to see people in context. That does not mean that decisions and recommendations can never be negative from the individual's point of view but that irrelevant influences are minimized as much as humanly possible.

The scope of the possible practice activities of the OBC psychologist is very broad—broader than that of any other professional psychologist. The nature of the problems, the types of organizations, and all possible multicultural and diversity factors encountered by an OBC psychologist create a set of permutations that exceeds anyone's capacity to document. Since OBC psychologists are well aware of legal issues, adverse impact, and the like, this chapter will not revisit all of them. Instead, it will present a few of the many types of situations with which the OBC psychologist can be presented.

Over half a century ago, Super (1957) pointed out that people's roles change over time. He described six roles; child, student, citizen, worker, leisurite, and homemaker. The last does not refer just to working around the house; it refers to the role of making the home—that is, creating the social environment that generates an acceptable living situation for all concerned. It includes parenting, a function that has never been entirely left to one or the other gender. The relative importance of each role waxes and wanes as the person's life changes. Super saw this as a somewhat predictable developmental sequence, but at least over the last few decades the developmental aspect may have become less critical to understanding the process. So, even though Holland (1997) complained that the research evidence supporting developmental theories of vocational choice was scant, the variation in priorities that Super described is apparent to anyone with the power of observation and the ability to meet and speak to people from a wide swath of life circumstances.

Holmberg's Mistake refers to the assumption made by a prominent historian that conditions in the Americas were stable and constant prior to the arrival of Columbus (Mann, 2005). They weren't. The physical and cultural environment was continually evolving. Psychologists, and other social scientists make two similar errors. First, we can assume that whatever walk of life a person is in now will remain the same for a long period. Second, we can assume that cultures, whether organizational or societal, are static, and that the "snapshots" we take in our studies represent the culture as it was, is, and will be.

As an example of the first error, we often assume that a person whose current spectrum of roles is dominated by, say, "worker," will continue in that vein for a prolonged period. Along comes a new baby, an aging and weakening parent, a personal trauma, or divorce, to name a few possibilities, and the mix of roles changes. In other cases a change could increase the worker role, such as reaching the "empty nest" stage when managing the lives of children is not such a priority. A consequence is that finely laid plans for teams, succession planning, workload allocation, and others can be disrupted through naturally occurring processes. In addition, new opportunities can arise. The failure of the organization to recognize, respond to, or adapt to these changes on a wholesale scale results in worker stress, particularly from work-family balance issues. The range of problems ensuing from an imbalance in family and work roles was reviewed by Hammer, Colton, Caubet, and Brockwood (2002).

For an OBC psychologist, working effectively with diversity issues may require the flexibility to find creative ways to achieve ends. An example that came to my attention a few years ago was a woman I'll refer to as Lea. Prior to her marriage, Lea had been involved in a number of small-scale entrepreneurial enterprises that had been as successful as Lea and her partner (her brother) had hoped. Following her marriage Lea worked in a few jobs to help make ends meet, but then, true to her religion, which emphasized staying home with children, she left the workforce for about 20 years to raise a number of children. When her youngest child was old enough Lea decided to rejoin the workforce. She applied for several jobs and won an interview at a large department store. The job was for a supervisory position and Lea wondered whether she had the necessary qualifications. She had been out of the workforce for a very long time; she felt out of date and out of practice. An astute interviewer, we'll call him Gary, recognized the situation and deviated from the carefully structured interview format to ask questions in a manner calculated to uncover information about Lea's actual qualifications. When Lea admitted she had little recent experience managing several people working on different things at once, Gary asked her to describe a typical day getting her children ready and off to school. Her answers showed that Lea could supervise and multitask as well as anyone. Lea thought she had no applicable budgeting experience. Gary asked how she planned to feed her large family on the money her husband earned. Lea was an expert at budgeting and making ends meet. The interview proceeded in this manner and Lea got the job. She was a successful supervisor for about 20 years before she retired. Gary was not a psychologist, but he was aware of diversity issues and how to use them to the company's advantage while respecting the people he hired. Gary took some risk; asking questions such as how Lea dealt with getting her children ready for school could be seen as a violation of EEO interviewing guidelines. He could have rigidly stayed with the interview format, probably not have hired Lea, and been considered successful due to his following procedure. Unfortunately, regulation and litigation stifle creativity and can prevent goal attainment.

Sexual orientation is listed in the ADDRESSING model but is nearly absent from the journals and handbooks typically read by OBC psychologists. This may be partly because sexual orientation in the workplace is not covered by federal discrimination laws other than the prohibition of sexual harassment. It is, however, increasingly covered by state and local statutes. One of the few studies examining sexual orientation in the workplace was reported by Ragins, Singh, and Cornwell (2007), who conducted a national survey of gay, lesbian, and bisexual employees. Of the 534 respondents, roughly a third reported that they had been discriminated against in a prior position due to their sexual orientation and slightly more reported that they had been discriminated against because of a perception of others regarding their orientation. Surprisingly, to me at least, only slightly over 10% had been physically harassed due to their sexual orientation. Those who had experienced past discrimination were more fearful of disclosure in the current workplace, but there was no relationship with actual disclosure rates. As expected, there were correlations of fear with job attitudes, psychological strain, perceptions of the work environment, and career outcomes. Today, with the internet and social networking, news travels fast and people may come out in one environment and quickly discover the information is common knowledge at work and in other venues of life. OBC psychologists who work with organizational culture and change, development and coaching, teams, and almost every other aspect of practice either do or will soon be expected to assist individuals, teams, and organizations on this issue.

Psychopathology has largely been ignored within OBCP (Thomas & Hite, 2002), with a consequence that little thought has been given to how persons with mental disorders fit into the workplace. Most current theories of organizing, leadership, and motivation assume a workforce that is fully functional in cognitive, emotional, behavioral, and interpersonal matters. The data reviewed by Thomas and Hite indicate that this assumption is not tenable; a meaningful proportion of the population suffers from diagnosable mental disorders at some point and many of those who do not are touched by the problems of family members and friends. Instead of concentrating on pathology, OBCP practitioners have found it more practical to concentrate on methods of coping used by individuals with varying degrees of functionality and dysfunctionality (Frew, 2004). Although many consulting psychologists have some background in counseling or clinical work, few I/O psychologists have any competence in this area at all, leading to a major diversity blind spot. Ideally, training programs will come to recognize this and begin to rectify the situation.

Diversity issues do not occur only at the employee level. A small manufacturing company was owned by the father and son team of the Browns. Unlike most family businesses, they had bought the company together; Senior Brown was the chairman and Junior Brown combined the positions of chief executive officer and chief operating officer. Senior Brown had hired a salesman, Mr. Smith, whom he had known for many years as they had both worked in the same industry. Mr. Smith was the worst salesperson in the company, selling a fraction of what other salespeople sold in a year. Due to his poor performance and other reasons that are too complex to present, any management consultant would have recommended that Mr. Smith be terminated as soon as possible as the only reasonable business move. However, Senior Brown had known him for a long time. In addition, the Browns were Catholics who took their faith and consequent responsibilities seriously. One of these responsibilities, as they interpreted it, was to be loyal and supportive of their community. Mr. Smith was part of the community. The proper business move of firing Mr. Smith would have created an unacceptable moral crisis for the Browns, particularly Senior Brown. The OBC psychologist was not qualified to examine the religious beliefs and help the Browns determine whether their religion was really restricted terminating Mr. Smith. All the psychologist could do was adopt an attitude of "Forget best practices" as the problem was to develop an intervention that would deal with Mr. Smith's ineptitude within the constraints set by the Browns' cultural and religious beliefs. The result was a program that did increase Mr. Smith's sales to a high level for a time until his alcoholism made it impossible for him to continue with the company. By then the Browns were comfortable with the outcome even though it had required financial risk and commitment most companies would not have considered.

Organizational Consulting Across Cultures

Gelfand, Erez, and Aycan (2007) reviewed the literature on cross-cultural organizational behavior and noted that cultures differ in the effects of such common organizational strategies as feedback, reward systems, and the impact of job and organizational characteristics. Studies show, for example, that managers in different cultures use reward systems differently (Zhou & Martocchio, 2001). Cultures also differ in the correlates of job satisfaction and in the nature of employee commitment. The issue is especially complicated because cultures obviously differ from one another to the point that what is important or desirable in one culture receives much less, or no, consideration in another culture. Cross-cultural psychologists distinguish between emics and etics. Emics are ideas and behaviors that are culture specific and etics are culture general or universal (Gelfand et al., 2007). In work organizations these are overlain by organizational and professional cultures. For example, American, Chinese, and Ukrainian physicists are apt to have more in common intellectually with each other than they do with their neighbors back home and to differ considerably from each other in terms of personal values, loyalties, emotional expression, and other affective factors.

The picture becomes yet more complex as cultures and the people within them evolve over time, sometimes rapidly. Culture can be seen as a dynamic system, not a static entity (Cohen, 2001; Kitayama, 2002). Some people are bicultural due to mixing cultures; others seem to have one foot in the past and the other in the present or future as their home culture changes rapidly. A worldwide example is the very rapid adoption of communications technologies by young people while their elders are mystified about the whys, wherefores, and desirability of social networking, Twittering, and whatever else is hot at the moment.

Two seemingly mundane examples of cultural difference are the influence of time and physical space and their effects on behavior across and within cultures. Time would seem a constant; we define a day as having 24 hours, an hour as being 60 minutes, and so on. Yet time changes its meaning depending on context; precision may or may not be significant. There is a continuum with clock time on one end and event time on the other (Brislin & Kim, 2003; Brislin & Low, 2006). Clock time simply refers to doing things as scheduled and when scheduled with strict adherence to the time of day indicated on a clock. If an hour appointment is set for 11:00 A.M., it begins at 11:00 and participants are expected to be there at that moment. In event time, things happen when it is appropriate for them to happen; a farmer knows that the harvest will occur in the fall, but he can't set the date months in advance, and a fisher is dependent on the tides, not the clock. Cultures that are more agrarian tend to rely more on event time; industrialized and postindustrial cultures run more on clock time.

But it's not that simple. Not all individuals in a particular culture utilize or are influenced by time the same way, and many switch back and forth between clock time and event time, depending on the circumstance. Time usage also gets confounded with other cultural factors, such as status. In some places the privilege of being late is confined to those in leadership positions; almost everyone is expected to arrive on time. In other places a person with status or prestige will be late as a rule. Only those who are insecure will be on time (Stone-Romero, Stone, & Salas, 2003). Thus, organizations with locations in far-flung locations or employees, customers, or suppliers from different cultures have to contend with the differing and inconsistent applications of time.

Space also seems a constant, yet people and cultures differ in how they divide it (or don't divide it), how meaning is ascribed to the spaces we occupy, and how we share space. Conflict over space use can arise even in culturally homogeneous environments, but throw in different meanings of space and things really get complicated (Ayoko & Härtel, 2003). Managements who see space as something people will adapt to as needed and as unimportant in maintaining productivity and civility are blindsided by conflict and inefficiency that become inexorable. A mix of cultures can derail the assumptions of architects. A colleague, Jon Frew, and I were asked by a neighboring county to survey mental health contractors on their ability to provide culturally appropriate mental health services to cultural minorities, the largest group of which comes from a growing Latino population. Typically the office of a psychotherapist can be designed and furnished to comfortably fit between two and four or five people when "families" are involved. The definition of "family" is different for many Latino clients and it is not uncommon for groups of a dozen or more to attend a family session. This also stretches the capacity of waiting rooms. Safety management can be a concern when members of rival gangs appear in common areas. This could happen in many employment settings as well.

It is easy to try to learn something about a culture and then generalize the results to everyone within the culture. Social scientists are as prone to this as anyone. A prime example is the concept of individualism versus collectivism, first described with regard to work behavior by Hofstede (1980). The concept has had an important influence on research and discussion in psychology, and there is a clear tendency to speak of this culture as "individualist" and that culture as "collectivist." Stereotyping is never a good strategy. When it works, it doesn't advance one's cause very much, and when a stereotype is wrong, as they usually are, the outcome can be disastrous. Not only are the constructs of individualist and collectivist scientifically questionable (Gelfand et al., 2007; Oyserman, Coon, & Kemmelmeier, 2002), but even if they stand it is not clear how they should be applied to residents of various cultures (Dien, 1999; Kitayama, 2002). Much of what passes for cross-cultural research is based on surveys of convenience samples. There are significant issues in data collection in these studies (Aycan & Kanungo, 2001), and the heavy reliance on a single data collection technique makes much of the cross-cultural research of questionable value. As a competent professional, you will always be better prepared if you find out who you are dealing with and how they think, what values they hold, what motivates them, what pleases and displeases them—just in general get to know them as individuals, team members, and organizational contributors rather than make assumptions, even with good intentions.

Mullin and Cooper (2002) presented a six-factor model for international consultation, adopted from an earlier model for multicultural training. In their model, the first level is to examine the "personal and interpersonal aspects of oneself that influence the consultant's self-awareness in a cultural context" (p. 554). It focuses on the person in relation to the interpersonal relationships and environment in which the person lives and works. The second level refers to technical and professional skills important for success in one's own culture. Third are factors that exist "beyond culture." Mullin and Cooper's list includes poverty, international relations, organizational health, and sexism. Fourth, consultants must understand their own culture and its impact on them. Fifth, the consultants should understand the extent to which their own culture is multi- or monocultural. The final level, six, consists of learning skills to work in a nonjudgmental and helpful manner in another culture.

One area that OBC psychologists are asked to work in is the selection, training, and socialization of expatriates—that is, employees who are sent to live and work in another culture. The recent reviews by Sinangil and Ones (2001) and Gelfand, Erez, and Aycan (2007) point to several factors that influence success of expatriates. Adjusting to the new environment, including ways of life and ways of working, is a critical factor. Adjustment can be conceptualized three ways: general or cultural, work, and interaction (Black, Mendenhall, & Oddou, 1991). Gelfand et al. (2007) described several general and specific predictors of adjustment. It is important to note that the adjustment of not just the employee but also the employee's family is critical and that socialization experiences must extend to all members of the family. According to Gelfand et al., expatriate job satisfaction is related to factors such as task significance, autonomy, authority, teamwork, and similarity. Of course, each of these may be defined somewhat differently in each culture. If the organization values an expatriate experience, the employee is apt to show higher organizational commitment, as might be expected since being assigned to a showplace versus a backwater is commonly seen as a career maker or breaker. Language concerns and networking opportunities and relationships with host company nationals are important components of success. Expatriate performance is very important to organizations that work globally, yet few consider much more than technical competence in making selections for expatriate positions (Sanchez & Levine, 2001). The selection, training, and socialization of expatriates is an area that relatively few OBC psychologists practice in and may be best seen as a subspecialty that requires particular forms of competence.

THIRTEEN

Interpersonal Interactions

The interpersonal side of OBC psychology is not often discussed in books and journals. It does not even appear in the lists of competencies promulgated by the Society for Industrial and Organizational Psychology (SIOP), the Society for Consulting Psychology (SCP), and the American Psychological Association (APA). Clearly, many functions of the OBC psychologist require excellent interpersonal skills; marketing one's services, making presentations to clients, engaging in process consultation and other helping actions, doing individual development and assessments, gathering information via interviews and focus groups, and many other activities necessitate an ability to develop rapport, develop trust, understand another's position, adapt one's professional demeanor to fit organizational cultures, make frank comments and give negative and positive feedback without losing the faith of the client, and similar skills. On the other hand, it is probably true that an I/O psychologist could choose to live as a hermit, away from all personal human contact, and so long as there was Internet access and clients willing to utilize questionnaires, surveys, and web-based assessment instruments, could be successful in providing a limited range of services. So we cannot say these interpersonal skills are absolute necessities, but success as a consultant would be unlikely without them. I do not believe it is possible to describe how an OBC psychologist can develop these interpersonal competencies in a book. These are best learned in person from a mentor. This chapter covers some areas of interpersonal competence that are not often recognized in the OBC psychology literature.

Maintaining Professional Boundaries

Psychologists who provide mental health services must be concerned with maintaining appropriate role boundaries with clients and the families of clients. It is an ethical imperative because if personal relationships develop between the psychologist and the client, the clinical relationship can deteriorate and the client can be harmed. These psychologists are warned not to self-disclose personal information, not socialize with clients, and for maintenance of confidentiality, not address the client should they meet in a public setting unless the client initiates the contact. In recent years clinicians have discovered that when they work with clients from certain other cultures these rules have to be modified (LaRoche & Christopher, 2010). Similarly, organizations and business represent another culture in which the nature of personal relationships and boundaries changes. Client meetings may be held in restaurants, airport lounges, the client organization's offices, and other public places. Indeed, some OBC psychologists will meet a person over lunch or coffee rather than in the person's office as a way of maintaining the privacy of the contact (e.g., Winum, 2005). A clinician could never play golf or tennis with a client, yet such encounters are common in the business world. Indeed, once you get into an executive's contact list there is a high probability you will get invited to a charity auction, golf tournament, or similar function in which socializing and making financial contributions are expected. An ethical dilemma that sometimes arises is what to do when the executive insinuates that further work with the company is dependent on a good donation to the charity.

The type of relationship between the consultant and the client organization impacts what the psychologist does, how it is received, and how the client can use the information. This can be illustrated using the example of conducting a program evaluation, but the principles extend to all sorts of projects. In a dependent mode, the consultant is involved with the design and development of the program, assists with implementation, provides immediate feedback, and suggests revisions to be incorporated in the program. In this mode the consultant essentially becomes part of the program, with all the intellectual and emotional investment that accompanies identifying with the product. The client organization can benefit because the OBC psychologist's expertise creates a better program, and since program staff know, trust, and are working directly with the consultant, they may be more likely to utilize the information. The downside of the dependent mode is that the consultant may find it difficult to provide objective, bottom-line assessments of program success and of program personnel.

In a semi-independent role, the consultant is heavily involved with observations, interviews, and other data gathering, feeding back information and recommendations on a periodic but not immediate basis. Since the consultant is less intimately involved with the program there may be less of a problem with passing on negative information. However, the consultant is less knowledgeable of the daily operation and of the staff. Although the consultant may be a known entity, trust in him or her by the staff may not be as high as with a consultant who is more closely involved in daily activities. Semi-independent relationships are necessarily less flexible than dependent ones; with these, it is necessary to have more detailed plans at the beginning and most information to be gathered identified at the outset. In an independent evaluation, the consultant and members of the client organization plan the data gathering at the beginning of the project, the program runs its course, and the consultant collects and analyzes the data. With little knowledge of program personnel and no stake in the program, the consultant has little trouble with "objective" evaluations. However, as the program runs, the data thought important at the beginning may come to appear to be no longer as relevant as other data that could have been gathered had the consultant been aware of the changes. In addition, the psychologist is unknown to program personnel and possibly management, so it is relatively easy to dismiss his or her conclusions and recommendations. The fully independent role is useful for established programs for which a summative evaluation is desired. It is not very useful for formative evaluation purposes. The consultant's role and relationship with the client organization and its personnel has to be consciously managed. The consultant has more degrees of freedom than the clinician has, but the added complexity creates a greater cognitive, emotional, and possibly financial burden on the psychologist.

Working With and Supervising New Psychologists

Professional skills in OBC psychology are largely learned after graduate school and on the job (Silzer et al., 2008). It is a role of more senior and seasoned practitioners to assist new psychologists in this learning and skill development process. OBC psychology is alone among fields of professional psychology in that it does not have a literature or tradition relating to supervision. Indeed, the term has different meanings; for OBC psychology, supervision commonly means having an administrative or leadership position, that is, being the boss. For clinicians, the term encompasses specific training, mentoring, and evaluative tasks, some of which are specific to the field (Shallcross, Johnson, & Lincoln, 2010). Clinicians, particularly those who are less experienced, may suffer secondary traumatization listening to the histories and narratives of their clients. An important role of the supervisor is to help the junior psychologist function in his or her position without internalizing the client's problems. In addition, some clinicians in training are able to perform effectively in the classroom but have psychological characteristics that interfere with their ability to practice in an ethical and effective manner. These are not such common occurrences in OBC psychology, which may explain why special attention to supervision has not been an issue of interest in the field. This is somewhat unfortunate considering that clinical psychology has developed detailed descriptions of the developmental trajectory of competence development in junior psychologists and for supervisors (Shallcross, Johnson, & Lincoln, 2010). OBC psychology has no such standards. In this situation we have to fall back on the competencies in training and development described in chapter 7 to guide and judge an OBC psychologist's competence in supervision.

Working with Professionals From Other Disciplines

OBC psychologists often find themselves collaborating with professionals trained in very different fields, including accounting, law, finance, engineering, marketing, and human resources. These professionals may be subject to licensing or professional standards, just as psychologists are. There is a potential for inadvertent conflict because of differing requirements and expectations regarding confidentiality, billing, and other business matters. For example, an OBC psychologist working with an industrial engineer may discover that the engineer in the normal course of working with the client contact is compromising information gained from members of the client organization. To maintain an ethical practice the psychologist and the other professionals need to clarify the legal, ethical, and professional standards they must adhere to and form an agreement on how these obligations will be met by the team. In addition, they should create a plan for dealing with unanticipated problems as they develop.

Telecommunications, Internet, and Other Distance Communications

In today's environment the OBC psychologist needs to be competent in working with individuals and groups over long distances using a variety of technologies. These technologies are rapidly evolving, so any attempt to enumerate them would be quickly obsolete. Historically, new communications technologies have been adopted earlier in some industries than others, meaning the OBC psychologist must be aware of these technologies and adoption rates in the industries served and adapt to their use as necessary.

Travel

Unless the OBC psychologist lives in one of the largest cities in the country, business travel will be a fact of life. There are two interpersonal challenges associated with this. First, the consultant must be able to adapt to new climes and time zones and be able to meet with clients without showing the effects of jet lag. Even within the same nation there are varying expectations regarding formality, dress, and other cultural artifacts and the psychologist must be able to either conform or, at least, not offend clients. Second, constant travel can put a strain on the consultant's personal life. If the psychologist has a family, some sort of accommodations have to be made. This is up to the individual and family members; from the perspective of competence, the psychologist has to find a way to prevent spillover from family issues from impacting his or her work performance.

Practice Organization

Nevis (1987) ended his book on organizational consulting with a unique chapter discussing whether the consultant is better off working as an individual or as part of a group. An OBC psychologist can work independently, as part of a small group practice, as a member of a large national or international firm, or as an internal consultant to a large organization; there are also those who work for government or the military. Nevis raised a number of issues, including finding a balance between personal needs for independence and autonomy and those of collegiality and stability. Finding a solution will depend on a number of individual factors, such as work style, competing priorities such as having young children, the nature of the consultant's skills and background, and market conditions. According to Nevis, being affiliated with a group brings some advantages such as a sense of belongingness, the opportunity to work on projects that are much larger than one can do alone, and availability of a support system. The price one pays for this is less control over activities, time, and decisions. Going it alone brings more opportunity to do things your own way and to make your own reputation. Among the costs are possible loneliness, smaller projects, and less opportunity to see the big picture. Nevis points out that since there is no single right answer, the work of the consultant will always involve some degree of stress.

The OBC psychologist who chooses to work independently will still want to develop a network of colleagues with whom the psychologist can discuss ideas, reflect on new developments, and use as a sounding board and for consultation on ethical dilemmas. This is so important it should be a part of the consultant's business plan or practice management system.

FOURTEEN

Professional Identity

After 13 chapters it should be evident that OBC psychology and the two traditions it consolidates cover a great breadth of subject matter and practice. This is more apparent when one considers the material and forms of practice that have been left out of this volume to keep it within reasonable limits. Because of the breadth of the field, it may seem that any professional identity that fits all would be so superficial as to have no meaning. That is not the case. There are common elements throughout that bring us together. Obviously one of these elements is an interest in work, the workplace, and the people who do the work. The O*NET describes I/O psychologists with four of the six Holland codes: investigative, enterprising, artistic, and social, yet it is clear that the psychologist must be able to sustain interest in the other two types, realist and conventional, as well if the consultant is to successfully understand and advise people in all types of work. The OBC consultant must be results oriented, even when the project focuses on process. There are two reasons organizations call in a consultant. Either they do not know what to do and need direction, or they know what to do but don't have the guts to do it. If the money spent on the consultant is not to be wasted, the consultant must be committed to working with the client to achieve an ethical and practical resolution to the problem. There is a degree of common educational background between the two fields even though it continues to evolve with new findings in psychology.

Lowman (2002, p. 2) writes that there is a common commitment to three features that differentiate consulting psychology from business administration or organizational development. First is an "insistence on measurement," second an "insistence on assessment," and third a concern with ethics and values. I do not think he meant that all OBC psychologists insist on precision in measurement to the nth degree in every circumstance because they clearly do not do that. Nor does he imply that every assessment is formal and ritualized. What he does mean is an obligation to evaluate every situation on its merits and formulate a plan of intervention based on the needs of the client as opposed to selling a solution without regard for the problem, as a mere vendor might (Church & Waclawski, 1998).

There has been a conflict between research and practice in I/O psychology, and to a lesser extent, consulting psychology, for decades (Blanton, 2000; Viswesvaran, Sinangil, Ones, & Anderson, 2001). This results partly from the vastly different reinforcement contingencies for academics and practitioners and partly from the difference in time scale at which each operates. Academics are rewarded for publishing in the "top tier" journals, which requires the latest analytical techniques to be applied in theory tests. Practitioners are rewarded for getting the job done. Science is, or should be, for the ages, while practice concentrates on the here and now. Unfortunately, as experienced practitioners recognize, effective practice in the here and now can make scientific generalizations obsolete before the future arrives.

That does leave us with the question of where OBC psychology lies within the pantheon of psychology in general. Drenth, Thierry, and de Wolff (1998) ask a rhetorical question of whether it is an application of four core areas of psychology: experimental, personality (individual differences), developmental, and behavioral (the integration of the others plus social and cultural psychology). Their answer is an emphatic "no." There is, for some, a stigma attached to a discipline that is merely "applied," but that doesn't seem to be the driving force behind the conclusion of Drenth et al. (1998). They see two major differences that separate OBC psychology from the other fields. First, the field has "gone its own way" (p. 4) in that much theorizing and subsequent research have been inspired by problems encountered in settings unvisited by other branches of psychology. Second, OBC psychology has built on many multidisciplinary relationships, leading to different insights and means of solving problems.

To these perspectives we can add a third. OBC psychologists, along with other professional psychologists, help solve problems. They do this regardless of whether the science has caught up with the issue; so often, they are having to utilize professionally informed judgment and extrapolating from existing knowledge. Some psychologists cannot accept this risk; they do not dare to venture into application until all questions are answered by science (cf. de Wolff, 1998). Consulting is not for the faint of heart or those who lack confidence. This is not to justify the overconfident consultant who lacks insight into the degree of support—or lack of it—for the work being done. Competence implies having a well thought out plan that utilizes the knowledge of the field as much as possible as well as the experience and reason of the psychologist.

Professional Affiliations

Psychologists benefit from affiliation and contact with other psychologists. In addition, membership in professional bodies can benefit the profession as these groups publish journals and books, arrange conferences and continuing education, and advocate for the profession to government and other influential bodies. The primary national and international organizations are the American Psychological Association (apa.org) and the International Association of Applied Psychology (IAAP; iaapsy.org). Each of these associations holds yearly conferences and publishes journals, and APA and IAAP have divisions of special interest to OBC psychologists. APA is by far the largest of the these organizations and has the most comprehensive set of standards, including ethical standards.

Specialty organizations for OBC psychologist include APA divisions; the Society for Industrial and Organizational Psychology (siop.org), the Society for Consulting Psychology (SCP; div13.org), Applied Experimental and Engineering Psychology (http://www.apa.org/divisions/div21/), and APA Division 5 Evaluation, Measurement, and Statistics (http://www.apa.org/about/division/div5.html). SIOP and SCP are generally the most relevant for OBC psychology.

There are other organizations that attract the interest of OBC psychologists, including the Society of Psychologists in Management (SPIM; spim.org), which requires that a potential member work in management in some capacity, and the Human Factors and Ergonomics Society (HFES, hfes.org). The latter organization is composed of professionals from a wide range of disciplines working in the area of human factors and human-technology interaction. Many OBC psychologists also belong to the Society for Human Resource Management (shrm.org), the American Society for Training and Development (astd.org), American Statistical Association (asa.org), or the OD Network (odnetwork.org), depending on their areas of practice and interest. Academically inclined OBC psychologists may belong to the Academy of Management (aomonline.org).

Licensure and Certification

Psychologists who practice need to obtain a license. That is true in all 50 states. I/O psychology as a field has not encouraged I/O psychologists to obtain licenses to practice, although Blanton (2006) gives four good reasons to become licensed: It is the law in most jurisdictions, it increases credibility, it protects the psychologist from certain legal hazards and allows the purchase of liability insurance, and having a license allows the psychologist to protect a client's confidential information.

Unfortunately, there has been a good deal of confusion about licensure in the I/O psychology community. The confusion stems from a long-standing aversion to licensing and program accreditation within SIOP. The current SIOP position (downloaded from http://siop.org/licensure/licensure.aspx, May 19, 2009), adopted in 1996, is this:

> SIOP recognizes that some states require that certain areas of I-O practice be licensed. SIOP members should be allowed to be licensed in these states if they desire, and SIOP should provide guidance to state licensing boards on how to evaluate the education and training of an I-O psychologist.

It is not a strong statement in favor of licensing but was the best the society could get passed (I was chair of the State Affairs Committee at the time). Unfortunately, the reluctance to become deeply involved in the licensing process means that I/O psychologists have not been influential in designing models that work for the field. This is currently changing, and a prominent SIOP member and practitioner, Judith Blanton, is a member of the APA task force developing a new model licensing act. In the most recent drafts of the model act, I/O psychologists are explicitly included in the scope of practice and are listed as requiring licensure (American Psychological Association, 2009a). Getting licensed requires the psychologist to clear several hurdles (Blanton, 2006).

It is easier to obtain a license if the psychologist's doctoral program was accredited by the American Psychological Association or at least listed in the National Register of Health Service Providers in Psychology. APA does not accredit I/O psychology programs and few are listed in the National Register,[1] even though accomplishing the latter is not difficult or expensive.

---

[1]   In March 2008 I searched for selected high-profile I/O psychology programs in the National Register. I found the University of Akron, University of Tennessee (management), and CUNY-Baruch. Programs that were not listed included Bowling Green, Maryland, Ohio State, Michigan State, Wayne State, Houston, Georgia, Auburn, Tulane, Tulsa, Penn State, and Portland State. There were no programs listed in the following states and district: California, Colorado, District of Columbia, Florida, Illinois, Massachusetts, Michigan,

Thus, graduates of I/O programs need to demonstrate that their program meets the basic standards of licensing agencies. In addition, some 3,000 to 4,000 hours of supervised experience are required (Blanton, 2006). For most psychologists this is accomplished in an internship and postdoctoral residency. Again, it is easier to get licensed if the internship is accredited by APA or by the Association of Psychology Post-Doctoral and Internship Centers (APPIC). Since neither of these bodies accredits internships in I/O psychology, meeting this requirement is the most complicated part of obtaining a license. According to Blanton (2006), several states, APA, and the Association of State and Provincial Psychology Board (ASPPB) are attempting to find suitable means for graduates to meet this requirement. One has to pass the Examination for Professional Practice in Psychology (EPPP), developed under the auspices of ASPPB. Finally, in many states the candidate for licensure must pass a written or oral examination covering ethics and legal issues.

Mobility of a license across state lines is a critical issue (Blanton, 2003). Many, if not most, OBC psychologists work across state and international boundaries. The definition of "psychologist" and scope of practice vary from state to state, making it complicated to know whether a project that is not subject to license requirements in one state is within a licensee's scope of practice in another. Many OBC psychologists who hold a psychologist license take advantage of exceptions in licensing laws that permit practice for a limited time in a state by a psychologist licensed in another state. The time limitation varies from 7 to 60 days. Professional organizations are working to increase this time for OBC psychologists and to expand the potential for mobility. Two actions a psychologist can take to minimize mobility problems are (1) to register with the Certificate of Professional Qualification with the ASPPB and (2) to become a certified specialist with the American Board of Professional Psychology.

Once licensed, the next logical step is to obtain specialty certification from the American Board of Organizational and Business Consulting Psychology (ABOBCP), a specialty board of the American Board of Professional Psychology (ABPP). Specialty certification adds to the benefits of licensure, particularly credibility. It also demonstrates a commitment to working at the highest levels of professional competence. Yet another advantage is the ease of movement of license between states once the ABPP is earned. There is now a trend for states to require certification for a

Minnesota, North Carolina, or South Carolina. I did not check all 50 states, but this list indicates that few programs are listed.

psychologist to be designated a specialist. If that trend continues, psychologists will need ABOBCP diplomas to refer to themselves as I/O or OBC psychologists. Full information on how to become board certified is available online at ABPP.org and in Nezu, Finch, and Simon (2009). Basically, the process consists of a credential review to verify that the applicant meets the requirements of ABPP and of ABOBCP. Next is the preparation and submission of the practice sample. Applicants with 15 or more years in practice may elect a senior option, which changes the practice sample requirement somewhat. Applicants indicate three to five subspecialities in which they primarily practice and choose to be examined on. Once the practice sample is approved, an oral examination can be scheduled. The oral exam lasts 3 to 4 hours and consists of a presentation of the practice sample followed by questions, then a section on subspecialty areas (including current research and theory, method of practice, and how competence was developed and is maintained), and finally an examination on ethical standards and practice. Successful candidates are invited to a convocation held at the next APA conference where their achievement is recognized and celebrated.

REFERENCES

Adams, J. S. (1965). Inequity in social exchange. In L. Berkowitz (Ed.), *Advances in experimental social psychology* (Vol. 2, pp. 267–299). San Diego, CA: Academic Press.

Aditya, R. N. (2004). Leadership. In J. C. Thomas (Ed.), *Comprehensive handbook of psychological assessment: Vol. IV. Industrial and organizational assessment* (pp. 216–239). New York: Wiley.

Aditya, R. N. (2006). Personality and the transformational leader. In J. C. Thomas & D. Segal (Eds.), *Comprehensive handbook of personality and psychopathology: Vol. I. Personality and everyday functioning* (pp. 345–363). New York: Wiley.

Aguinis, H., & Cascio, W. F. (2008). Narrowing the science-practice divide: A call to action. *The Industrial-Organizational Psychologist, 46*(2), 27–36.

Aguinis, H., & Kraiger, K. (2009). Benefits of training and development for individuals and teams, organizations, and society. *Annual Review of Psychology, 60*, 451–474.

Aguinis, H., Pierce, C. A., Bosco, F. A., & Muslin, I. S. (2009). First decade of *Organizational Research Methods*: Trends in design, measurement, and data-analysis topics. *Organizational Research Methods, 12*(1), 69–112.

Alderfer, C. P. (1969). An empirical test of a new theory of human needs. *Organizational Behavior and Human Performance, 4*, 142-175.

Alliger, G. M. & Janak, E. (1989). Kirkpatrick's levels of training criteria: Thirty years later. *Personnel Psychology, 42*, 331–343.

Allport, G. W. (1937). *Personality: A psychological interpretation.* New York: Henry Holt.

American Board of Professional Psychology. (2007). *Standards for specialty board certification,* revised. Savannah, GA: Author.

American Educational Research Association, American Psychological Association, & National Council on Measurement in Education. (1999). *Standards for educational and psychological testing.* Washington, DC: American Educational Research Association.

American Psychiatric Association. (1987). *Diagnostic and statistical manual of mental disorders* (3rd ed., rev.). Washington, DC: Author.

American Psychiatric Association. (2000). *Diagnostic and statistical manual of mental disorders* (4th ed., text revision). Washington, DC: Author.

American Psychological Association. (2000). *Report of the task force on test user qualifications.* Downloaded from www.apa.org/science/tuq.pdf, May 20, 2009.

American Psychological Association. (2001). *Publication manual of the American Psychological Association.* Washington, DC: Author.

American Psychological Association. (2002). Ethical principles of psychologists and code of conduct. *American Psychologist, 57*(12), 1060–1073.

American Psychological Association. (2003). Guidelines on multicultural education, training, research, practice, and organizational change for psychologists. *American Psychologist, 58,* 377–402.

American Psychological Association. (2007). Guidelines for education and training at the doctoral and postdoctoral levels in consulting psychology/organizational consulting psychology. *American Psychologist, 62*(9), 980–992.

American Psychological Association. (2009a). Model act for state licensure: Public comment. Downloaded from http://forms.apa.org/practice/modelactlicensure/mla-review-2009. pdf, May 19, 2009.

American Psychological Association. (2009b). *Publication manual of the American Psychological Association* (6th ed.). Washington, DC: Author.

American Psychological Association. (n.d.). *Rights and responsibilities of test takers: Guidelines and expectations.* Downloaded from www.apa.org/science/ttrr.html, May 20, 2009.

American Psychological Association Task Force on Evidence-Based Practice. (2006). Evidence-based practice in psychology. *American Psychologist, 61*(4), 271–286.

Amundson, N. E., Harris-Bowlsbey, J., & Niles, S. G. (2010). *Essential elements of career counseling.* Upper Saddle River, NJ: Pearson.

Antoniou, A.-S. G., & Cooper, C. L. (Eds.). (2005). *Research companion to organizational health psychology.* Cheltenham, UK: Edward Elgar.

Armenakis, A. A., & Bedeian, A. G. (1999). Organizational change: A review of theory and research in the 1990s. *Journal of Management, 25*(3), 293–315.

Arthur, W. J., Bennett, W. J., Edens, P., & Bell, S. T. (2003). Effectiveness of training in organizations: A meta-analysis of design and evaluation features. *Journal of Applied Psychology, 88*(2), 234–245.

Arthur, W. J., Day, E. A., & Woehr, D. J. (2008). Mend it, don't end it: An alternative view of assessment center construct-related validity evidence. *Industrial and Organizational Psychology, 1*(1), 105–111.

Ashkanasy, N.M., & Jackson, C.R.A. (2001). Organizational culture and climate. In N. Anderson, D. S. Ones, H. K. Sinangil, & C. Viswesvaran (Eds.), *Handbook of industrial, work, and organizational psychology: Vol. 2. Personnel psychology* (pp. 398-415). Thousand Oaks, CA: Sage.

Ashkanasy, N. M., Zerbe, W. J., & Härtel, C. E. J. (2002). *Managing emotions in the workplace.* Armonk, NY: M. E. Sharp.

Association of State and Provincial Psychology Boards. (2005). *Code of conduct, revised.* Downloaded from www.asppb.net/i4a/pages/index.cfm?pageid=3353.

Austin, J. T., & Villanova, P. (1992). The criterion problem: 1917–1992. *Journal of Applied Psychology, 77,* 836–874.

Avolio, B., Walumbwa, F. O., & Weber, T. J. (2009). Leadership: Current theories, research, and future directions. *Annual Review of Psychology, 60,* 421–450.

Aycan, Z., & Kanungo, R. N. (2001). Cross-cultural industrial and organizational psychology: A critical appraisal of the field and future directions. In N. Anderson, D. S. Ones, H. K. Sinangil, & C. Viswesvaran (Eds.), *Handbook of industrial, work, and organizational psychology: Vol. 1. Personnel psychology* (pp. 385–408). Thousand Oaks, CA: Sage.

Ayoko, O. B., & Härtel, C. E. J. (2003). The role of space as both a conflict trigger and a conflict control mechanism in culturally hetereogeneous workgroups. *Applied Psychology: An International Review, 52*(3), 383–412.

Babiak, P. (1995). When psychopaths go to work: A case study of an industrial psychopath. *Applied Psychology: An International Review, 44,* 171–188.

Balzer, W. K., Greguras, G. J., & Raymark, P. H. (2001). Multisource feedback. In J. C. Thomas (Ed.), *Comprehensive handbook of psychological assessment: Vol. IV. Industrial and organizational assessment* (pp. 390–411). New York: Wiley.

Bandura, A. (1977). *Social learning theory.* Englewood Cliffs, NJ: Prentice-Hall.

Bandura, A. (2001) Social cognitive theory: An agentic perspective. *Annual Review of Psychology, 52,* 1–26.

Barbazette, J. (2006). *Training needs assessment: Methods, tools, and techniques.* San Francisco: Pfeiffer.

Barlow, D., & Nock, M. (2009). Why can't we be more idiographic in our research? *Perspectives on Psychological Science, 4*(1), 19–21.

Barlow, D. H., Nock, M. K., & Hersen, M. (2009). *Single case experimental designs: Strategies for studying behavior change* (3rd ed.). Boston: Pearson.

Barnes-Farrell, J. (2001). Performance appraisal: Person perception processes and challenges. In M. London (Ed.), *How people evaluate others in organizations* (pp. 135–153). Mahwah, NJ: Lawrence Erlbaum.

Barnett, J. E. (2008). Impaired professionals: Distress, professional impairment, self-care, and psychological wellness. In M. Hersen & A. M. Gross (Eds.), *Handbook of clinical psychology: Vol. 1. Adults* (pp. 857–884). New York: Wiley.

Baron, H. (1996). Strengths and limitations of ipsative measurement. *Journal of Occupational and Organizational Psychology, 69,* 49–56.

Barrett, G. V. (2008). Practitioner's view of personality testing and industrial-organizational psychology: Practical and legal issues. *Industrial and Organizational Psychology, 1,* 299–302.

Barrett, G. V., Phillips, J. S., & Alexander, R. A. (1981). Concurrent and predictive validity designs: A critical analysis. *Journal of Applied Psychology, 25,* 499–513.

Barrett, R. S. (1992). Content validation form. *Public Personnel Management, 21*(1), 41–52.

Bass, B. M. (1981). *Stogdill's handbook of leadership* (Revised and expanded). New York: Free Press.

Bauer, T. N., & Taylor, S. (2001). Toward a globalized conceptualization of organizational socializations. In N. Anderson, D. S. Ones, H. K. Sinangil, & C. Viswesvaran (Eds.), *Handbook of industrial, work, and organizational psychology: Vol. 1. Personnel psychology* (pp. 409–423). Thousand Oaks, CA: Sage.

Bauer, T. N., Truxillo, D. M., & Paronto, M. E. (2004). The measurement of applicant reactions to selection. In J. C. Thomas (Ed.), *Comprehensive handbook of psychological assessment: Vol. IV. Industrial and organizational assessment* (pp. 482–506). New York: Wiley.

Beckhard, R. (1969). *Organization development: Strategies and models.* Reading, MA: Addison-Wesley.

Berra, Y. (1998) *The Yogi book: I really didn't say everything I said.* New York: Workman.

Berry, C. M., Sackett, P. R., & Wiemann, S. (2007). A review of recent developments in integrity test research. *Personnel Psychology, 60*(2), 271–302.

Bickel, R. (2007). *Multilevel analysis for applied research: It's just regression.* New York: Guilford.

Birch, J. (2008). Pass rates for the Farnsworth D 15 colour vision test. *Ophthalmic and Physiological Optics, 28*(3), 259–264.

Black, J. S., Mendenhall, M., & Oddou, G. (1991). Toward a comprehensive model of international adjustment: An integration of multiple theoretical perspectives. *Academy of Management Review, 16*, 291–317.

Blake, R. R., & McCanse, A. A. (1991). *Leadership dilemmas: Grid solutions.* Houston, TX: Gulf.

Blake, R. R., & Mouton, J. S. (1964). *The managerial grid.* Houston, TX: Gulf.

Blanton, J. S. (2000). Why consultants don't apply psychological research. *Consulting Psychology Journal: Practice and Research, 52*(4), 235–247.

Blanton, J. S. (2003). Mobility for industrial-organizational and consulting psychologists. *Professional Psychology: Research and Practice, 34*(5), 476–479.

Blanton, J. S. (2006). License issues for industrial/organizational psychologists and other non-health service providers. In T. J. Vaughn (Ed.), *Psychology licensure and certification: What students need to know* (pp. 145–154). Washington, DC: American Psychological Association.

Borden, L. W., & Sharf, J. C. (2007). Developing legally defensible content valid selection procedures. In D. L. Whetzel & G. R. Wheaton (Eds.), *Applied measurement: Industrial psychology in human resources management* (pp. 385–401). Mahwah, NJ: Lawrence Erlbaum.

Borman, W. C., & Motowidlo, S. J. (1993). Expanding the criterion domain to include elements of contextual performance. In N. Schmidt & W. C. Borman (Eds.), *Personnel selection* (pp. 71–98). San Francisco: Jossey-Bass.

Bracken, D. W., & Timmreck, C. J. (1999). Guidelines for multisource feedback when used for decision making. *The Industrial-Organizational Psychologist, 36*(4). Downloaded from www.siop.org/tip/backissues/Tipapr99/7Bracken.aspx, April 12, 2009.

Brands, H. W. (1997). *T.R.: The last romantic.* New York: Basic Books.

Brannick, M. T., Levine, E. L., & Morgeson, F. P. (2007). *Job and work analysis: Methods, research, and applications for human resource management.* Thousand Oaks, CA: Sage.

Brickman, P., Coates, D., & Janoff-Bulman, R. (1978). Lottery winners and accident victims: Is happiness relative? *Journal of Personality and Social Psychology, 36*(8), 917–927.

Brislin, R. W., & Kim, E. S. (2003). Cultural diversity in people's understanding of time. *Applied Psychology: An International Review, 52*(3), 363–383.

Brislin, R. W., & Low, K. D. (2006). Culture, personality, and people's uses of time: Key interrelationships. In J. C. Thomas & D. Segal (Eds.), *Comprehensive handbook of personality and psychopathology: Vol. I. Personality and everyday functioning* (pp. 44–64). New York: Wiley.

Broverman, D. M. (1962). Normative and ipsative measurement in psychology. *Psychological Review, 69*(4), 295–305.

Brown, K. G., & Ford, J. K. (2002). Using computer technology in training: Building an infrastructure for active learning. In K. Kraiger (Ed.), *Creating, implementing, and managing effective training and development: State-of-the-art lessons for practice* (pp. 192–233). San Francisco: Jossey-Bass.

Burke, W. W. (2006). Where did OD come from? In J. V. Gallos (Ed.), *Organizational development* (pp. 13–38). San Francisco: Jossey-Bass.

Burns, J. M. (1978). *Leadership.* New York: Harper & Row.

Burns, T., & Stalker, G. M. (1961). *The management of innovation.* London: Tavistock.

Buster, M. A., Roth, P. L., & Bobko, P. (2005). A process for content validation of education and experienced-based minimum qualification: An approach resulting in federal court approval. *Personnel Psychology, 58*, 771–799.

Campbell, J. P. (1986). Labs, fields, and straw issues. In E. A. Locke (Ed.), *Generalizing from laboratory to field settings* (pp. 269–279). Lexington, MA: Lexington.

Campbell, J. P., & Dunnette, M. D. (1968). Effectiveness of T-group experiences in managerial training and development. *Psychological Bulletin, 70*(2), 73–102.

Cannon-Bowers, J., & Salas, E. (1998). *Making decisions under stress: Implications for individual and team training.* Washington, DC: American Psychological Association.

Cascio, W. F., & Aguinis, H. (2008). Research in industrial and organizational psychology from 1963 to 2007: Changes, choices, and trends. *Journal of Applied Psychology, 93*(5), 1062–1081.

Cascio, W. F., Alexander, R. A., & Barrett, G. V. (1988). Setting cut-off scores: Legal, psychometric, and professional issues and guidelines. *Personnel Psychology, 41*, 1–24.

Chao, G. T., Walz, P. M., & Gardner, P. D. (1992). Formal and informal mentoring relationships: A comparison of mentoring functions and contrast with nonmentored counterparts. *Personnel Psychology, 45*, 619–636.

Church, A. H., & Waclawski, J. (1998). The vendor mind-set: The devolution from organizational consultant to street peddler. *Consulting Psychology Journal: Practice and Research, 50*(2), 87–100.

Cleveland, J. N., Murphy, K. R., & Williams, R. E. (1989). Multiple uses of performance appraisal: Prevalence and correlates. *Journal of Applied Psychology, 74*(1), 130–135.

Cohen, D. (2001). Cultural variation: Considerations and implications. *Psychological Bulletin, 127*(4), 451–471.

Cohen, M. D., March, J. G., & Olsen, J. P. (1972). A garbage can model of organizational choice. *Administrative Science Quarterly, 17*, 1–25.

Cooper, G. L., & Marshall, J. (1978). *Understanding executive stress.* London: Macmillan.

Cornwell, J. M. (2004). Basic skills. In J. C. Thomas (Ed.), *Comprehensive handbook of psychological assessment: Vol. IV. Industrial and organizational assessment* (pp. 87–106). New York: Wiley.

Cronbach, L.J., & Meehl, P. (1955). Construct validity in psychological tests. *Psychological Bulletin, 52*, 281-302.

Cullen, M. J., & Sackett, P. R. (2004). Integrity testing in the workplace. In J. C. Thomas (Ed.), *Comprehensive handbook of psychological assessment: Vol. IV. Industrial and organizational assessment* (pp. 149–165). New York: Wiley.

De Beuckelaer, A., & Lievens, F. (2009). Measurement equivalence of paper-and-pencil and internet organizational surveys: A large scale examination in 16 countries. *Applied Psychology: An International Review, 58*(2), 336–361.

Dekker, S. (2006). *The field guide to understanding human error.* Burlington, VT: Ashgate.

De Wolff, C. J. (1998). The role of the work and organizational psychologist. In P. J. D. Drenth, H. Thierry, & C. J. de Wolf (Eds.), *Handbook of work and organizational psychology* (2nd ed.): *Vol. 1. Introduction to work and organizational psychology* (pp. 47–69). London: Psychology Press.

Dien, D., S.-f. (1999). Chinese authority-directed orientation and Japanese peer-group orientation: Questioning the notion of collectivism. *Review of General Psychology, 3*(4), 372–385.

Dipboye, R. L., Wooten, K., & Halverson, S. K. (2004). Behavioral and situational interviews. In J. C. Thomas (Ed.), *Comprehensive handbook of psychological assessment: Vol. IV. Industrial and organizational assessment* (pp. 297–316). New York: Wiley.

Donnay, D. A. C., Morris, M. L., Schaubhut, N. A., &, Thompson, R. C. (2005). *Strong interest inventory manual* (Rev. ed.). Mountain View, CA: Consulting Psychologists Press.

Dorans, N. J., Pommerich, M., & Holland, P. W. (Eds.). (2007). *Linking and aligning scores and scales.* New York: Springer.

Doverspike, D., Cober, A. B., & Arthur, W. A., Jr. (2004). Multiaptitude test batteries. In J. C. Thomas (Ed.), *Comprehensive handbook of psychological assessment: Vol. IV. Industrial and organizational assessment* (pp. 35–55). New York: Wiley.

Doyle, M. (2000). Managing careers in organizations. In A. Collin & R. A. Young (Eds.), *The future of career* (pp. 228–243). Cambridge, UK: Cambridge University Press.

Drenth, P. J. D., Thierry, H., & de Wolff, C. J. (1998). What is work and organizational psychology? In P. J. D. Drenth, H. Thierry, & C. J. de Wolf (Eds.), *Handbook of work and organizational psychology* (2nd ed.): *Vol. 1. Introduction to work and organizational psychology* (pp. 1–10). London: Psychology Press.

Druckman, D., Singer, J. E., & Van Cott, H. (Eds.). (1997). *Enhancing organizational performance*. Washington, DC: National Academy Press.

Dubois, D. A. (2002). Leveraging hidden expertise: Why, when, and how to use cognitive task analysis. In K. Kraiger (Ed.), *Creating, implementing, and managing effective training and development: State-of-the-art lessons for practice* (pp. 80–116). San Francisco: Jossey-Bass.

Dunnette, M. D. (1966). Fads, fashions, and folderol in psychology. *American Psychologist, 21*(4), 343–352.

Edgington, E. S., & Onghena, P. (2007). *Randomization tests* (4th ed.). Boca Raton, FL: Taylor & Francis.

Edmondson, A. C., Bohmer, R. M., & Pisano, G. P. (2001). Disrupted routines: Team learning and new technology implementation in hospitals. *Administrative Science Quarterly, 46*, 685–716.

Education and Training Committee, Division 13, Society of Consulting Psychology, American Psychological Association. (2002). Principles for education and training at the doctoral and postdoctoral level in consulting psychology/organizational. *Consulting Psychology Journal: Practice and Research, 54*(4), 213–222.

Fiske, D. W. (1951). Values, theory, and the criterion problem. *Personnel Psychology, 4*, 93–98.

Flanagan, J. C. (1954). The critical incident technique. *Psychological Bulletin, 51*, 327–358.

Fleishman, E. A., & Reilly, M. E. (1992). *Handbook of human abilities: Definitions, requirements, and job task requirements*. Palo Alto, CA: Consulting Psychologists Press.

Flexner, J. T. (1974). *Washington: The indispensable man*. Boston: Little-Brown.

Fouad, N. A. (2007). Work and vocational psychology: Theory, research, and applications. *Annual Review of Psychology, 58*, 543–564.

Frechtling, J. A. (2007). *Logic modeling methods in program evaluation*. San Francisco: Jossey-Bass.

Freedman, A. M., & Bradt, K. H. (Eds.). (2009). *Consulting psychology: Selected articles by Harry Levinson*. Washington, DC: American Psychological Association.

Freedman, D., Pisani, R., & Purves, R. (2007). *Statistics* (4th ed.). New York: Norton.

French, J. R. P., & Raven, B. H. (1959). The bases of social power. In D. Cartwright (Ed.), *Studies in social power* (pp. 150–167). Ann Arbor, MI: Institute for Social Research.

Frew, J. (2004). Motivating and leading dysfunctional employees. In J. C. Thomas & M. Hersen (Eds.), *Psychopathology in the workplace* (pp. 293–312). New York: Brunner-Routledge.

Freyd, M. (1923). Measurement in vocational selection: An outline of a research procedure. *Journal of Personnel Research, 2*, 215–249, 268–284, 377–385.

Frost, D. (2004). The psychological assessment of emotional intelligence. In J. C. Thomas (Ed.), *Comprehensive handbook of psychological assessment: Vol. IV. Industrial and organizational assessment* (pp. 203–215). New York: Wiley.

Gelfand, M. J., Erez, M., & Aycan, Z. (2007). Cross-cultural organizational behavior. *Annual Review of Psychology, 58*, 479–514.

Gellerman, S. W. (1992). *Motivation in the real world: The art of getting extra effort from everyone—including yourself.* New York: Dutton.

Gerhart, B., & Milkovich, G. T. (1992). Employee compensation: Research and practice. In M. D. Dunnette & L.M. Hough (Eds.), *Handbook of industrial and organizational psychology* (2nd ed., Vol. 3, pp. 481–570). Palo Alto, CA: Consulting Psychologists Press.

Ghiselli, E. E. (1966). *The validity of occupational aptitude tests.* New York: Wiley.

Gigerenzer, G. (1993). The superego, the ego, and the id in statistical reasoning. In G. Keren & C. Lewis (Eds.), *A handbook for data analysis in the behavioral sciences: Methodological issues* (pp. 311–340). Mahwah, NJ: Lawrence Erlbaum.

Gigerenzer, G. (2008). *Rationality for mortals.* New York: Oxford University Press.

Gigerenzer, G., & Selthon, R. (2001). *Bounded rationality: The adaptive toolbox.* Cambridge, MA: MIT Press.

Gilbert, T. (1994). A question of performance: The PROBE model. In P. J. Dean (Ed.). *Performance engineering at work* (pp. 43–62). Batavia, IL: International Board of Standard for Training, Performance, and Instruction.

Guion, R. (1965). *Personnel testing.* New York: McGraw-Hill.

Guion, R. (1974). Open a new window: Validities and values in psychological measurement. *American Psychologist, 29*, 287–296.

Guion, R. (1998). *Assessment, measurement, and prediction for personnel decisions.* Mahway, NJ: Lawrence Erlbaum.

Guion, R., & Gottier, R. F. (1965). Validity of personality measures in personnel selection. *Personnel Psychology, 18*, 135–164.

Gustavsen, B. (2008). Action research, practical challenges and the formation of theory. *Action Research, 6*(4), 421–437.

Griffith, R. L., & Peterson, M. H. (2008). The failure of social desirability measures to capture applicant faking behavior. *Industrial and Organizational Psychology, 1*, 308–311.

Grubb, W. L. III, Whetzel, D. L., & McDaniel, M. A. (2004). General mental ability tests in industry. In J. C. Thomas (Ed.), *Comprehensive handbook of psychological assessment: Vol. IV. Industrial and organizational assessment* (pp. 7–20). New York: Wiley.

Hackman, J. R., & Lawler, E. E. (1971). Employee reactions to job characteristics. *Journal of Applied Psychology, 55*, 259–286.

Hackman, J. R., & Oldham, G. R. (1976). Motivation through the design of work: Test of a theory. *Journal of Applied Psychology, 60*, 159–170.

Hammer, L. B., Colton, C. L., Caubet, S., & Brockwood, K. J. (2002). The unbalanced life: Work and family conflict. In J. C. Thomas & M. Hersen (Eds.), *Handbook of mental health in the workplace* (pp. 83–102). Thousand Oaks, CA: Sage.

Hansen, J. C., & Dik, B. J. (2004). Measures of career interests. In J. C. Thomas (Ed.), *Comprehensive handbook of psychological assessment: Vol. IV. Industrial and organizational assessment* (pp. 166–191). New York: Wiley.

Harrison, R. (1974). Some criteria for choosing the depth of organizational intervention strategy. In D. A. Kolb, I. M. Rubin, & J. M. McIntyre (Eds.), *Organizational psychology: A book of readings* (pp. 387–399). Englewood Cliffs, NJ: Prentice-Hall. (Originally presented in 1968).

Harvey, J. L., Anderson, L. E., Baranowski, L. E., & Morath, R. A. (2007). Job analysis: Gathering job-specific information. In D. L. Whetzel, & G. R. Wheaton (Eds.), *Applied measurement: Industrial psychology in human resources management* (pp. 57–95). Mahwah, NJ: Lawrence Erlbaum.

Hays, P. A. (2001). *Addressing cultural complexities in practice: A framework for clinicians and counselors.* Washington, DC: American Psychological Association.

Henderson, N. D., Berry, M. W., & Matic, T. (2007). Field measures of strength and fitness predict firefighter performance on demanding tasks. *Personnel Psychology, 60*(2), 431–473.

Heneman, R. L., Fay, C. H., & Wang, Z.-M. (2001). Compensation systems in the global context. In N. Anderson, D. S. Ones, H. K. Sinangil, & C. Viswesvaran (Eds.), *Handbook of industrial, work, and organizational psychology: Vol. 2. Organizational psychology* (pp. 76–92). Thousand Oaks, CA: Sage.

Herman, J. B. (1973). Are situational contingencies limiting job attitude-job performance relationships? *Organizational Behavior and Human Performance, 10*, 208–224.

Herold, D. M., Fedor, D. B., & Caldwell, S. D. (2007). Beyond change management: A multilevel investigation of contextual and personal influences on employee's commitment to change. *Journal of Applied Psychology, 92*(4), 942–951.

Herzberg, F. (1966). *Work and the nature of man.* Chicago: World Publishing.

Herzberg, F. I., Mausner, B., Peterson, R. O., & Capwell, D. R. (1957). *Job attitudes: Review of research and opinion.* Pittsburgh, PA: Psychological Service of Pittsburgh.

Heuvel, L. N., Lorenzo, D. K., Jackson, L. O., Hanson, W. E., Rooney, J. J., & Walker, D. A. (2009). *Root cause analysis handbook: A guide to efficient and effective incident investigations* (3rd ed.) Brookfield, CT: Rothstein.

Hofstede, G. (1980). *Culture's consequences: International differences in work-related values.* Beverly Hills, CA: Sage.

Hogan, J. (1991a). Physical abilities. In M. D. Dunnette & L. M. Hough (Eds.), *Handbook of industrial and organizational psychology* (2nd ed., Vol. 2, pp. 753–831). Palo Alto, CA: Consulting Psychologists Press.

Hogan, J. (1991b). Structure of physical performance in occupational tasks. *Journal of Applied Psychology, 76*, 495–507.

Hogan, R. (1994). Trouble at the top: Causes and consequences of managerial incompetence. *Consulting Psychology Journal, 46*(1), 1061–1087.

Hogan, R., & Hogan, J. (2001). Assessing leadership: A view from the dark side. *International Journal of Selection and Placement, 9*(1/2), 40–51.

Hogan, R., & Warrenfeltz, R. (2003). Educating the modern manager. *Academy of Management Learning and Education, 2*(1), 74–84.

Holland, J. L. (1997). *Making vocational choices: A theory of vocational personalities and work environments* (3rd ed.). Odessa, FL: Psychological Assessment Resources.

Hough, L. (1992). The "big five" personality variables-construct confusion: Description vs. prediction. *Human Performance, 5*, 139–155.

Hough, L., & Oswald, F. L. (2008). Personality testing and industrial-organizational psychology: Reflections, progress, and prospects. *Industrial and Organizational Psychology, 1*, 272–290.

House, R. J. (1976). A 1976 theory of charismatic leadership. In J. G. Hunt & L. L. Larson (Eds.), *Leadership: The cutting edge* (pp. 189–207). Carbondale: Southern Illinois University Press.

Howard, A. (2008). Making assessment centers work the way they are supposed to. *Industrial and Organizational Psychology, 1*(1), 98–104.

Huffcutt, A. I., Weekley, J. A., Wiesner, W. H., Degroot, T. G., & Jones, C. (2001). Comparison of situational and behavior description interview questions for higher-level positions. *Personnel Psychology, 54*, 619–644.

Jawahar, I. M., & Williams, C. R. (1997). Where all the children are above average: The performance appraisal purpose. *Personnel Psychology, 50*(4), 905–925.

Jeanneret, R. (2005). Professional and technical authorities and guidelines. In F. J. Landy (Ed.), *Employment discrimination litigation: Behavioral, quantitative, and legal perspectives* (pp. 47–100). San Francisco: Jossey-Bass.

Johns, G. (2002). Absenteeism and mental health. In J. C. Thomas & M. Hersen (Eds.), *Handbook of mental health in the workplace* (pp. 437–457). Thousand Oaks, CA: Sage.

Jones, J. W., & Arnold, D. W. (2008). Protecting the legal and appropriate use of personality testing: A practitioner perspective. *Industrial and Organizational Psychology, 1,* 296–298.

Judge, T. A., Thoresen, C. J., Bono, J. E., & Patton, G. K. (2001). The job satisfaction-job performance relationship: A qualitative and quantitative review. *Psychological Bulletin, 127*(3), 376–407.

Katona, G. (1953). Rational behavior and economic behavior. *Psychological Review, 60*(5), 307–318.

Katz, D., & Kahn, R. L. (1966). *The social psychology of organizations.* New York: Wiley.

Katz, D., & Kahn, R. L. (1978). *The social psychology of organizations* (2nd ed.). New York: Wiley.

Kaufman, J. D., & Borman, W. C. (2004). Citizenship performance in organizations. In J. C. Thomas (Ed.), *Comprehensive handbook of psychological assessment: Vol. IV. Industrial and organizational assessment* (pp. 412–424). New York: Wiley.

Keegan, J. (1978). *The face of battle.* New York: Penguin Books.

Keegan, J. (1988). *The mask of command.* New York: Penguin Books.

Kehoe, J. F., & Olson, A. (2005). Cut scores and employment discrimination litigation. In F. J. Landy (Ed.), *Employment discrimination litigation: Behavioral, quantitative, and legal perspectives* (pp. 410–449). San Francisco: Jossey-Bass.

Kendler, H. (1993). Psychology and the ethics of social policy. *American Psychologist, 48,* 1046–1053.

Kilburg, R. R. (2000). *Executive coaching: Developing managerial wisdom in a world of chaos.* Washington, DC: American Psychological Association.

King, L. M., Hunter, J. E., & Schmidt, F. E. (1980). Halo in a multidimensional forced-choice performance evaluation scale. *Journal of Applied Psychology, 65,* 507–516.

Kirkpatrick, D. M. (1959a). Techniques for evaluating training programs. *Journal of ASTD, 13*(11), 3–9.

Kirkpatrick, D. M. (1959b). Techniques for evaluating training programs: Part 2—learning. *Journal of ASTD, 13*(12), 21–26.

Kirkpatrick, D. M. (1960a). Techniques for evaluating training programs: Part 3—behavior. *Journal of ASTD, 14*(1), 13–18.

Kirkpatrick, D. M. (1960b). Techniques for evaluating training programs: Part 4—results. *Journal of ASTD, 14*(2), 28–32.

Kitayama, S. (2002). Culture and basic psychological processes—Toward a system view of culture: Comment on Oyserman et al. (2002). *Psychological Bulletin, 128*(1), 89–96.

Klann, G. (2007). *Building character: Strengthening the heart of good leadership.* San Francisco: Jossey-Bass.

Klein, G. (1998). *Sources of power: How people make decisions.* Cambridge, MA: MIT Press.

Klein, G. (2009). *Streetlights and shadows: Searching for the keys to adaptive decision making.* Cambridge, MA: MIT press.

Koopman, P. L., Broekhuijsen, J. W., & Wierdsma, A. F. M. (1998) In P. J. D. Drenth, H. Thierry, & C. J. de Wolf (Eds.), *Handbook of work and organizational psychology* (2nd ed.): *Vol. 4. Organizational psychology* (pp. 357–386). East Sussex, UK: Psychology Press.

Koppes, L. (Ed.). (2007). *Historical perspectives in industrial and organizational psychology.* Mahwah, NJ: Lawrence Erlbaum.

Kozlowski, S., Chao, G., & Morrison, R. F. (1998). Games raters play: Politics, strategies, and impression management in performance appraisal. In J. W. Smithers (Ed.), *Performance appraisal: State of the art in practice* (pp. 163–208). San Francisco: Jossey-Bass.

Kozlowski, S., & Ilgen, D. (2006). Enhancing the effectiveness of work groups and teams. *Psychological Science in the Public Interest, 3*(7), 77–124.

Kraiger, K. (2008). Transforming our models of learning and development: Web-based instruction as enabler of third-generation instruction. *Industrial and Organizational Psychology, 1*(4), 454–467.

Kroeck, K. G., & Brown, K. W. (2004). Work applications of the big five model of personality. In J. C. Thomas (Ed.), *Comprehensive handbook of psychological assessment: Vol. IV. Industrial and organizational assessment* (pp. 109–129). New York: Wiley.

Krug, J. A., & Hegarty, W. H. (1998). Postacquisition turnover among U.S. top management teams: An analysis of the effects of foreign vs. domestic acquisitions of U.S. targets. *Strategic Management Journal, 18*(8), 667–675.

Kurpius, D. J. (1985). Consultation interventions: Successes, failures, and proposals. *Journal of Counseling Psychology, 13*(3), 368–389.

Landy, F. J. (Ed.). (2005). *Employment discrimination litigation: Behavioral, quantitative, and legal perspectives.* San Francisco, CA: Jossey-Bass.

Landy, F. J., & Farr, J. (1980). Performance rating. *Psychological Bulletin, 87*, 72–107.

Lance, C. E. (2008). Why assessment centers do not work the way they are supposed to. *Industrial and Organizational Psychology, 1*(1), 84–97.

LaRoche, M. J., & Christopher, M. C. (2010). Cultural diversity. In J. C. Thomas & M. Hersen (Eds.), *Handbook of clinical psychology competencies: Vol. 1. General competencies (pp. 95–122).* New York: Springer.

Latham, G. P., & Budworth, M.-H. (2007). The study of work motivation in the 20th century. In L. L. Koppes (Ed.), *Historical perspectives in industrial and organizational psychology* (pp. 353–381). Mahwah, NJ: Lawrence Erlbaum.

Latham, G. P. & Pinder, C. C. (2005). Work motivation theory and research at the dawn of the twenty-first century. *Annual Review of Psychology, 56*, 485–516.

Lawrence, P. R., & Lorsch, J. W. (1967). *Organization and environment.* Boston: Harvard.

Leahy, R. L. (2003). *Psychology and the economic mind: Cognitive processes and conceptualizations.* New York: Springer.

LeBreton, J. M., Binning, J. B., & Adorno, A. J. (2006). Subclinical psychopaths. In J. C. Thomas & D. Segal (Eds.), *Comprehensive handbook of personality and psychopathology: Vol. I. Personality and everyday functioning* (pp. 388–412). New York: Wiley.

Ledford, G. E., Mohrman, S. A., Mohrman, A. M., Jr., & Lawler, E. E. (1989). The phenomenon of large scale organizational change. In A. M. Mohrman, Jr., S. A. Mohrman, G. E. Ledford, T. G. Cummings, & E. E. Lawler (Eds.), *Large scale organizational change* (pp. 1–32). San Francisco: Jossey-Bass.

Lent, R. W., Brown, S. D., & Hackett, G. (1996). Career development from a social cognitive perspective. In D. Brown & L. Brooks (Eds.), *Career choice and development* (3rd ed., pp. 373–421).

Leong, F. T. L., Cooper, S., Huang, J. L. (2008). Selected bibliography on diversity consulting: Supplement to the special issue on culture, race, and ethnicity in organizational consulting psychology. *Consulting Psychology Journal: Practice and Research, 60*(2), 215–226.

Levine, E. L., Ash, R. A., & Levine, J. D. (2004). In J. C. Thomas (Ed.), *Comprehensive handbook of psychological assessment: Vol. IV. Industrial and organizational assessment* (pp. 269–296). New York: Wiley.

Levine, E. L., Maye, D. M., Ulm, R. A., & Gordon, T. R. (1997). A methodology for developing and validating minimum qualifications (MQs). *Personnel Psychology, 50,* 1009–1023.

Levinson, H. (1996). Executive coaching. *Consulting Psychology Journal: Practice and Research,* 48, 115–123.

Levinson, H. (2002). Psychological consultation to organizations: Linking assessment and intervention. In R. L. Lowman (Ed.), *California School of Organizational Studies handbook of organizational consulting psychology* (pp. 415–449). New York: Wiley.

Lewin, K. (1947). Frontiers in group dynamics. II. Channels of group life; social planning and action research. *Human Relations, 1,* 143–153.

Levy, P. E., Cober, R. T., & Norris-Watts, C. (2004). Specific personality measures. In J. C. Thomas (Ed.), *Comprehensive handbook of psychological assessment: Vol. IV. Industrial and organizational assessment* (pp. 130–148). New York: Wiley.

Likert, R. (1961). *New patterns of management.* New York: McGraw-Hill.

Locke, E. A., & Latham, G. A. (1990). *A theory of goal setting and task performance.* Englewood Cliffs, NJ: Prentice-Hall.

London, M. (2003). *Job feedback: Giving, seeking, and using feedback for performance improvement.* Mahwah, NJ: Lawrence Erlbaum.

Lord, R. G., Hanges, P., & Godfrey, E. G. (2003). Integrating neuro networks into decision making and motivational theory: Rethinking VIE theory. *Canadian Psychology, 44,* 21–38.

Low, K. S. D., & Rounds, J. (2006). Vocational interests. In J. C. Thomas & D. Segal (Eds.), *Comprehensive handbook of personality and psychopathology: Vol. 1. Personality and everyday functioning* (pp. 251–267). New York: Wiley.

Lowman, R. L. (2002). Introduction. In R. L. Lowman (Ed.), *California School of Organizational Studies handbook of organizational consulting psychology* (pp. 1–2). New York: Wiley.

Lowman, R. L. (2005). Executive coaching: The road to Dodoville needs paving with more than good intentions. *Consulting Psychology Journal: Practice and Research, 57*(1), 90–96.

Lowman, R. L. (Ed.). (2006). *The ethical practice of psychology in organizations* (2nd ed.). Washington, DC: American Psychological Association and Society for Industrial and Organizational Psychology.

Lykken, D. (1995). *The antisocial personalities.* Mahwah, NJ: Lawrence Erlbaum.

Machin, M. A. (2002). Planning, managing, and optimizing transfer of training. In K. Kraiger (Ed.), *Creating, implementing, and managing effective training and development: State-of-the-art lessons for practice* (pp. 263–301). San Francisco: Jossey-Bass.

Maddi, S. R. (2006). Hardiness: The courage to be resilient. In J. C. Thomas & D. Segal (Eds.), *Comprehensive handbook of personality and psychopathology: Vol. 1. Personality and everyday functioning* (pp. 306–321). New York: Wiley.

Mann, C. C. (2005). *1491: New revelations of the Americans before Columbus*. New York: Vintage Books.

Mann, F. (1951). Changing superior-subordinate relationships. *Journal of Social Issues, 7,* 56–63.

Marks, M. L. (2002). Mergers and acquisitions. In J. W. Hedge & E. D. Pulakos (Eds.), *Implementing organizational interventions: Steps, processes, and best practices* (pp. 43–77). San Francisco: Jossey-Bass.

Markus, L. H., Cooper-Thomas, H. D., & Allpress, K. N. (2005). Confounded by competencies? An evaluation of the evolution and use of competency models. *New Zealand Journal of Psychology, 34*(2), 117–126.

Marrow, A. J., Bowers, D. G., & Seashore, S. E. (1967). *Management by participation.* New York: Harper & Row.

Maslow, A. H. (1943). A theory of human motivation. *Psychological Review, 50,* 370–396.

Mayer, J. D., & Salovey, P. (1997). What is emotional intelligence? In P. Salovey & D. J. Sluyter (Eds.), *Emotional development and emotional intelligence: Educational implications* (pp. 3–34). New York: Basic Books.

Mayer, R. E. (2008). Applying the science of learning: Evidence-based principles for the design of multi-media instruction. *American Psychologist, 63*(8), 760–769.

McCauley, C. D., & Hezlett, S. A. (2001). Individual development in the workplace. In N. Anderson, D. S. Ones, H. K. Sinangil, & C. Viswesvaran (Eds.), *Handbook of industrial, work, and organizational psychology: Vol. 1. Personnel psychology* (pp. 313–335). Thousand Oaks, CA: Sage.

McCormick, E. J. (1976). Job analysis. In M. D. Dunnette (Ed.), *Handbook of industrial and organizational psychology* (pp. 651–696). Chicago: Rand McNally.

McCormick, E. J. (1979). *Job Analysis: Methods and applications.* New York: AMACOM.

McCormick, E. J., Jeanneret, P. R., & Meacham, R. C. (1969). *The position analysis questionnaire.* West Lafayette, IN: Purdue Research Foundation.

McGinnis, J. L., Vignovic, J., DuVernet, A., Behrend, T., Poncheri, R., & Hess, C. (2008). TIP-TOPics for students: All aboard: Navigating the waters of professional ethics. *The Industrial-Organizational Psychologist, 46*(2), 93–99.

McIntyre, R. M., & Tedrow, L. (2004). A theory-based approach to team performance assessment. In J. C. Thomas (Ed.), *Comprehensive handbook of psychological assessment: Vol. IV. Industrial and organizational assessment* (pp. 443–454). New York: Wiley.

McLaughlin, J. A., & Jordan, G. B. (2004). Using logic models. In J. S. Wholey, H. P. Hatry, & K. E. Newcomer (Eds.), *Handbook of practical program evaluation* (pp. 7–32). San Francisco: Jossey-Bass.

McPhail, S. M. (Ed.). (2007). *Alternative validation strategies: Developing new and leveraging existing validity evidence.* San Francisco: Jossey-Bass.

Meeke, H. (2009). *Desired characteristics and competencies organizational and business consulting firms seek when hiring I/O psychologists.* Unpublished manuscript.

Meyer, H. (1991). A solution to the performance appraisal feedback enigma. *Academy of Management Executive, 5,* 68–76.

Michaelson, G. A. (2001). *Sun Tzu: The art of war for managers.* Avon, MA: Adams Media Corporation.

Mills, J. (1999). Improving on the 1957 version of dissonance theory. In E. Harmon-Jones & J. Mills (Eds.), *Cognitive dissonance: Progress on a pivotal theory in social psychology.* Washington, DC: American Psychological Association.

Miner, J. B. (1993). *Role motivation theories.* London: Routledge.

Miner, J. B. (2006). Role motivation theories. In J. C. Thomas & D. Segal (Eds.), *Comprehensive handbook of personality and psychopathology: Vol. 1. Personality and everyday functioning* (pp. 233–251). New York: Wiley.

Mischel, W. (1977). The interaction of person and situation. In D. Magnussen & N. S. Endler (Eds.), *Personality at the crossroads: Current issues in interactional psychology* (pp. 333–352). Hillsdale, NJ: Lawrence Erlbaum.

Mirvis, P. H. (2006). Revolutions in OD: The new and new, new things. In J. V. Gallos (Ed.), *Organization development* (pp. 39–88). San Francisco: Jossey-Bass.

Moscoso, S., & Salgado, J. F. (2004). "Dark side" personality styles as predictors of task, contextual, and job performance. *International Journal of Selection and Placement, 12*(4), 356–362.

Muchinsky, P. M. (2004). Mechanical aptitude and spatial ability testing. In J. C. Thomas (Ed.), *Comprehensive handbook of psychological assessment: Vol. IV. Industrial and organizational assessment* (pp. 21–34). New York: Wiley.

Mullin, V., & Cooper, S. (2002). Cross-cultural skills in international organizational consultation. In R. L. Lowman (Ed.), *California School of Organizational Studies handbook of organizational consulting psychology* (pp. 545–561). New York: Wiley.

Murphy, K. R. (2009). Content validation is useful for many things, but validity isn't one of them. *Industrial and Organizational Psychology: Perspectives on Science and Practice, 2* (4), 453–464

Murphy, K. R. & Balzer, W. K. (1989). Rater errors and rating accuracy. *Journal of Applied Psychology, 74,* 619–624.

Murphy, K. R., Jako, R. A., & Anhalt, R. L. (1993). Nature and consequences of halo error: A critical analysis. *Journal of Applied Psychology, 78,* 218–225.

Murphy, T. P. (2006). Judgment: The foundation of professional success. *Consulting Psychology Journal: Practice and Research, 58*(4), 185–194.

Nevis, E. C. (1987). *Organizational consulting: A Gestalt approach.* New York: Gardner Press.

Newman, D. A., Kinney, T., & Farr, J. L. (2004). Job performance ratings. In J. C. Thomas (Ed.), *Comprehensive handbook of psychological assessment: Vol. IV. Industrial and organizational assessment* (pp. 373–389). New York: Wiley.

Newman, J. L., Robinson-Kurpius, S. E., & Fuqua, D. R. (2002). Issues in the ethical practice of consulting psychology. In R. L. Lowman (Ed.), *California School of Organizational Studies handbook of organizational consulting psychology* (pp. 733–758). New York: Wiley.

Neuman, G. A., Edward, J. E., & Raju, N. S. (1989). Organizational development interventions: A meta-analysis of their effects on satisfaction and other attitudes. *Personnel Psychology, 42,* 461–489.

Nezu, C. M., Finch, A. J., & Simon, N. (Eds.). (2009). *Becoming certified by the American Board of Professional Psychology.* New York: Oxford University Press.

Nord, W. R. (1969). Beyond the teaching machine: The neglected area of operant conditioning in the theory and practice of management. *Organizational Behavior and Human Performance, 4,* 375–401.

Northouse, P. G. (2007). *Leadership: Theory and practice* (4th ed.). Thousand Oaks, CA: Sage.

Oliver, C., Shafiro, M., Bullard, P., & Thomas, J. C. (in press). Use of integrity tests may reduce worker's compensation costs. *Journal of Business and Psychology.*

O*NET On-Line. (2009a). Details report for 19-3032.00–Industrial-Organizational Psychologists. Downloaded October 10, 2008, from http://online.onetcenter.org/link/details/19-3032.00.

O*NET On-Line. (2009b). Summary report for 19-3032.00–Industrial-Organizational Psychologists. Downloaded October 10, 2008, from http://online.onetcenter.org/link/summary/19-3032.00.

Osborne, W. L., Brown, S., Niles, S., & Miner, C. U. (1997). *Career development assessment and counseling: Applications of the Donald E. Super C-DAC approach.* Alexandria, VA: American Counseling Association.

Oyserman, D., Coon, H. M., & Kemmelmeier, M. (2002). Rethinking individualism and collectivism: Evaluation of theoretical assumptions and meta-analysis. *Psychological Bulletin, 128*(1), 3–72.

Owens, W. A. (1976). Background data. In M. D. Dunnette (Ed.), *Handbook of industrial and organizational psychology* (pp. 609–644). Chicago: Rand McNally.

Parsons, F. (2005). *Choosing a vocation.* Broken Arrow, OK: National Career Development Association. (Originally published 1909).

Patton, M. Q. (2009). *Utilization focused evaluation* (4th ed.). Thousand Oaks, CA: Sage.

Persons, J. B., & Silberschatz, G. (1998). Are results of randomized controlled trials useful to psychotherapists? *Journal of Consulting and Clinical Psychology, 66,* 126–135.

Peterson, C. (2009). Minimally sufficient research. *Perspectives on Psychological Science, 4*(1), 7–9.

Peterson, D. B. (2002). Management development: Coaching and mentoring programs. In K. Kraiger (Ed.), *Creating, implementing, and managing effective training and development: State-of-the-art lessons for practice* (pp. 160–191). San Francisco: Jossey-Bass.

Peterson, N. G., & Jeanneret, P. R. (2007). Job analysis: Overview and description of deductive methods. In D. L. Whetzel & G. R. Wheaton (Eds.), *Applied measurement: Industrial psychology in human resources management* (pp. 13–56). Mahwah, NJ: Lawrence Erlbaum.

Petroski, H. (1985). *To engineer is human.* New York: St. Martin's Press.

Petroski, H. (2003). *Small things considered: Why there is no perfect design.* New York: Vintage Press.

Pittenger, D. J. (2005). Cautionary comments regarding the Myers-Briggs Type Indicator. *Consulting Psychology Journal: Research and Practice, 57*(3), 210–221.

Posthuma, R. A., Morgeson, F. P., & Campion, M. A. (2002). Beyond employment interview validity: A comprehensive narrative review of recent research and trends over time. *Personnel Psychology, 55,* 1–81.

Prien, E. P., Goodstein, L. D., Goodstein, J., Gamble, L. G., Jr. (2009). *A practical guide to job analysis.* San Francisco: Pheiffer.

Prien, E. P., Schippmann, J. S., & Prien, K. O. (2003). *Individual assessment: As practiced in industry and consulting.* Mahwah, NJ: Lawrence Erlbaum.

Prochaska, J. O. (1999). How do people change, and how can we change to help many more people? In M. A. Hubble, B. L. Duncan, & S. D. Miller (Eds.), *The heart and soul of change: What works in therapy* (pp. 227–258). Washington, DC: American Psychological Association.

Pulakos, E. D. (2007). Performance measurement. In D. L. Whetzel & G. R. Wheaton (Eds.), *Applied measurement: Industrial psychology in human resources management* (pp. 293–317). Mahwah, NJ: Lawrence Erlbaum.

Quick, J. C., & Tetrick, L. E. (Eds.). (2003). *Handbook of occupational health psychology*. Washington, DC: American Psychological Association.

Ragins, B. R., Singh, R., & Cornwell, J. M. (2007). Making the invisible visible: Fear and disclosure of sexual orientation at work. *Journal of Applied Psychology, 92*(4), 1103–1118.

Ravina, M. (2004). *The last samurai: The life and battles of Saigō Takamura*. New York: Wiley.

Raymond, M. R., Neustel, S., & Anderson, D. (2007). Retest effects on identical and parallel forms in certification and licensure testing. *Personnel Psychology, 60*(2), 367–396.

Rayson, M., Holliman, D., & Belyavin, A. (2000). Development of physical selection procedures for the British Army. Phase 2: Relationship between physical performance tests and criterion tasks. *Ergonomics, 43*(1), 73–105.

Reason, J. (2008). *The human contribution: Unsafe acts, accidents, and heroic recoveries*. Burlington, VT: Asgate.

Rock, M. L. & Berger, L. A. (Eds.). (1991). *The compensation handbook: A state-of-the-art guide to compensation strategy and design* (3rd ed.). New York: McGraw-Hill.

Rodolfa, E., Bent, R., Eisman, E., Nelson, P., Rehm, L., & Ritchie, P. (2005). A cube model for competency development: Implications for psychology educators and regulators. *Professional Psychology: Research and Practice, 36*(4), 347–354.

Rogelberg, S. G. (2004). *Handbook of research methods in industrial and organizational psychology*. Malden, MA: Blackwell.

Rogers, E. (2003). *Diffusion of innovations* (5th ed.). New York: Free Press.

Rogers, L. L., & Peterson, C. W. (2002). Beg, borrow, and steal: How the best training professionals keep up. In K. Kraiger (Ed.), *Creating, implementing, and managing effective training and development: State-of-the-art lessons for practice* (pp. 3–10). San Francisco: Jossey-Bass.

Roth, P. L., Bevier, C. A., Bobko, P., Switzer, F.S. III, & Tyler, P. (2001). Ethnic group differences in cognitive ability in employment and educational settings: A meta-analysis. *Personnel Psychology, 54*, 297–330.

Roth, P. L., Van Iddekinge, C. H., Huffcutt, A. I., Eidson, C. E., Jr., & Bobko, P. (2002). Corrections for range restriction in structured interview ethnic group differences: The values may be larger than researchers thought. *Journal of Applied Psychology, 87*(2), 369–376.

Rothe, H. (1978). Output rates among employees. *Journal of Applied Psychology, 63*, 40–46.

Ryan, A. M., & Sackett, P. R. (1987). A survey of industrial assessment practices by I/O psychologists. *Personnel Psychology, 40*, 455–480.

Rynes, S. L., Gerhart, B., & Parks, L. (2005). Personnel psychology: Performance evaluation and pay for performance. *Annual Review of Psychology, 56*, 571–600.

Salas, E., Burke, C. S., Fowlkes, J. E., & Priest, H. A. (2004). On measuring teamwork skills. In J. C. Thomas (Ed.), *Comprehensive handbook of psychological assessment: Vol. IV. Industrial and organizational assessment* (pp. 427–442). New York: Wiley.

Salas, E., & Cannon-Bowers, J. A. (2001). The science of training: A decade of progress. *Annual Review of Psychology, 52*, 471–501.

Sanchez, J. I., & Levine, E. L. (2001). The analysis of work in the 20th and 21st centuries. In N. Anderson, D. S. Ones, H. K. Sinangil, & C. Viswesvaran (Eds.), *Handbook of industrial, work, and organizational psychology: Vol. 1. Personnel psychology* (pp. 71–89). Thousand Oaks, CA: Sage.

Sapolsky, R. (2004). *Why zebras don't get ulcers* (3rd ed.). New York: Henry Holt.

Saunderson, R. (2005). Survey findings of the effectiveness of recognition in the public sector. *Public Personnel Management, 33*(3), 255–275.

Savickas, M. L. (2000). Renovating the psychology of careers for the twenty-first century. In A. Collin, & R. A. Young (Eds.), *The future of career* (pp. 53–68). Cambridge, UK: Cambridge University Press.

Scarborough, D., & Somers, M. J. (2006). *Neural networks in organizational research: Applying pattern recognition to the analysis of organizational behavior.* Washington, DC: American Psychological Association.

Schwartz, N. (1999). Self-reports: How the questions shape the answers. *American Psychologist, 54,* 93–105.

Schneider, B., Goldstein, H. W., & Smith, D. B. (1995). The ASA framework: An update. *Personnel Psychology, 48,* 747–773.

Schein, E. H. (1993). *Career anchors: Discovering your real values.* San Francisco: Pheiffer.

Schein, E. H. (1999). *Process consultation revisited.* Reading, MA: Addison-Wesley.

Schein, E. H. (2004). *Organizational culture and leadership* (3rd ed.). New York: Wiley.

Schein, E. H. (2009). *Helping: How to offer, give, and receive help.* San Francisco: Berrett-Koehler.

Schmidt, F. L., & Kaplan, L. B. (1971). Composite vs. multiple criteria: A review and resolution of the controversy. *Personnel Psychology, 24,* 419–434.

Schippmann, J. S. (1999). *Strategic job modeling.* Mahwah, NJ: Lawrence Erlbaum.

Schippmann, J. S., Ash, R. A., Battista, M. A., Carr, L., Eyde, L. D., Hesketh, B., Kehoe, J., Pearlman, K., Prien, E. P., & Sanchez, J. I. (2000). The practice of competency modeling. *Personnel Psychology, 53,* 703–740.

Schwartz, N. (1999). Self-reports: How the questions shape the answers. *American Psychologist, 54*(2), 93–105.

Shallcross, R., Johnson, W. B., & Lincoln, S. H. (2010). Supervision. In J. C. Thomas & M. Hersen (Eds.), *Handbook of clinical psychology competencies: Vol. 1. General competencies,* (pp. 503–548). New York: Springer.

Silzer, R., Erickson, A., Robinson, G., & Cober, R. (2008). Practitioner professional development. *The Industrial-Organizational Psychologist, 46*(2), 39–56.

Simon, H. A. (1955). A behavioral model of rational choice. *Quarterly Journal of Economics, 69,* 99–118.

Simon, H. A. (1956). Rational choice and the structure of the environment. *Psychological Review, 63,* 129–138.

Sinangil, H. K., & Ones, D. S. (2001). Expatriate management. In N. Anderson, D. S. Ones, H. K. Sinangil, & C. Viswesvaran (Eds.), *Handbook of industrial, work, and organizational psychology: Vol. 1. Personnel psychology* (pp. 424–444). Thousand Oaks, CA: Sage.

Smith, B. H. (2006). Rear end validity: A caution. In R. R. Bootzin & P. E. McKnight (Eds.), *Strengthening research methodology: Psychological measurement and evaluation* (pp. 233–248). Washington, DC: American Psychological Association.

Smith, C. S., Sulsky, L. M., & Uggerslev, K. L. (2002). Effects of job stress on mental and physical health. In J. C. Thomas & M. Hersen (Eds.), *Handbook of mental health in the workplace* (pp. 61–82). Thousand Oaks, CA: Sage.

Smith, P. C. (1976). Behaviors, results, and organizational effectiveness: The problem of criteria. In M. D. Dunnette (Ed.), *Handbook of industrial and organizational psychology* (pp. 745–775). Chicago: Rand McNally.

Society for Industrial and Organizational Psychology (SIOP). (1998). *Guidelines for education and training at the doctoral level in industrial/organizational psychology.* Dayton, OH: Author.

Society for Industrial and Organizational Psychology (SIOP). (2003). *Principles for the validation and use of personnel selection measures.* Bowling Green, OH: Author.

Somerville, K. (1998). Where is the business of business psychology headed? *Consulting Psychology: Research and Practice, 50*(4), 237–241.

Spector, P. E. (2001). Research methods in industrial and organizational psychology: Data collection and data analysis with special consideration to international issues. In N. Anderson, D. S. Ones, H. K. Sinangil, & C. Viswesvaran (Eds.), *Handbook of industrial, work, and organizational psychology: Vol. 1. Organizational psychology* (pp. 10–26). Thousand Oaks, CA: Sage.

Strachey, L. (1921). *Queen Victoria.* New York: Harcourt, Brace, & World.

Stajkovic, A. D., & Luthans, F. (1997). A meta-analysis of the effects of organizational behavior modification on task performance, 1975–95. *Academy of Management Journal, 40*(5), 1122–1149.

Stayer, R. (1990). How I learned to let my workers lead. *Harvard Business Review*, reprint number 90610.

Sterns, H., & Subich, L. M. (2002). Career development at mid-career. In D. C. Feldman (Ed.), *Work careers: A developmental perspective* (pp. 186–213). San Francisco: Jossey-Bass.

Stober, D. R., & Grant, A. M. (Eds.). (2006). *Evidence based coaching handbook: Putting best practices to work with your clients.* Hoboken, NJ: Wiley.

Stokes, G. S., & Cooper, L. A. (2004). Biodata. In J. C. Thomas (Ed.), *Comprehensive handbook of psychological assessment: Vol. IV. Industrial and organizational assessment* (pp. 243–268). New York: Wiley.

Stone, A. A., Turkkan, J. S., Bachrach, C. A., Jobe, J. B., Kurtzman, H. S., & Cain, V. S. (2001). *The science of self report: Implications for research and practice.* Mahwah, NJ: Lawrence Erlbaum.

Stone-Romero, E. F., Stone, D. L., & Salas, E. (2003). The influence of culture on role conceptions and role behavior in organizations. *Applied Psychology: An International Review, 52*(3), 328–364.

Stroh, L. K., & Johnson, H. H. (2006). *The basic principles of effective consulting.* Mahwah, NJ: Lawrence Erlbaum.

Sutherland, V. J., & Cooper, C. L. (2002). Models of job stress. In J. C. Thomas & M. Hersen (Eds.), *Handbook of mental health in the workplace* (pp. 33–59). Thousand Oaks, CA: Sage.

Super, D. E. (1957). *The psychology of careers.* New York: Harper & Row.

Suutari, V., & Viitala, R. (2007). Management development of senior executives: Methods and their effectiveness. *Personnel Review, 37*(4), 375–392.

Svyantek, D. J., & Bott, J. P. (2004). Organizational culture and organizational climate measures: An integrative review. In J. C. Thomas (Ed.), *Comprehensive handbook of psychological assessment: Vol. IV. Industrial and organizational assessment* (pp. 507–523). New York: Wiley.

Taleb, N. N. (2005). *Fooled by randomness: The hidden role of chance in markets and life* (2nd ed.). New York: Random House.

Taleb, N. N. (2007). *The black swan: The impact of the highly improbable.* New York: Random House.

Tannenbaum, S. (2002). A strategic view of organizational training and learning. In K. Kraiger (Ed.), *Creating, implementing, and managing effective training and development: State-of-the-art lessons for practice* (pp. 10–53). San Francisco: Jossey-Bass.

Thomas, J. C. (Ed.). (2004). *Comprehensive handbook of psychological assessment: Vol. IV. Industrial and organizational assessment.* New York: Wiley.

Thomas, J. C. (2006, December 6). Does coaching work? Who knows? [Review of the book *Evidence based coaching handbook: Putting best practices to work with your clients*], *Psyc-CRITIQUES-Contemporary Psychology: APA Review of Books, 51*(49), Article 6.

Thomas, J. C. (2008). Statistical considerations. In M. Hersen & A. M. Gross (Eds.), *Handbook of clinical psychology: Vol. 1. Adults* (pp. 205–224). New York: Wiley.

Thomas, J. C., & Hite, J. (2002). Introduction: Mental health in the workplace. In J. C. Thomas & M. Hersen (Eds.), *Handbook of mental health in the workplace* (pp. 3–14). Thousand Oaks, CA: Sage.

Thomas, J. C., & Meeke, H. (2010). Rater error. In I. B. Weiner & W. E. Craighead (Eds.), *The Corsini Encyclopedia of Psychology* (4th ed.). New York: Wiley.

Thorndike, R. L. (1949). *Personnel selection: Test and measurement techniques.* New York: Wiley.

Thornton, G. C. III, & Mueller-Hanson, R. A. (2004). *Developing organizational simulations: A guide for practitioners and students.* Mahwah, NJ: Lawrence Erlbaum.

Thornton, G. C. III, & Rupp, D. E. (2004). Simulations and assessment centers. In J. C. Thomas (Ed.), *Comprehensive handbook of psychological assessment: Vol. IV. Industrial and organizational assessment* (pp. 319–344). New York: Wiley.

Tiffin, J. (1943). *Industrial psychology.* New York: Prentice-Hall.

Todman, J. B., & Dugard, P. (2001). *Single-case and small-n experimental designs: A practical guide to randomization tests.* Mahwah, NJ: Erlbaum.

Truax, P., & Thomas, J. C. (2003). Effectiveness vs. efficacy studies. In J. C. Thomas & M. Hersen (Eds.), *Understanding research in clinical and counseling psychology* (pp. 343–377). Mahwah, NJ: Erlbaum.

Truxillo, D. M., Donahue, L. M., & Kuang, D. (2004). Work samples, performance tests, and competency testing. In J. C. Thomas (Ed.), *Comprehensive handbook of psychological assessment: Vol. IV. Industrial and organizational assessment* (pp. 345–370). New York: Wiley.

Tuckman, B. W. (1965). Developmental sequences in small groups. *Psychological Bulletin, 63,* 384–399.

Tversky, A., & Kahneman, D. (1974). Judgement under uncertainty: Heuristics and biases. *Science, 185,* 1124–1131.

Uniform Guidelines on Employee Selection Procedures. 29 C.F.R. § 1607 *et seq.* (1978).

U.S. Department of Labor. (1991). *Dictionary of occupational titles* (4th ed., rev.). Washington, DC: U.S. Government Printing Office.

Üsdiken, B., & Leblebici, H. (2001). Organization theory. In N. Anderson, D. S. Ones, H. K. Sinangil, & C. Viswesvaran (Eds.), *Handbook of industrial, work, and organizational psychology: Vol. 2. Organizational psychology* (pp. 377–397). Thousand Oaks, CA: Sage.

van Eijnatten, F. M. (1998). Developments in socio-technical systems design (STSD). In P. J. D. Drenth, H. Thierry, & C. J. de Wolff (Eds.), *Handbook of work and organizational psychology* (2nd ed.): *Vol. 4. Organizational psychology* (pp. 61–88). East Sussex, UK: Psychology Press.

Vinchur, A. J., & Koppes, L. L (2007). Early contributors to the science and practice of industrial psychology. In L. L. Koppes (Ed.), *Historical perspectives in industrial and organizational psychology* (pp. 37–60). Mahwah, NJ: Lawrence Erlbaum.

Viswesvaran, C. (2001). Assessment of individual job performance: A review of the past century and a look ahead. In N. Anderson, D. S. Ones, H. K. Sinangil, & C. Viswesvaran

(Eds.), *Handbook of industrial, work, and organizational psychology: Vol. 1. Personnel psychology* (pp. 110–126). Thousand Oaks, CA: Sage.

Viswesvaran, C., Sinangil, H. K., Ones, D. S., & Anderson, N. (2001). Where we have been, where we are, (and where we could be). In N. Anderson, D. S. Ones, H. K. Sinangil, & C. Viswesvaran (Eds.), *Handbook of industrial, work, and organizational psychology: Vol. 1. Organizational psychology* (pp. 1–9). Thousand Oaks, CA: Sage.

Wallace, S. R. (1965). Criteria for what? *American Psychologist, 20,* 411–417.

Walsh, J. P. (1988). Top management turnover following mergers and acquisitions. *Strategic Management Journal, 9*(2), 173–183.

Wang, P., & Walumba, F. O. (2007). Family-friendly programs, organizational commitment, and work withdrawal: The moderating role of transformational leadership. *Personnel Psychology, 60*(2), 397–427.

Warr, P. (2007). *Work, happiness, and unhappiness.* Mahwah, NJ: Lawrence Erlbaum.

Weitz, J. (1961). Criteria for criteria. *American Psychologist, 16*(5), 228–231.

Westermeyer, J. F. (1998). Predictors and characteristics of mental health among men at mid-life: A 32 year longitudinal study. *American Journal of Orthopsychiatry, 68,* 265–273.

White, L. A., Young, M. C., Hunter, A. E., & Rumsey, M. G. (2008). Lessons learned in transitioning personality measures from research to operational settings. *Industrial and Organizational Psychology, 1,* 291–295.

Wilkinson, L., & the Task Force on Statistical Inference. (1999). Statistical methods in psychology journals: Guidelines and explanations. *American Psychologist, 54,* 594–604.

Winum, P. (2005). Effectiveness of a high-potential African American executive: The anatomy of a coaching engagement. *Consulting Psychology Journal, 57,* 71–89.

Zaccaro, S. J. (2007). Trait-based perspectives on leadership. *American Psychologist, 62,* 6–17.

Zhang, L. (2009). An exchange theory of money and self-esteem in decision making. *Review of General Psychology, 13*(1), 66–76.

Zhou, J., & Martocchio, J. J. (2001). Chinese and American managers' compensation award decisions: A comparative policy-capturing study. *Personnel Psychology, 54,* 115–145.

Zickar, M. J., & Gibby, R. E. (2007). Four persistent themes throughout the history of I-O psychology in the United States. In L. L. Koppes (Ed.), *Historical perspectives in industrial and organizational psychology* (pp. 61–80). Mahwah, NJ: Erlbaum.

KEY TERMS

Action research—working with the client organization to gather information through surveys, focus groups, interviews, or other means, analyzing the information, and using it to plan the next phase of change.

Behavior description interview (BDI)—asking applicants to relate what they did in a specific situation; that is, BDI focuses on actual behavior.

Competency modeling—the activity of determining the specific competencies that are characteristic of high performance and success in a given job.

Critical incident technique (CIT)—collecting a number of examples of effective or ineffective job behaviors by questioning individuals who have firsthand knowledge of the incidents.

Formative evaluation—a method of judging the worth of a program while the program activities are forming or happening.

Ipsative measurement—measurement system for comparing a person's relative level of multiple characteristics within the person rather than individual characteristics compared against other people.

Job analysis—the process used to collect information about the duties, responsibilities, necessary skills, outcomes, and work environment of a particular job.

Job modeling—taking the job analysis results and augmenting them with additional information to allow strategic planning of the workforce.

KSAOs—the knowledge, abilities, skills, and other characteristics (KSAOs) that are needed to perform well in a task, job, or profession.

Mergers and acquisitions (M&A)—the successful combination of two organizations. In an acquisition one company takes over another, and the latter firm ceases to exist. In a merger two companies decide to go forth as a single entity.

Normative measurement—measurement system for comparing scores of one person to scores of other people within a defined group.

Organizational development (OD)—a planned, organization-wide effort to increase an organization's effectiveness and viability.

Position Analysis Questionnaire (PAQ)—a standardized instrument for conducting job analysis.

Process consultation (PC)—the most commonly used OD technique wherein the consultant does not try to help the client as an expert but instead helps the client to help himself.

Situational interview (SI)—focuses on what applicants **would** do in a specific situation.

Subject matter expert (SME)—an individual who understands a business process or area well enough to answer questions from people in other groups who are trying to help.

Summative evaluation—a method of judging the worth of a program at the end of the program activities.

Task analysis—the analysis of how a task is accomplished, including a detailed description of the factors involved in or required for one or more people to perform a given task.

INDEX

Note: Page number followed by "*t*" denote tables.

ABOUT THE AUTHOR

Jay C. Thomas, PhD, ABPP, is distinguished university professor and assistant dean in the School of Professional Psychology at Pacific University, Portland, Oregon. He received his PhD from the University of Akron in industrial and organizational psychology and holds a diplomate from the American Board of Professional Psychology in that specialty and in organizational and business consulting psychology. He is a former president of that board and is a member of the ABPP Board of Trustees. After many years as a consultant and in private practice he joined Pacific's School of Professional Psychology teaching statistics, research methods, program evaluation, and courses in organizational behavior and consultation, organizational assessment, and career development. His research interests include program evaluation, methodology for field studies, outcome research, and integrating findings and concepts across industrial/organizational and clinical/counseling psychology. He also has a consulting team that provides organizational consulting to several institutions. He is co-editor of 14 books and is on the editorial boards of *Aggression and Violent Behavior, Journal of Anxiety Disorders*, and *PsycCRITIQUES*. He has also published several papers in industrial/organizational psychology, program evaluation, and mental health.